Pius XII and the
Second World War

Pius XII and the Second World War

According to the Archives of the Vatican

PIERRE BLET, S.J.

Translated by Lawrence J. Johnson

PAULIST PRESS
New York, N.Y. • Mahwah, N.J.

Jacket design by Kokopelli Design Studio.

Jacket photograph by AP/Wide World Photos.

Library of Congress Cataloging-in-Publication Data

Blet, Pierre.
    [Pie XII et la Seconde Guerre Mondiale. French]
    Pius XII and the Second World War : according to the Archives of the Vatican / by Pierre Blet ; translated by Lawrence J. Johnson.
       p. cm.
    Includes bibliographical references and index.
    ISBN 0-8091-0503-9 (alk. paper)
    1. World War, 1939–1945—Diplomatic history. 2. Pius XII, Pope, 1876–1958.
3. Catholic Church—Foreign relations. 4. World War, 1939–1945—Vatican City.
I. Title.
D749.B4841   1999
940.53´2545634—dc21   99-24020
                                                                                    CIP

Published by Paulist Press
997 Macarthur Boulevard
Mahwah, New Jersey 07430 USA

www.paulistpress.com

Printed and bound in the
United States of America

Contents

~.~

Abbreviations
Used in the Notes

~·~

ADSS = *Actes et Documents du Saint-Siège relatifs à la Seconde Guerre mondiale*
Akten = *Akten zur deutschen auswärtigen Politik (1918–1945)*
DDI = *Documenti diplomatici italiani*
DBFP = *Documents on British Foreign Policy 1919–1939*
FRUS = *Foreign Relations of the United States, Diplomatic Papers*

*   *   *

Actes et Documents du Saint-Siège relatifs à la Second Guerre mondiale, edited by Pierre Blet, Robert A. Graham, Angelo Martini, Burkhart Schneider, Libreria Editrice Vaticana, Vatican City, 1965–1981, 12 volumes:

1. *Le Saint-Siège et la guerre en Europe, 1939–1940*

2. *Lettres de Pie XII aux évêques allemands, 1939–1944*

3. *Le Saint-Siège et la situation religieuse en Pologne et dans les Pays baltes, 1939–1945*, 2 volumes

4. *Le Saint-Siège et la guerre en Europe, juin 1940–juin 1941*

5. *Le Saint-Siège et la guerre mondiale, juillet 1941–octobre 1942*

6. *Le Saint-Siège et les victimes de la guerre, mars 1939–décembre 1940*

7. *Le Saint-Siège et la guerre mondiale, novembre 1942–décembre 1943*

8. *Le Saint-Siège et les victimes de la guerre, janvier 1941–décembre 1942*

9. *Le Saint-Siège et les victimes de la guerre, janvier–décembre 1943*

10. *Le Saint-Siège et les victimes de la guerre, janvier 1944–juillet 1945*

11. *Le Saint-Siège et la guerre mondiale, janvier 1944–mai 1945*

Preface

~·~

One discerns only in the 1960s a qualitative and quantitative leap of scholarly interpretative writings on World War II. But the headache of the historians of this dense period continues: sifting more available but limited data, projecting and interrelating the conditions and causes of events, and determining the agents. Even at the end of the twentieth century the scrupulous scholar heeds the warning of Walter Raleigh: Any writer of modern history who treads too closely on the heels of events may get his or her teeth knocked out. And one ponders the calm reply of Chou En-lai when a European intellectual had asked the premier of China what he thought of the eighteenth-century French Revolution: "It's too early to tell."

In this context looms large the role of Pope Pius XII, the Vatican and the local Catholic churches, their hierarchies and faithful in Europe and elsewhere, in particular, as they faced the Shoah, the unique holocaust of six million Jews. Always the haunting questions: When did who know what? What did one do or not do with what one knew? And why? The descriptions find ominous words: *denial, collaboration, passivity, silences*. Historians argue their cases.

In 1963 controversy entered the more public arena through a German play. During the first session of Pope John XXIII's Vatican Council II in 1962, observant Christians and Jews knew that at the next autumn session the council bishops would discuss a draft dealing with the relations of the Roman Catholic Church to the Jews. But first, on 20 February 1963, Rolf Hochuch's *Der Stellvertreter* premiered on a Berlin stage. It set off an international argument with wide publicity. Through caricatured dramatic license the play stunningly condemned God's "deputy" or "representative," Pius XII, for his failure publicly and vigorously to act against the mass murders of Jews under Hitler. Accompanied by picketing and efforts toward censorship, the drama seemed to compel its viewers and so many others to choose sides—for or against Pope Pius XII, for or against the Catholic Church's role during World War II. Reactions did not strictly follow religious lines.

Cardinal Archbishop Montini of Milan, Pius XII's close Vatican associate during the war years, had prepared a defense that the London *Tablet* (29 June 1963) published shortly after Montini had been elected the successor of John XXIII (23 June). He accused the thirty-one-year-old Lutheran playwright of "an inadequate grasp of the psychological, political realities" in "those appalling conditions of war and Nazi oppression." The wartime pope tried "so far as he could fully and courageously to carry out the mission entrusted to him." For Pius XII to have adopted "an attitude of protest and condemnation would have been *not only futile but harmful.*"

Although translated in over twenty languages, *Der Stellvertreter* (*The Deputy,* New York: Grove, 1964) was soon forgotten, but not the question. Soon after he had become pope, Paul VI bypassed the strict time restraint (75 years) governing access to the Vatican Secretariat of State Archives. He initiated for eventual publication direct research of the years 1936–1945. Three Jesuit church historians assumed the burden—Pierre Blet, Angelo Martini, and Burkhart Schneider. Joining them in 1967 was the American, Robert A. Graham.

In his initial years of research, Father Graham and I occasionally found ourselves together in a quiet restaurant near our separate Vatican offices. He related the agony of total unhampered access to the Archives, going through boxes and boxes on shelves and shelves, unsorted materials in year-by-year general categories. The foursome's obedience was not to order and index the entire massive documentation but to select what they judged to pertain to Pius XII and his Secretariat of State during World War II. Also burdensome was their selection for publication of those materials (public statements, correspondence, cablegrams, notations, and memoranda) that were essential and illustrative but not repetitive, and that would still accurately reflect the total documentation.

The labors resulted in twelve volumes completed between 1965 and 1981: *Actes et Documents du Saint Siège relatifs à la Seconde Guerre Mondiale,* published by the Vatican Press. The narrative is in French, but the documents are kept in their original Italian, French, German, Spanish, Latin, and English. The four Jesuits did not editorialize, accuse, excuse, interpret motives, delineate personalities, or describe the explosive, unstable mixtures of religion, nation, and self.

They seldom correlated their materials with other available documents from other archival sources, whether of foreign state departments and military headquarters or of bishops and other church people. Other scholars can do such complementation and interpretation.

Some did, but they are few. Demands for a volume-by-volume summary and for translations of texts prompted Father Blet in the 1990s to do so. He finished the book in 1997 (Paris: Perrin), and now Paulist Press has produced an English translation. Blet was handicapped insofar as his three collaborators could offer no counsel; they had passed away. Only he is responsible for the accuracy of the summary. But he goes beyond rigid guidelines. He uses only a few other published archival sources. And he defends Pius XII's quiet diplomacy and his "silences."

In an address to nurses in May 1952, Pius XII asked himself: "What should we have done that we have not done?" Pierre Blet judges that "insofar as the documents allow anyone to probe the human heart of another," they do support the same conclusion of Pius XII regarding these years of fire and sword: "He was conscious of what he had done to prevent war, to alleviate sufferings, to reduce the number of its victims, everything he thought he could do." The pope saw himself between contradictory pastoral demands: "reserve and prudent silence, or resolutely speaking out and vigorous action" (March 1944). As Pius wrote in February 1941 to the German bishops: "Where the pope wants to cry out loud and strong, it is expectation in silence that are unhappily imposed on him; where he would act and give assistance, it is patience and waiting [that are imposed]." For Father Blet, what "makes difficult the task of understanding his policy and personality" are Pius XII's "high ideals, transcending as they did opposing interests and rival passions." Not "neutrality" or passive indifference, but "impartiality" amidst warring countries, "judging things according to truth and justice."

The evaluation confirms Paul VI's general judgement in June 1963, before the secret archives had been explored by Father Blet and his three colleagues. But there still is no consensus among the historians of Pius XII and the Holy See in the war years.

The more recent provocation was a lengthy footnote in *We Remember: A Reflection on the Shoah*, published on 16 March 1998 by the Vatican Commission for Religious Relations with the Jews. Addressed to "our brothers and sisters of the Catholic Church throughout the world," the *Reflection* attempts, all too briefly, to delineate the history of relations between Jews and Christians; Nazi anti-Semitism and the Shoah; "anti-Jewish prejudices imbedded in some Christians' minds and hearts," which supported the Nazi's Final Solution; the muffled voices of protest; the assistance of Christians "to those being persecuted, and in particular to the persecuted Jews"; and "the heavy burden of conscience," which "must be a call to penitence."

Pope Pius XII, states the document, "personally or through his representatives" saved "hundreds of thousands of Jewish lives." The footnote cites examples to support the claim that Jewish leaders often publicly acknowledged "the wisdom of Pope Pius XII's diplomacy." Immediate reactions were almost as pro and con and mixed as had been those 1963 responses to Hochuch's stark portrayal in *Der Stellvertreter.* Was such a footnote even necessary? Was the unqualified commendation a classic example of selective use of history and thus implicitly a denial? The plea surfaced: "Open the Vatican archives," mostly by those who never even suspected that direct research had already resulted in twelve such available volumes.

The mid-March publication was shortly followed by the sixteenth meeting of the International Catholic-Jewish Liaison committee (ILC) between the Holy See and the International Jewish Committee on Interreligious Consultations, in the Vatican, 23–26 March 1998. In discussion of those "Jewish demands for impartial access to the relevant archival material," Cardinal Edward I. Cassidy, president of the Vatican Commission for Jewish relations, suggested that, first, a joint team of Jewish and Catholic scholars review the twelve volumes of the Secretariat of State records during World War II. "If questions still remained, they should seek further clarification." In response through a joint communiqué, the ILC intends, in more general terms, "to establish a joint working group of historians and theologians, to pursue further studies on the period of the Shoah, and to seek together a "healing of memory."

Meanwhile, on 3 December 1998 Dr. Joaquin Navarro-Valls, director of the Vatican Press Office, referred to the twelve volumes and firmly declared: "The exhaustive perusal *(spoglio)* of the documents of the Vatican archives permits to affirm that there is nothing—repeat: nothing—to add to what is already published."

A personal note. I can only wonder if all possible archival delving would ever reach a scholarly consensus about the person of

Eugenio Pacelli, an ambiguous person in even more ambiguous circumstances as a wartime pope, "a prisoner in the Vatican." What-ifs are not the stuff of history. Can historians ever agree on what more the pope could have done, and where, and with whom, and how? As an intentional diplomatic peacemaker "by the universal paternity proper to our office," Pius XII's judgments about public statements, quiet diplomacy, and "silences" seem, in hindsight, not between good and evil but between two evils in the midst of Evil. In either case, lives would be lost. And whose lives? "The greater evil is to be avoided *[majora mala vitanda]*." Diplomacy, the art of the possible, exacts its own price. Can it ever be boldly prophetic or heroic?

And the Shoah? It imposes silence, yet demands speech. Defying all solutions and meanings, it calls for responses and for responsibility. Obscenely historical, it rejects explanatory facts. Can one disagree with the historian Christopher Browning: "The Holocaust is a story with many victims and not too many heroes. I think we are naïve if we think that one more hero could have stopped it."

Pope John Paul II unambiguously claims that "the crime which has become known as the Shoah remains an indelible stain on the history of the century that is coming to a close.... [The Church] calls for sons and daughters to place themselves humbly before the Lord and examine themselves on the responsibility which they too have of the evils of our time."

Thomas F. Stransky, Paulist

Thomas F. Stransky was an original staff member of the Vatican Secretariat for Christian Unity (1960–70), and rector of the Tantur Ecumenical Institute for Theological Studies, Jerusalem.

Introduction

~·~

IN DECEMBER 1965 the Libreria Editrice Vaticana published the first volume of *Actes et Documents du Saint-Siège relatifs à la Seconde Guerre mondiale.* Many collections of diplomatic history had long been in existence, and any number of them were concerned with the Second World War: *Documenti diplomatici italiani; Documents on British Foreign Policy; Foreign Relations of the United States, Diplomatic Papers; Akten zur deutschen auswärtigen Politik (1918–1945).* In light of these collections it seemed right that historians, once they were acquainted with Vatican materials, could undertake a very critical study of the documents pertaining to the Holy See's role and activity during this period.

It was easy enough for the historiography of modern times to have been completely silent regarding the papacy's role in international affairs, although at times there were but brief references to this activity. For example, despite several in-depth studies devoted to Benedict XV's initiatives to limit the First World War and to hasten its conclusion, modern works only mention Benedict's work in summary fashion.

As to the Second World War, since 1964–1965 a wave of systematic disparagements concerning the person and activity of Pius XII has been added to the silence of the chronicler. Immediately following his death on 9 October 1958 the pope was the object of praise, admiration, and gratitude. Yet several years later he became the hero of a *légende noire:* it was said that during the war, whether for reasons of policy or timidity, he, emotionless and silent, watched crimes against humanity, crimes that words from his lips could have stopped (!).

There is only one way of returning from fiction to reality, from legend to history, and that is by going back to the original documents, for these directly reveal what the pope did and said. And so Pope Paul VI, who, as the substitute in the Vatican's Secretariat of State, had been one of Pius XII's closest collaborators, authorized the publication of the Holy See's documents regarding the war.

1

Indeed, the archives of the Secretariat of State preserve documents that allow us to follow day after day, at times hour by hour, the activity of the pope and his associates. Contained in the archives is the information received by the Vatican, proposals of the secretary of state and his collaborators, decisions made by the pope, instructions sent to the nuncios, and notes given to various ambassadors. The material can essentially be classified into five categories: (1) the pope's speeches and messages; (2) letters the pope exchanged with civil and ecclesiastical dignitaries; those originating in the Vatican are usually conserved under the form of rough drafts, which the pope corrected by hand; (3) notes from the Secretariat of State as well as minutes redacted by subordinates for their superiors in order to communicate information or proposals; in addition, private notes, especially those of Monsignor Tardini, who was accustomed, and very fortunately so for the historian, to reflect with pen in hand; (4) diplomatic notes exchanged between the Secretariat of State and the ambassadors or other ministers accredited to the Holy See; (5) correspondence exchanged between the Secretariat of State and the Holy See's representatives abroad, namely, nuncios, internuncios, and apostolic delegates. Many of these papers bear the signature of the secretary of state or that of the secretary of the first section of the Secretariat of State; very few carry the signature of the pope himself. Documents of this sort do not reflect the mind of the person who signed them but indicate the mind of the pope, who was responsible for all final decisions.

This is the material that has been published in the *Actes et Documents du Saint-Siège relatifs à la Seconde Guerre mondiale* (12 volumes, including the 2 volumes that form the third book in the collection). The documents it contains offer the historian a means of ascertaining what was really the attitude and activity of the pope and the Holy See during the Second World War. Such documentation permits us to see the pope during a world in conflict, with the more or less complete information he received, with the appeals being made to his moral or religious influence, which some imagined to be unlimited and which all sought to use for their own purposes, with his efforts to do everything possible while preserving his impartiality toward the belligerents. It allows us to view the steps the pope took to ward off the calamity, his attempts to contain the conflict when it turned into a European and then a world war, and finally his efforts to alleviate suffering and to assist the victims.

Surely no archival collection, not even the most complete, can ever account for the whole reality. For example, it is only by way of exception that the Vatican archives reveal what actually took place during papal audiences, the words exchanged between the pope and his visitor. Indeed the documents tell us, for example, that on 30 June 1944 Pius granted an audience to General de Gaulle, and *l'Osservatore Romano* specifies that it took place at nine in the morning, and yet these sources record not a word of the conversation; it is the general's *War Memories* that provide us with information here. Furthermore, the nuncios often sent Rome a chronicle of their daily activities. Yet these sources, witnessing as they do the many initiatives taken to save the victims of racial persecution, indicate very little in terms of results. In this respect what we most often find is the gratitude expressed to a particular nuncio by the beneficiaries of this action. Despite such limitations—known well by historians who work with archival material—these documents no less remain an essential and irreplaceable source for the history of the Holy See's activity during the Second World War.

Yet the experience of the fifteen years that have passed since the appearance of the last book in the series shows that the content of this collection, if not its very existence, has escaped the attention of many who speak and write about the Holy See during the war. This is why we have tried to give an overview of the collection's contents in this, a more manageable volume. Each book in the *Actes et Documents* is preceded by an introduction pointing out the essentials of the printed documents contained in the volume. With the authorization of the Secretariat of State, which is responsible for publishing the series, we have reproduced these introductions, although in a more synthetic form; furthermore, we have not refrained from including texts that we have already published.

To make the results of the work more accessible, we have reduced its dimensions, doing so at the risk of sacrificing numerous details and even entire areas of the Holy See's activities during the war, for example, the help it sent to the prison camps and to afflicted regions, its unsuccessful efforts to ease the blockades that resulted in people going hungry, its tireless efforts to establish an information service for prisoners of war and their families. In this regard those who desire more complete information or additional details—and we hope they are many—can easily have recourse to the complete series. It is in the same spirit that we have here reduced the critical apparatus that refers the reader to the sources that have been used; at the beginning of each chapter we indicate the volume or volumes in which these documents have been published; their chronological order and date should facilitate verification. Furthermore, in order to be faithful to the documents, we have taken care to retain their vocabulary in all the material that has been rewritten, a vocabulary that remains perfectly understandable today, and we have studiously avoided using more recent terminology, which so easily carries with it anachronistic understandings.

In concluding this introduction, I must do justice to the colleagues and confreres with whom I worked from 1965 to 1982 in preparing *Actes et Documents,* and from whose labors I now benefit: Fathers Robert A. Graham, Angelo Martini, and Burkhart Schneider. Two of these died, as it were, "in the saddle." Burkhart Schneider was a professor of church history at the Gregorian University, and to his duties as teacher and administrator he added that of editor, working on Pius XII's letters to the German bishops (volume 2); his activity especially extended to volumes 6, 8, and 9 till the day when illness took him from us in 1976. Angelo Martini, a contributor to *Civiltà Cattolica* and a recognized specialist in contemporary history, dedicated the last fifteen years of his life to this project. Although he did not see its final completion, he had in his hands the final proofs of the last volume. Robert Graham, who joined us in 1967, remained in Rome till July 1996, when he returned to his native California, where he died on 11 February 1997. Even though he was our senior in age, he continued working till the completion of the collection; during the last fifteen years of his life he was even able to supplement the series by his various writings, which most often appeared as articles in *Civiltà Cattolica.* They too are a source of information, one that historians of the Second World War can consult with profit.

CHAPTER 1

Vatican Diplomacy
against the War*

~·~

O
N THURSDAY 2 MARCH 1939, a little after six in the evening, Camillo Caccia Dominioni, the first cardinal of the order of deacons, announced from the central loggia of St. Peter's Basilica to the crowd gathered between Bernini's colonnades the news the people were impatiently awaiting: *Annuntio vobis gaudium magnum: habemus papam, Eminentissimum et Reverendissimum Dominum Eugenium Pacelli, qui sibi nomen imposuit Pium XII* ("It is with great joy that I announce to you that we have a pope: It is Eugenio Cardinal Pacelli, who has taken the name Pius XII."). The third round of voting in a conclave lasting less than twenty-four hours elected as Pius XI's successor Cardinal Pacelli, who for ten years had served as secretary of state. The next morning at eleven the third "adoration" of the cardinals took place in the Sistine Chapel. Having received the obedience of those who were his equals the previous day, the new pope delivered a message addressed not only to the princes of the church assembled before him but also to the whole world. He greeted the pastors of the church, its missionaries, priests, and faithful, and then all people, even those outside the Catholic Church. It was to all these that the pope wanted to extend a wish, a desire for peace, "peace, which all righteous people long for, peace, the fruit of charity and justice." From the very first day of his pontificate Pius XII gave proof that he intended to continue the task his predecessor had assigned to him, namely, defending the peace of the world.

In so doing Pius XII responded to a general expectation. His election was greeted by a concert of approvals. While Berlin was content

---

*Documentation for chapter 1: See *ADSS,* vol. 1. Add: *DBFP,* series 3, vols. 5, 6, and 7; *FRUS,* 1940, vols. 1 and 2; *DDI,* series 8, vols. 12 and 13; series 9, vol. 3; *Akten,* series D, vols. 6 and 7; Ciano, *Diario;* see also François Charles-Roux, *Huit ans au Vatican;* Owen Chadwick, *Britain and the Vatican.*

with a somewhat cold reserve, the United States, France, and England, praised Pacelli's election as a victory over the totalitarian states. From diverse points on the horizon there was an expectation that the new pope would ease the situation and take effective steps on behalf of peace. *Le Populaire,* the journal of the French Socialist party, spoke ironically about the attitude of the Italian press, which rejoiced over the election of the secretary of state, preferring this to the election of a religious pope ready to let loose lightening bolts upon those who favored war: "There is no need to strike with lightening today's dictators once they have declared war. What we fervently request is that someone help us in keeping them from running wild."

It was difficult to respond to everything people desired. At least Eugenio Pacelli had been exceptionally prepared for the diplomatic and religious task that the necessities of the time imposed upon the papacy. He seemed to unite in his very person the "religious pope" and the "political pope," which popular opinion liked to set in opposition. His ascetic appearance and his intense contemplation during the solemn ceremonies impressed even the least mystical of souls. On the other hand, his very sharp intelligence, served by a prodigious memory, had been brought to maturity by his outstanding diplomatic experience. Joining the Secretariat of State under Leo XIII, he was entrusted by Pius X with the dossier, the most delicate of all, of the Church of France, and he then became secretary of the Congregation for Extraordinary Ecclesiastical Affairs. Benedict XV sent him to the emperor of Austria and then to the emperor of Germany so that he might look into the possibilities of limiting World War I or of bringing it to a quick end. Nuncio in Munich in 1917, then in Berlin in 1925, he gained from his twelve years in Germany a direct understanding of the country's problems and a particular attachment to its people, who appreciated, as did he, punctuality and diligent work. In 1929 Pius XI recalled Pacelli to Rome, where he was appointed secretary of state. His missions to France allowed him to gain an intimate familiarity with French culture and tradition. Finally, he was the first pope to visit North America. His long tour of the United States began a personal correspondence with President Roosevelt, a correspondence that enriched the papal secretariat with some rather new ways of addressing the pope: "You, whom I have the privilege of calling an old and good friend," but a correspondence that for some time offered a chance for world peace.

These antecedents were not, in fact, accidental. Pius XI had intentionally prepared his secretary of state to succeed him in the pontifical office. In this regard the testimony of Monsignor Tardini is formal and precise. The secretary of the Congregation for Extraordinary Ecclesiastical Affairs wrote on 22 February 1939:

> Many times His Holiness Pius XI spoke to me about his successor. For him, there was no doubt. His secretary of state had to become the next pope. The Holy Father told me that it was to prepare him for the tiara that he often sent him abroad, and even to the two Americas. One day, in October-November 1936, when his Eminence [Cardinal Pacelli] was in the United States, Pius XI highly praised his secretary of state and, looking me straight in the eye with his penetrating eyes, concluded by saying: "He will be a magnificent pope." (*Sarà un bel papa.*) He did not say: "He would be" or "He could be" but "he will be" without admitting any doubt. He said this on 12 November.

After the papal election the diplomats anxiously awaited to see who would be appointed secretary of state. On 11 March, the eve of the coronation, the name was made public; it was Cardinal Maglione who assumed the post vacated when Cardinal Pacelli was raised to the chair of St. Peter. Luigi Maglione had joined the Secretariat of State during the last war. Sent to Switzerland as a representative of the Holy See, and then as apostolic nuncio, he was transferred in 1926 to the nunciature in Paris, a position he occupied for ten years and where he was happily remembered.

Immediately under Cardinal Maglione was Monsignor Domenico Tardini, who since 1937 filled the post of secretary of the Congregation for Extraordinary Ecclesiastical Affairs and the first section of the Secretariat of State. Tardini enjoyed speaking in a humorous way; he could be biting, and yet he loved to reflect while he wrote. The numerous notes he left testify to his untiring labor on behalf of transmitting the orders of the pope, whom he intended to serve with complete loyalty; they also show that he critically reflected on the problems of the day. The substitute in the Secretariat of State, who was in charge of the second section, was Monsignor Giovanni Battista Montini. In principle, diplomatic questions were taken up by Tardini, his colleague. Yet it was not seldom that an ambassador found a reason to explain his views to Monsignor Montini, with the hope of finding in him, as one ambassador wrote, "a generous comprehension."

INTERNATIONAL SITUATION AND THREATS OF WAR

But how could the pope and his associates have any hope of success in prolonging Pius XI's peace efforts? From the time Germany became the Third Reich, submitting to Adolf Hitler's dictatorship, Europe each day came nearer to the moment when it would have to choose between war or servitude. The believed guarantees that the Treaty of Versailles would surround the future peace had fallen one after another. The successes of the Führer increased his audacity and strengthened the confidence of his partisans and allies. Whereas France used only diplomatic notes to respond to German rearmament, to the remilitarization of the Rhineland, and to the absorption of Austria, the Italian government, embittered by consecutive sanctions in regard to its war in Ethiopia, saw its future only in an understanding with the Third Reich. Europe witnessed the formation of two blocs: one that of the rich democracies asleep upon their laurels of 1918, and the other that of the needy dictatorships whose economies were devoted to armaments. In September 1938 the clash between them failed to take place. At the last moment, when mobilization was underway, the Munich conference, inspired by Mussolini, seemed to save everything. Pope Pius XI, who addressed to the people a vibrant call for peace, was nevertheless not mistaken: For him Munich was not only capitulation but the bankruptcy of the democracies.

In fact, it was quickly understood that Hitler, far from being satisfied with his latest acquisitions in Czechoslovakia, "once again planned to escape from obligations whose ink was not yet dry." The fear of new attacks weighed heavily upon the world at the time Cardinal Pacelli reached the pontifical throne.

This fear was justified. Pius XII had hardly put on the tiara on 12 March before the delegations of thirty-five nations, coming from the four corners of the world, when once again thunder burst over Europe. On 15 March German troops marched into Prague. The note of protest brought by the French ambassador to Wilhelmstrasse received from Weizsäcker, the German secretary of state, only a haughty response. Several days later a German ultimatum forced Lithuania to surrender

8

the city of Memel to the Reich. And Poland, which in the previous year did not hesitate to share in the spoilation of Czechoslovakia, in turn found itself threatened. Warsaw received from Berlin a note about the return of Danzig to the Reich and about German communications with east Prussia. The nuncio in Warsaw reported this to the Secretariat of State, which responded by enjoining him not to hesitate to use the telegraph for important news.

The occupation of Prague provoked a "revolution in English politics." Opinion in England, disquieted by the growth of Germany's power, was shocked by the violation of an agreement freely consented to during the previous September. Henceforth England intended to show its opposition, by arms if need be, to any further annexations by the Reich. Considering Poland as the first country to be threatened, on 31 March Chamberlain told the House of Commons: "In the case of any action whatsoever that clearly endangers Polish independence and that the Polish government believes is in its vital interest to resist with national force, His Majesty's government considers itself as immediately bound to support Poland by all possible means." And on 13 April the French government specified: "France and Poland guarantee each other immediately and directly against all direct or indirect threats that might strike at their vital interests." That same day France and England extended this guarantee to Greece and Romania.

But already Italy, to compensate itself for the Reich's expansion in central Europe, turned toward the Balkans. On 7 April, Good Friday, Italian planes bombed Tirana, and Italy occupied Albania.

Two days later, on Easter Sunday, the pope celebrated a pontifical mass. To the prelates and the faithful gathered about him in St. Peter's Basilica, and beyond those present to all people wishing to hear him, the pope spoke of peace, of the dangers threatening it, and of the ways to preserve it. The troubles of the present seemed to portend far worse evils. Pius XII showed that the root of these troubles and dangers was found in the misery suffered by many people, in the evil distribution of natural resources, in the lack of mutual trust among nations, in the violation of treaties that were made and of the word that was given; each day it was becoming more and more difficult to limit the arms race and to calm the situation.

President Roosevelt in the United States attempted a more direct approach. He addressed a long message to Hitler and to Mussolini, remarking that people were living in the distress of aggression, and he

9

invited these leaders to bind themselves for a period of ten years not to attack any of the thirty-one nations on a list he presented. Meanwhile, the claims of the parties involved could be discussed and peacefully resolved. Roosevelt also requested that Pius XII intervene with Hitler and Mussolini to support the president's message of 14 April. The Vatican's reply to the president was that the pope was attentively following his efforts on behalf of peace, but that it was not possible for the pope to take any action at this time that would deal with Hitler in the way desired. As to Mussolini, with whom relations were more comfortable, the Holy See had taken measures, yet it had few illusions as to the outcome.

The Vatican's reserve proved to be justified. In a speech given on 28 April before the Reichstag, Hitler launched a new attack against Poland; his words were more menacing than before. He denounced the English-German naval agreement and ridiculed the message from the president of the United States.

In view of the storm appearing over the horizon, uneasy souls turned to the pope as to a last hope. An English lady who signed herself "a very ordinary English woman" wrote from Bournemouth: "I ask that you use your great authority as a power for peace." Others were not content with asking that he intervene, but they offered plans of all sorts: a new truce of God, a new league of nations with its own military forces and executive body. Among such rather fanciful ideas, one suggestion somewhat constantly recurred, namely, that the pope convoke a world conference to seek a peaceful solution to pending problems. In England the *Catholic Herald* issued a petition asking the pope to take the initiative in this regard, and many letters and telegrams supported this proposal.

PROPOSAL FOR A CONFERENCE

Faced with these requests and with the growing danger, Pius XII determined to put diplomacy to the test by suggesting that an international conference be called. On 21 April the pope called in Father Tacchi Venturi, who since the negotiation of the Lateran accords had often served as intermediary between the Vatican and the Venetian Palace. Two days later Tacchi Venturi wrote to Mussolini and requested an interview, which was granted on 1 May. It took the Jesuit only fifteen minutes to explain the pope's intentions to the Duce: Faced with the evident danger threatening peace, Pius XII had in mind to invite the five European powers—France, Germany, England, Italy, and Poland—to a conference that would permit a discussion of the contested points from which a general conflagration might arise. The Duce used the lateness of the hour as a pretext for postponing his response to the next day. Nevertheless, he clearly judged the situation: "Germany cannot but imagine that what it accomplished in Czechoslovakia it will also accomplish in Poland: yet Poland, defending itself, will be crushed by the superiority of the German forces; and we will have the beginning of a European war."

The following day Father Tacchi Venturi received a definitive response from Mussolini, who said that he agreed with Pius XII. According to the Duce, what the pope was proposing had to be approved by the civilized world.

The next day, 3 May, four telegrams were sent by Cardinal Maglione to the Holy See's representatives in France, Germany, England, and Poland. The nuncios or apostolic delegates were directed to inform the respective governments that the pope, "deeply disturbed by the continually growing danger of war breaking out, intended to send a message to the five powers—France, Germany, England, Italy, and Poland—inviting them to solve among themselves, through a conference, the questions that threatened to unleash the conflict." The purpose of the conference was to solve the questions that divided, on the one hand, Germany and Poland and, on the other hand, France and Italy. The telegram addressed to the nuncio in Warsaw also invited him to recommend to Colonel Beck the greatest moderation in his next speech.

The reception of this message was not what the head of the Italian government had anticipated. As to the western powers, the disillusions that followed the Munich conference were too recent to allow them to be enthusiastic about repeating the experience. The French government showed itself very reserved vis-à-vis the papal proposal. Moreover, the French courteously added that this was not a refusal: It would be better to preserve intact the pope's authority for a time when there would be no other means to preserve the peace. The response of the British government, which first had to consult with its French and Polish allies, expressed the same reservations.

The pope's initiative took a more spectacular form in Germany. On 4 May the nuncio in Berlin, Archbishop Orsenigo, urgently requested an interview with Hitler, who was at Berchtesgaden. The next day a special plane was sent for the nuncio's use, and on 5 May at four in the afternoon the Holy See's representative explained the pope's plan to the Führer. The meeting, at which Ribbentrop, the foreign minister, was also present, lasted an hour. The thanks expressed by the chancellor for the pope's skillfulness, as well as Hitler's assurances that for now there was no question in Europe that could not be solved without conflict, were naturally unable to dispel all anxiety. Even though he had not yet concluded a military alliance with Mussolini, Hitler declared himself completely in solidarity with Italy. In other words, a Franco-Italian conflict would result in German intervention. Then Hitler let loose against England. The British guarantee given to Poland was the true cause of present tension since it inflamed the Warsaw government's intransigence. Finally, the Reich's chancellor and his foreign minister, who was on his way to Milan, postponed their definitive response to the time when they would be able to come to terms with Italy.

The following day in Milan Ribbentrop met with Count Ciano, Mussolini's son-in-law and foreign minister. Among the numerous problems considered, they discussed the conference proposed by the pope; the notes of the session conclude with this point: "All agree that the pope is to be thanked for his initiative, and at the same time he is to be asked to forgo his appeal to the five powers." On 9 May the response was communicated to Cardinal Maglione by Italy's ambassador to the Holy See.

Finally, the Polish government also expressed a negative response: Warsaw feared that such a conference would fail, and this would rather increase the danger of war; preferred was a more discrete intervention on the part of the pope to promote bilateral conversations between Poland and Germany.

In short, neither the western powers, who retained the smarting memory of the Munich conference and all that followed it, nor Germany and Italy, who apparently no longer hoped to regain by chance what they had succeeded in obtaining the previous September, wanted any such conference. For the moment, Berlin and Rome were content with locking up their agreement; Poland was satisfied with the French-British guarantee; and the two western powers preferred to perfect their diplomatic preparations in the direction of Russia and the United States. Nonetheless, the reception given by the governments to the initial Vatican initiatives seemed to open a way to further interventions since all recognized that the Holy See's authority could be, at the most acute moment of the crisis, the final resort for preserving peace. The British government showed itself especially receptive. Lord Halifax, the foreign secretary, in asking the pope to abandon temporarily his invitation to a conference, said he did not mean to deprive the cause of peace from any help that papal diplomacy might bring at certain critical moments.

Since there was no conference of the five governments, only one way remained open: that of using the Holy See's resources to promote direct talks between Germany and Poland, as well as between France and Italy. During the following months, June and July, the Vatican's activity was oriented along these lines.

FURTHER EFFORTS TOWARD PEACE

The conversation that the nuncio in Berlin had with Ribbentrop on 17 May was not, however, sufficient to dissipate concerns occasioned by the interview at Berchtesgaden. The violence of the Nazi press that was unleashed against Poland seemed to be a prelude to a Wehrmacht offensive. The nuncio asked Ribbentrop whether he feared war with the western powers. The foreign minister replied with conviction that France and England would never overcome Germany's western defenses, that German submarines would challenge the British fleet, and that if Poland were ever so foolish as to go to war, it would be crushed in no time: "In the case of war with a people like our own, with eighty-five million inhabitants armed to the teeth, Poland will have very few days during which to wage battle; it will be overwhelmingly crushed since it will be simultaneously attacked from ten sides." Faced with such confidence, the nuncio dared to inquire as to Russia's attitude. Ribbentrop lifted up before the Holy See's envoy part of the veil shrouding German-Soviet negotiations: The only point of current disagreement between the Reich and Russia is that of Communist propaganda. But "if Russia renounces this propaganda, nothing forbids us from reaching an agreement." According to this, the reflections of Archbishop Orsenigo, the nuncio, were moderately optimistic.

Several days later, on 22 May, Ciano and Ribbentrop signed at Berlin, and in the presence of Hitler and Goering, a treaty of alliance, the famous pact of Acier. It said that "notwithstanding the desires and hopes of the contracting parties, if it happens that one of them finds itself engaged in military operations with one or many powers, the other party to the contract will immediately intervene as a side-by-side ally, and will give support with all its military forces, on the ground, on sea, and in the air." And yet Mussolini, before signing the pact, informed Hitler that Italy would not be ready to engage in war before 1943.

So it was that, on the one hand, the French-English guarantees on behalf of Poland and Romania and, on the other hand, the Rome-Berlin axis increasingly tended to pitch the hostile blocs against each other. Nonetheless, this situation seemed to offer a possibility for work toward peace. At the time some believed that Mussolini, having great influence over Hitler, could exercise a restraining action on him. It was with this hope that François Poncet left the French embassy in Berlin for the Farnese Palace. This was also a hope for the Vatican. The pope wanted to bring France and Italy closer together, not only to avoid conflict between the two nations but also in the expectation of winning Mussolini over to the cause of peace in general.

On 22 May Cardinal Maglione, receiving Charles-Roux, who was the French ambassador to the Holy See, requested that France engage in a twofold effort: inviting Poland to be moderate in its relationship with Germany and improving France's own relationship with Italy, "the only power having a non-negligible influence on Germany and capable of restraining it." In the mind of the cardinal, Mussolini basically desired only peace, but the press had to avoid irritating him by its attacks.

After this initiative in regard to France, the Vatican turned its attention to Italy. The intermediary was again Father Tacchi Venturi. The secretary of state sent him a note whose substance was to be orally communicated to the head of the Italian government:

> It would greatly help the cause of peace if the head of the Italian government, His Excellency M. Mussolini, would use his great influence on Chancellor Hitler and on the German government so that the question of Danzig might be treated with a calm made ever more necessary by the delicate international situation.

On 6 June Father Tacchi Venturi again met with Mussolini. The Duce's reception was icy. Without saying a word Mussolini listened to

14

the statement of the Jesuit who, controlling the uneasiness that was taking hold of him, finally said: "But Your Excellency, do you believe that war is inevitable?"

"Most assuredly," replied the Duce.

"Perhaps because, as is believed, Russia is in the process of concluding a treaty with France and England?"

"A treaty means absolutely nothing," responded Mussolini. "What it does is completely indifferent."

Pius XII, not taking seriously Mussolini's bad temper, concluded that the Duce wanted to provoke the Holy See to a new intervention.

But Germany pursued its claims regarding Poland, and it appeared clear that the western powers, more and more confident in their military preparations and also hoping to reach an agreement with Russia, would no more yield to Hitler's threats. On 10 June the nuncio in Paris met with Léger, who was the general secretary at the Quai d'Orsay and who represented the most belligerent faction within the French government. Léger did not want to hear any talk about a conference with the totalitarian powers, and he was completely optimistic on the question of a conflict. Germany's internal situation was becoming more critical each day; the people there were poorly nourished and physically weak. Should war break out, there would not be a general mobilization. The nuncio's polite skepticism did not appear to disturb his own conviction.

Three days later the nuncio to Italy met with Count Ciano. Here the news was better. Ciano categorically stated that in six months' time there would be no danger of war, for Germany had no intention of attacking Poland. In his opinion Poland was the only danger since "in its fear of being attacked, it can from one moment to the next do something foolish"; and so it was in regard to Poland that the pope, according to Ciano, had to use his powers of persuasion.

Ciano was heard, and Archbishop Cortesi, the nuncio, received orders to renew the counsels of moderation that the pope had already addressed to the Poles and also to intervene with Poland's cardinal primate so that clergy and faithful be advised to remain calm. After this Cardinal Maglione turned to Berlin and informed Archbishop Orsenigo of the steps that had been taken concerning Poland; furthermore, the Holy See had reason to hope that the German government would do everything possible to avoid provocation, to avoid any incident that could lead to conflict. On 30 June Archbishop Borgongini Duca, the nuncio to Italy, had another audience with Count Ciano. The nuncio told him how the Holy See, on its own, had intervened to exhort the Polish government to prudence. And the Holy See was now counting on Italy to exercise a moderating influence on Hitler. The minister's response was most reassuring: "Germany will not move without our consent, and neither Mussolini nor I want war." But these affirmations could mean not that Hitler was relinquishing his plans regarding Danzig, but simply that he counted on accomplishing them without starting a war.

Yet neither Paris nor London intended it in this way. The ambiguity could be fatal. Again on 30 June the British ambassador to France communicated to his government some news that had reached Paris: Hitler was ready to organize a popular movement in Danzig; it was to proclaim the city's attachment to the Reich. The Führer was convinced that neither France nor England would do anything and that they would even force Poland to accept a fait accompli. According to Daladier, the president of the French council, the only way to abort these plans was a very firm declaration on the part of the French and English: Berlin was to be warned that it was deluding itself in this regard and that an armed attack on Danzig would mean a general war.

Osborne, the British representative to the Holy See, was surely informed immediately. He came to tell Cardinal Maglione that perhaps Italy was deluding itself in its belief that if Hitler occupied Danzig, England would not react; on the contrary, in such a case England would begin hostilities. The precedent of Germany in 1914 declaring war on France and counting on British neutrality was in the minds of all. Cardinal Maglione called in the Italian ambassador and on 3 July informed him of England's decision.

The next day, in Paris, Archbishop Valeri drew up a report on the international situation. In general, French opinion was very favorable to the pope's initiatives on behalf of peace. But the nuncio had the impression that neither France nor England was preaching moderation to Warsaw. "The two major western powers, as has been publicly stated, are thus ready to march side by side with Poland when Poland, to defend its rights which are threatened, decides to take up arms against Germany. And so it is into Poland's hands that France and England have handed over the decision in regard to *casus belli*." The French government, under no illusions, was completing its military preparations. And the nuncio, who had already signed his report, added a postscript. He recently learned from Italy's ambassador that the Italian foreign minister had sent a note to the German ambassador, informing him of France's and England's irrevocable decision to come to Poland's aid if Poland were attacked. In spite of this, the German ambassador himself feared that Hitler's entourage was deluded in this respect. And so Germany would repeat its error of 1914. The nuncio's letter was dated 4 July.

CRISIS OVER DANZIG AND THE GERMAN-SOVIET TREATY

During the morning of 7 July, upon orders from the pope, the secretary of state again told the Italian ambassador that England as well as France would defend Poland and Danzig. The cardinal here was repeating the very words of Valeri: "There are still people around Hitler who are misguided here. An error of judgment like that of 1914 would be fatal for Germany and...for Italy." That very day the Italian ambassador informed his government of this.

Nevertheless, July passed with relative calm in the Vatican. But in August the situation again took a turn for the worse. For a long time the Danzig senate reluctantly supported the Polish custom agents and attempted to impede them. On 4 August the Polish government sent an inflammatory note to the president of the free city's senate. It stated that the Polish government had learned that the local authorities would oppose any inspections carried out by Polish custom agents, a measure already communicated to those agents. The Polish government set six in the evening of 5 August as a deadline for rescinding this order. Meanwhile, the Polish agents, with guns, carried out their functions. On 9 August the Polish chargé d'affaires in Berlin received from Weizsäcker, the German secretary of state, a note of protest: It was with great surprise that the German government had learned of Warsaw's intervention with the Danzig senate. Warsaw's reply had the same tone: The Polish government "had learned with the greatest surprise" of the German declaration. Henceforth it would consider as acts of aggression any steps taken by the Reich to the detriment of Polish rights and interests. During this exchange of notes the senate placed the city in a state of defense, and some "tourists," coming from the Reich, arrived to increase the strength of the movement whose purpose was to declare that the free city be returned to Germany.

17

On 11 August Hitler held a meeting at Berchtesgaden with Burckhardt, the high commissioner of the League of Nations in Danzig. The Reich's chancellor was extremely irritated at the Poles. Nonetheless, he reaffirmed that the definitive role of the territorial questions could be postponed, but it was necessary that the German minorities living in Polish territory should no longer be harassed by the Poles since this involved a question of German honor.

The pope had not yet learned of this conversation when on 14 August the nuncio in Warsaw telegraphed the Vatican that for the last fifteen days Germany had been massing troops on the Polish frontier. The first thing Cardinal Maglione did on the following day was to telegraph Cortesi requesting that he "discretely ask this government [namely, Warsaw] if it believed that the Secretariat of State could do something, and if so what." While awaiting a reply, the cardinal secretary of state on 16 August received the Polish ambassador: In the eyes of the latter, the question of Danzig was a pretext to attack Poland in order to reach the Ukraine and Romania's oil fields, but Poland was calmly awaiting an attack, certain that it would be defended by the western powers. As to Russia, the ambassador had no misgivings, but the cardinal was not so tranquil. Other information—the note does not specify its source—confirmed for him that Hitler was using Danzig only as a pretext for attacking Poland, but the source also warned that Russia had a secret understanding with Germany as to a new division of Poland. Nonetheless, Berlin still nourished the fatal illusion that England and France would allow this to happen.

In fact on 11 August, 12 August, and 13 August Ciano met in Salzburg with Hitler and Ribbentrop, who no longer concealed that an attack on Poland was imminent. In vain did Ciano try to persuade them to solve the problem of Danzig through diplomacy. Osborne, who communicated this news to Monsignor Tardini in a note dated 19 August, admitted viva voce that he no longer saw how war could be avoided.

A month earlier the French ambassador in London sent to the British Foreign Office a memorandum emphasizing the urgency of concluding a treaty of mutual assistance with Russia. Should these negotiations fail," he wrote, "every initiative on behalf of French-English security in Europe will be shaken...the result of the negotiations will, in a definitive way, hold the balance between war and peace in the weeks ahead." But on 21 August, late in the evening, the German press agency, the Deutsches Nachrichtenbüro, issued the following announcement:

> The German and Soviet governments have agreed to establish a mutual non-aggression pact. Herr von Ribbentrop, the foreign minister, will travel to Moscow on Monday, 23 August, to conclude the negotiations.

It was easy to draw conclusions such as those indicated earlier in the French memorandum. As early as the next day Daladier, president of the council, told the British ambassador that he believed Hitler would march on Poland within two or three days. It was true, as Ciano noted in his diary on 23 August, that "France and England are making it known everywhere that they will likewise intervene in an eventual conflict." The Warsaw government pretended to receive the news with a great deal of detachment, and Papée, the ambassador, sent the secretary of state a note stating that he did not attach much importance to the German-Soviet pact: Russia wanted to remain outside the conflict and would not move against Poland.

In the Vatican, which for some time anticipated such a pact, a more realistic judgment was being made. On 22 August, in the evening, Osborne sent the papal secretary of state a note from Lord Halifax on what the Holy See was doing "to avert the catastrophe that seems to be approaching." The British government was ready to do everything in its power to facilitate an equitable solution to the pressing problems by means of open negotiations between Germany and Poland. But an unexpected event could prevent the British government from using diplomacy. Halifax hoped that in such a case the pope would bring to bear the full weight of his authority through a final appeal to reason. The following day Osborne returned to Monsignor Tardini with his suggestion for a solemn radio message in which Lord Halifax was placing his last hope.

On the same day, 23 August, Neville Henderson, the British ambassador in Berlin, flew to Berchtesgaden to give Hitler a letter from Chamberlain and to notify him that Great Britain would go to war in order to defend Poland if the latter were attacked. Once it gave its guarantee to Poland, Great Britain had to keep its word, which throughout the ages it had never broken. It would cease to be England if it did so. And so the dictator should not delude himself in thinking that he could swallow up Poland and still avoid a European war. The warning could not be more clear; it could not be said that England was responsible for war because of any ambiguous position. Yet on the following day Henderson wrote that "the conversation I had with him [Hitler] yesterday has confirmed my belief that it is quite useless to have any discussion with him." Henderson had no less of a liking for the Poles, whose behavior was foolish, or for the Russians, whose treachery placed England in a very unfavorable position. It was indeed a time for a last call to reason, a call the pope could still issue.

APPEAL OF 24 AUGUST

In the Vatican and in other capitals 24 August 1939 was a day of trepidation and feverish work. The morning witnessed a line of ambassadors at the Secretariat of State. At quarter to ten it was Charles-Roux, the French ambassador, who was quite pessimistic. Either today or tomorrow Hitler will attack Poland. The pope has to condemn aggression against a Catholic country. At half past ten the English minister returned for at least the third visit in three days: He gave Monsignor Tardini a summary of Chamberlain's letter warning Hitler of England's irrevocable decision to assist Poland if the latter were attacked. After Osborne there was the Marquess Giustiniani, a counselor at the Italian embassy to the Holy See. He admitted that after the German-Soviet pact Italy no longer had the means to intervene effectively, and he did not see how war could be avoided. At quarter past twelve in the afternoon the Polish ambassador arrived and repeated that Poland had never counted on Russia's assistance. He wanted the Holy Father to condemn the impending aggression. At one o'clock the minister from Yugoslavia again came looking for information.

During the day a telegram arrived from the nuncio in Berlin. Archbishop Orsenigo reported on Henderson's meeting with Hitler and on the fury of the latter who, after twenty years of trying to bring England and Germany closer to each other, saw England opposing all his country's claims. Berlin saw war as imminent, and there was already talk of an armistice to keep the peace.

FINAL EFFORTS AND PEACE PROPOSALS

While Monsignor Tardini was receiving the diplomats—and they all confirmed the approaching danger—the Secretariat of State was preparing the text of a papal radio message in which people would see the ultima ratio for peace. At least four different drafts were prepared and submitted to the pope, who in turn chose the text written by Monsignor Montini, the substitute, and corrected it with his own hand. At seven that evening Pius XII addressed the world with his call for negotiations and peace:

> Once again a grave hour sounds for the whole human family, an hour of terrible deliberations. Our heart cannot be disinterested in this, nor can the spiritual power given Us by God to guide souls along the paths of justice and of peace.

Having no arms other than the word of truth, yet speaking in the name of God, who is the Father of all people, and in the name of Christ, in whom all are brethren, and in the Spirit of love, the sovereign pontiff requested governments to seek out in peaceful negotiations the solution to the problems placing humanity at the brink of a dreadful conflict:

> Justice prevails through reason and not through arms. Empires not based on peace are not blessed by God. Politics divorced from justice betrays those who wish it so.

> The danger is imminent, but there is still time.

> Nothing is lost with peace. Everything can be lost by war....

> May those who are strong hear us so that they do not become weak through injustice. May those who are powerful hear us if they desire their power to be not destruction but support for peoples and a protection of tranquility in order and work. We appeal to them through the blood of Christ whose strength, victorious over the world, was sweetness in life and in death....

It was not to be expected that the pope's speech would deeply resound in the hearts of the leaders of the Third Reich. Nonetheless, Hitler, who had decided to attack Poland during the night of the 25th

21

or 26th of August, hesitated at the last moment and suspended the order to move forward. He wanted to make one last attempt to separate England and France from Poland. On 25 August at half past one in the afternoon the chancellor of the Reich sent a verbal note to the British ambassador and repeated his offer of friendship. Coulondre, the French ambassador, received a similar notice. Then, on the same day, Ciano telephoned to the Italian ambassador in Berlin a letter from Mussolini to Hitler, and at half past five Attolico brought it to Wilhelmstrasse. The Duce explained to the Führer that Italy was not in a position to provide military support in any conflict that might break out immediately after a German attack on Poland. The pope's appeal was followed by a respite on the way leading to disaster.

The diplomats used this interval to try to resume negotiations, which Pius XII also, again, tried to get underway. Telegrams crisscrossed between the Vatican and the nunciatures in Berlin and Warsaw with proposals on the fate of the ethnic minorities, which at the time appeared to be the crucial point. But on 28 August Monsignor Tardini had to inform Archbishop Orsenigo that such a plan was not feasible.

On the same day the French ambassador brought Monsignor Montini an article by George Goyau on Poland and its Catholic loyalty down through the centuries. Charles-Roux wanted at least a sign, a public statement, from the pope on behalf of Poland "before it undergoes the great ordeal that will pounce upon it." This request was transmitted to Pius XII, whose response was noted by Monsignor Tardini: "His Holiness says that this would be overdoing it. We cannot forget that forty million Catholics live in the Reich. What would happen to them after such an action on the part of the Holy See? The pope has already spoken and clearly so."

Nonetheless, Pius XII was not yet ready to give up. On 29 August the cardinal secretary of state communicated the pope's instructions to Father Tacchi Venturi, who was to tell Mussolini: (1) that the pope was very happy with everything that Mussolini had increasingly done for the sake of peace; (2) that the pope was asking the Duce to intensify these efforts now that the danger was increasing. On the same day at five in the afternoon Mussolini received Tacchi Venturi. This time the Duce appeared to be flattered by the appeal the pope was making to his good offices. Mussolini himself declared that it would be a crime to unleash, on account of Danzig, a war that could mark the end of present civilization. But Germany was now very strong, stronger than in

1914, when it had taken the whole world to overthrow it. Yet he believed that there was only one way out, namely, if Poland made substantial concessions to Germany. The Duce personally had drawn up a draft to be used as a basis for negotiations between Poland and Germany. On the one hand, Poland would not be opposed to Danzig being returned to the Reich; on the other hand, Poland would request that direct discussions begin with Germany in regard to the conditions for Polish commerce in the port of Danzig, on the question of the Corridor, and on the situation of the minorities. Mussolini then asked the pope to send, by means of the papal nuncio in Warsaw, a message to the president of the Polish republic explaining to him that, faced with imminent peril, he must examine these proposals. Mussolini believed that Hitler should and would accept them. If the German leader refused to do so, then the whole world would stand against him, and Poland would find itself in a very favorable situation. Father Tacchi Venturi was also instructed to raise the question of Italian neutrality in case war should occur. He did not fail to do so, this second part of his mission being even easier than the first. As soon as he raised the topic, he learned that Mussolini, "without betraying the Axis, had already considered how he would excuse himself from entering the field of battle."

Once the Secretariat of State had received Mussolini's response, Pius XII had a telegram prepared for Warsaw. Doing so, the Vatican was undertaking an initiative whose risks it did not conceal, and Monsignor Tardini believed he should emphasize its drawbacks in a personal letter addressed to the cardinal secretary of state. In the first place, "the Holy See would seem to be playing Hitler's game. Hitler could still eat up quite a mouthful, namely, Danzig, and next spring he would again begin at zero." Second:

> The Holy See would seem to have brought about a new Munich, which consisted in the following: Hitler complaining loudly, threatening, and then obtaining everything he wanted. And so, in regard to Danzig, Hitler's complaints and threats would obtain, under the auspices of the Holy See, that city's return to the Reich, something impossible to obtain through peaceful negotiations. Third, the Holy See would seem to be a little too closely linked to Mussolini since everyone will know that he had suggested this idea.

Nonetheless, in a last attempt to keep peace, the head of the first section of the Secretariat of State did not reject the proposal. The telegram containing Mussolini's ideas was sent on 30 August. Speaking in the name of the Holy Father, the nuncio in Warsaw made it the subject of a personal communication with Moscicki, the president of the Polish republic. And before sending the telegram, Cardinal Maglione communicated its substance to Great Britain's representative, who, agreeing with the Holy See's initiative, informed his government of it.

The following day, 31 August, the reply of the nuncio in Warsaw reached the Vatican: In his opinion it was difficult to request an audience with the president of the republic, who was not effectively in control. Furthermore, a general mobilization had already been called for, and the nuncio did not believe that the idea of the concessions proposed would be favorably received. Pius XII did not give up, and once again two telegrams were sent to Warsaw: The nuncio was to bring to the president of the council the communication that had been sent to him for the president of the republic; and the nuncio was to insist that the Polish government allow, in principle, an international control regarding the alleged mistreatment of German minorities.

Finally, the same day, 31 August, the pope repeated, but under a less solemn form, his appeal of 24 August. He sent a final call for negotiations and peace to the five powers that were directly involved as well as to the ambassador of Spain, and even, bypassing any scruples of protocol, to the U.S. ambassador at the Quirinal. Not all bridges had been destroyed between Berlin, Rome, London, and Paris, and a Polish negotiator was waiting in Berlin. The pope did not want to give up hope.

> His Holiness, in the name of God, consequently entreats the German and Polish governments to do whatever they can to avoid any incident and to refrain from undertaking any measure that might aggravate the present tension. The governments of England, of France, and of Italy are asked to support his request.

This message was sent to its intended recipients on 31 August, between twenty after one and quarter to two. In fact, the time for bargaining had passed. What took place on 31 August at half past six between Ribbentrop and the Polish ambassador at Wilhelmstrasse was only a sham. From Warsaw, at eleven thirty in the evening, Archbishop

Cortesi, the nuncio, informed the Vatican that he had passed the last message of the Holy See to the government and that he was awaiting a reply to be given on the next day.

When this response reached Rome on 1 September, the German armies had already invaded Polish territory. Also, when during the morning of 1 September the French ambassador came to request from the cardinal secretary of state an explicit condemnation of German aggression, Maglione replied "that the documents and the facts speak for themselves."

For a long time Hitler believed that war would be confined to the east. But the general mobilization ordered in France made him understand that the western powers would keep the promises they had made to Poland. On 2 September Mussolini contacted Hitler with the idea of holding a conference on 5 September. But England and France let it be known that as a condition for doing so the German troops had to return to their home bases. Mussolini withdrew his proposal, and the next day, 3 September, England and France declared war on Germany.

On 9 September, Sir d'Arcy Osborne, Great Britain's minister to the Holy See, wrote to Cardinal Maglione:

> During our last conversation you asked whether I believed that the Holy See had done everything possible on behalf of peace. Without hesitation I responded that I was convinced this was true. I reported our conversation to Lord Halifax, who instructed me to inform Your Eminence that he completely agrees with what I told you.

CHAPTER 2

Pius XII, Roosevelt, and Mussolini*

~.~

A T THE VERY MOMENT when the roaring of guns appeared to impose silence on all other voices, Pius XII did not cease speaking out on behalf of peace. The objectives of his diplomacy during this time of war were to limit the conflict and to proceed as quickly as possible to peace with justice and security.

First, he strove to resist any extension of the war. Till the beginning of September 1939 the pope's dealings with Mussolini were geared toward maintaining peace in Europe. Mussolini and Ciano had in fact tried, although in vain, to restrain Hitler and Ribbentrop from going down the path of war. The Duce and his foreign minister had at least informed the Führer that under present circumstances Italy would be unable to enter the war as Germany's ally. In this respect Pius XII's wishes were granted. Nonetheless, he had to reckon with Mussolini's old grudges against the Allies, with the ideological divergences separating Fascist Italy from the western democracies, and finally with the pact of Acier. In addition, while requesting Mussolini's help on behalf of world peace, the Holy See was also concerned about what Italy itself would do. When on 29 August Father Tacchi Venturi had, in the pope's name, asked the Duce to undertake a final effort regarding peace, Mussolini showed very little hope, but he was completely reassuring on the question of Italian neutrality. Two days later Archbishop Borgongini Duca, the nuncio, met with Ciano, who said that he and Mussolini were fighting like lions to prevent war. The nuncio asked with all frankness: "Am I to think that, no matter what happens, Italy will refrain from taking action?" The minister smiled and replied:

*Documentation for chapter 2: See *ADSS,* vol. 1. Add *FRUS,* 1940, vols. 1 and 2; DDI, series 9, vols. 3 and 4. Also see Owen Chadwick, *Britain and the Vatican,* with special reference to the archives of the Foreign Office: F.O. 800 / 318; Ciano, *Diario;* André François-Poncet, *Au palais Farnèse.*

"That's a different question. Before doing so, Italy will look twice." And in fact on 1 September, at the very moment when German troops were invading Poland, Italy announced its nonbelligerence.

Nonetheless, disturbing rumors were reaching the Vatican. On 5 September Prince Aldobrandini told undersecretary Monsignor Montini that, according to Ciano himself, Italian neutrality was still very uncertain. There was no agreement on this within the government. The foreign minister and the undersecretaries for war, for the navy, and for the air force were in favor of neutrality, but Mussolini and some of his ministers wanted to align themselves immediately with Germany, and the initial German successes in Poland aroused the Duce's desire for war. On the morning of 6 September Pius XII called in Father Tacchi Venturi and instructed him to relay the pope's congratulations to Mussolini for what he had done for peace and to urge him to continue to remain neutral.

That very evening at quarter to eight Tacchi Venturi was received by Ciano, to whom he had been sent by Mussolini. Ciano, on behalf of the head of the government, informed the Jesuit of the following: (1) Italy's 1 September declaration of nonbelligerency "truly and correctly is equivalent to a statement of neutrality; (2) this declaration remains firm, and it is Mussolini's intention that it remain so till the conclusion of the conflict, which, it must be added, could end in several weeks time, namely, once the war against Poland ceases; (3) it cannot be humanly foreseen what events might oblige Italy, in spite of its present intention to remain neutral, to adopt another course of action." Ciano added that it was true that some government members were said to favor Italy's participation in the conflict, but that he himself continued to defend, and strongly so, neutrality just as he had supported it in the past.

Thus assured by Rome as to the immediate future, the Holy See began to pay close attention to the positions of the other governments. On 11 September Valerio Valeri, the nuncio in Paris, met with Georges Bonnet, the French foreign minister. From this meeting the nuncio concluded that the French government was confident that Italy would remain neutral and that it did not share the opinion of those who were hoping that Italy would join the conflict; even more, Bonnet was ready to listen to Italy's requests or desires. The nuncio did not fail to stress that the Holy See had already done and was still doing everything possible to restrict the conflict and that it attached the greatest importance to good relations between France and Italy.

But the following week Daladier, the president of the council, replaced Bonnet at the Quai d'Orsay: A "war cabinet" had to be formed. It was anticipated that the neutral countries would be pressured to take sides. Also feared was the influence of those who believed that France would gain by engaging in war with Italy. Furthermore, some claimed that Daladier still held a personal grudge against Mussolini, whom he accused of having deceived him at Munich as to Hitler's true intentions.

To this disturbing information of 15 September, Valeri added on 21 September and 28 September much more reassuring news, which he corroborated in the following report: "As to Italy, at least for now, thanks be to God, the outlook continues to be good, and it is even said that it might sell airplanes and engines to France."

A letter from the nuncio to Italy, directly addressed to the pope, coincided with the news from Paris. On 28 September Borgongini Duca was received by Count Ciano and conveyed the pope's thanks for the work that had been done on behalf of peace. Ciano perfectly understood the meaning of these good wishes and again affirmed that he would continue "to battle vigorously for peace in general and for peace as regards Italy in particular." The conversation continued with Anfuso, the head of the cabinet, who unequivocally stated: "Set your mind at rest. There will be no military operations. In all confidence I tell you that there will be no war since we have nothing and since the Italian people do not want war. Ciano has done wonders along these lines."

Nonetheless, Pius XII did not overlook any opportunity to support the neutrality of the Italian government. On 7 December he received the diplomatic credentials of Dino Alfieri, the new Italian ambassador to the Vatican. In his response to the diplomat, Pius XII stigmatized doctrines that "humanize the divine and divinize the human"; it was not very difficult to recognize here the national-socialist ideology and that of the communists. The pope did not hesitate to predict their collapse: "Each of these errors, as in general all error, has its time: a time of expansion and a time of decline, its noon and its twilight or its dizzy fall." Then the pope expressed confidence that his concerns on behalf of peace with justice would always find an echo "in the courageous, strong, and hard-working Italian people, whose wise leaders and their own inner feelings have till now happily preserved them from the danger of being implicated in the war."

This public statement praising Italian neutrality was soon

repeated by the pope at a more solemn occasion when, two weeks later, on 21 December, he received at the Vatican the king and queen of Italy. The sovereign pontiff directly addressed to Victor Emmanuel the words of praise he uttered fifteen days earlier before the king's ambassador regarding the preservation of peace in Italy:

> At a time when other people are caught up in the war or are threatened by it, and when tranquility and peace have been expelled from the hearts of so many people, Italy, on the other hand, always watchful and strong under the majestic and wise hand of its emperor-king, and through the clear-sighted direction of its rulers, remains in peace.

During this visit Count Ciano was decorated with the Pontifical Order of the Golden Spur, and the certificate, signed by the cardinal secretary of state, stressed at great length what Ciano had done to preserve peace.

Deviating from protocol, Pius XII decided to go to the Quirinal and himself visit the Italian sovereigns whom he had received at the Vatican. On 28 December 1939 he entered the palace built by his predecessors and which, since 1870, had been the residence of the kings of Italy. The welcome given by the royalty was equal to this historic occasion. And the blessing invoked by the pope upon his royal hosts was again a blessing of peace. "May the peace that keeps Italy strong and respected before the world, a peace safeguarded by the wisdom of those directing it, become a stimulus and an invitation to future agreements for those who presently engaged in combat on land, in the air, and on the seas." Such brief allusions, enclosed in his public speeches, show that the pope had used his private meetings with the king and queen to insist that Italy remain at peace, as he had said to the French ambassador.

CHRISTMAS MESSAGES AND PRESIDENT ROOSEVELT

Between the king's visit to the Vatican and that of the pope to the Quirinal, Pius XII had other opportunities for returning to the major issue of peace. Christmas 1939 did not bring a truce to a Europe at war, as some were hoping. In fact, the minimal military activity taking place at the time would have made such a truce something of a formality.

Rather, the feast saw a new message from Pius XII. On 24 December at half past ten in the morning, directly addressing the prelates of the Roman Curia and through them the whole world, the pope spoke of peace. He did not call for negotiations or for the cessation of hostilities. What he requested was a long-term preparation for a future peace, both solid and lasting. After dwelling on the ultimate causes of war, on the horrors and the violations of law accompanying the present conflict, Pius XII listed under five headings the indispensable presuppositions for establishing world peace with order and justice:

1. Assuring each nation, whether large or small, its right to life and independence;
2. Freeing nations from the burden of an arms race through a mutually agreed upon, organic, and progressive disarmament;
3. Rebuilding and creating international institutions while bearing in mind the weaknesses of previous ones;
4. Recognizing, especially in the interests of European order, the rights of ethnic minorities;
5. Finally, recognizing above all human laws and conventions "the holy and immovable divine law."

At the conclusion of this message, which remained on a theoretical level, Pius XII changed his tone. He was happy, he said, to relay some good news to his listeners. The president of the United States had decided to establish official relations between the White House and the Vatican, and it would not be long before the president's personal representative came to Rome.

While Hitler's Germany was represented at the Vatican by an ambassador who, by reason of seniority, was dean of the diplomatic corps, the United States had no official representative to the pope. In fact, the intermediary between the Vatican and the White House was the apostolic delegate in Washington, Archbishop Amleto G. Cicognani, who was the pope's representative to the Catholic Church in the United States. When on 31 August 1939 the pope wanted to inform the American government about his previous message on behalf of peace, he had to instruct his nuncio to Italy to give it to the American ambassador at the Quirinal. To avoid such an awkward situation, Roosevelt decided to send to the Vatican a diplomat who would represent not the United States but the president, and he chose the Christmas season as a time for making his plan public and for appointing Myron C. Taylor as his emissary. In a cable dated 23 December and addressed to Pius XII, the U.S. president began by recalling the sad conditions of a world at war. He nonetheless took heart, he said, by remembering that it was during an equally disordered world that the prophet Isaiah had foretold the birth of Christ. And he continued to have confidence in the spiritual forces that always restored order and light after the darkest periods of human history. The president sent his Christmas message to the heads of the principal religious communities in the United States, Protestant and Jewish, but the cable sent to Rome was different since its conclusion announced the appointment of the president's representative to the pope "in order that our parallel endeavors for peace and the alleviation of suffering might be assisted."

The president's message was given to Archbishop Spellman of New York, who had been urgently called to Washington. Taking it to the apostolic delegation, he requested that it be immediately sent to the Vatican by means of an uncoded cable. The message arrived during the day on 23 December. And so Pius XII concluded his Christmas message by informing the Sacred College of Myron Taylor's appointment as President Roosevelt's personal envoy. The pope concluded:

> This news could not have made Us more happy since it represents, on the part of the eminent leader of such a great and powerful nation, a valuable and promising contribution toward what is of concern to us, namely, obtaining both a just and honorable peace as well as a more effective and broader means of alleviating the sufferings of the victims of war. We strongly desire to express our best wishes and sentiments of gratitude for this noble and generous act by President Roosevelt.

The pope's response to the handwritten letter that followed the cable did not wait till after Myron Taylor's arrival. On 7 January Pius XII wrote Roosevelt that his message had given light, with the beam of consolation, hope, and confidence, to all who were distressed by the war. As for himself, the vicar on earth of the Prince of Peace, he had dedicated all his efforts toward preserving and restoring peace, and he intended to pursue the path laid out by his apostolic mission. That the head of the great North American federation thus stood in the vanguard of those defending peace was something the pope greeted with grateful joy and increased confidence.

MUSSOLINI'S LETTER TO HITLER

Two days earlier a letter from Mussolini had left Rome, this time in the direction of the Reich. The head of the Italian government was not present at the meetings between Pius XII and the Italian sovereigns. Nonetheless, after the pope's repeated appeals on behalf of Italian neutrality, the Duce believed he had to reassure Hitler as to his own intentions. In a letter dated 5 January Mussolini, using the occasion of the new year, wrote to the Führer:

> The recent exchange of visits between the king and the pope were primarily of an internal, not international, nature. The conversations were brief and general, without producing any decision or proposals, and it could not have been otherwise.

And yet, after having dismissed the idea of the pope being able to influence Italian policy, Mussolini informed Hitler of his own concerns about the question of combat, and he suggested that the reconstitution of an independent Polish state, under the protection of the German Empire could lead to peace. Would this not eliminate the reason why the French and English entered the war? Surely he knew that the democracies would not capitulate to the Führer's Germany. "But it is not certain that the Allies can be brought to their knees or even divided. To believe so is to delude oneself. The United States will not allow the democracies to be completely defeated." Better, then, to forgo the risks and sacrifices of a massive offensive on the western front if peace can be obtained through an agreement based on recognizing Poland as a free state.

Hitler and Ribbentrop were little prepared to listen to such language. Giving an account of the audience during which Italy's ambassador presented Mussolini's letter to Hitler, the Italian diplomat wrote to Ciano: "They are sure that 1940 will bring us victory."

THE GERMAN GENERALS

Pius XII, however, was still hopeful in regard to Germany. On 11 January 1940 he summoned Great Britain's minister and explained that he had met with an envoy from some German military leaders. A grand offensive was being prepared for mid-February or even earlier. But if England could give the generals an assurance of a peace that would be neither a new Compiègne nor a peace à la Wilson, they were ready to replace the present government with a regime that could be dealt with; the basis for this would be the reestablishment of Poland and Czechoslovakia, yet keeping Austria as part of the Reich. Pius XII said that he trusted the good faith of the envoy, although he could not guarantee that of those who sent him or their ability to bring about a change in the regime.

The following month Osborne, England's ambassador, sent Lord Halifax a new message from the pope. Every precaution was taken to ensure secrecy. During the evening of 6 February the *maestro di camera,* who was in charge of escorting visitors to the pope, asked Osborne to come the next day to his office, from which the diplomat would be discretely led to the pope's apartment. Osborne was not to come dressed for an audience, and nothing would be made public. The visit took place, and Pius XII told the diplomat that he had received an intermediary, someone worthy of confidence, from German military circles; an important general was involved in this, and so the matter should be taken very seriously. The message received by the pope was that a notable part of the army wanted to rid itself of Hitler. The action would occur outside Berlin, and so it was possible that for a time there could be two governments, possibly even a civil war. The new regime would be moderate and conservative, although in the beginning it would be a military dictatorship. Germany would move to a federal and decentralized government. What the authors of the plan wanted from the pope was the British government's assurance that Austria's union with the Reich be retained as a starting point for negotiations. Despite his repugnance to pass on this information, Pius XII felt obliged in conscience not to let it slip away, no matter how little chance there was to save lives. The pope asked for no reply. And yet it was requested that if Osborne had anything to communicate to the pope, it should be passed on through the *maestro di camera* since the cardinal secretary of state had not been informed of all this.

Faithful to the pope's instructions to guarantee secrecy, Osborne himself typed the letter that was to be sent to Lord Halifax, and he kept no copy of it. Eight days later Halifax replied that if the designers of the plan were in a position to follow through with it, conditions for peace would have to be discussed with the French government. What he could say was that henceforth the Allies viewed the war's purpose as not the division of Germany but the achievement of European security, and in this regard the establishment of a federal government was of great interest. As to Austria, the country itself had to decide by means of a referendum whether it wanted to be part of this federation.

TAYLOR, WELLES, AND RIBBENTROP IN ROME

At the end of the month President Roosevelt's personal representative arrived in Rome. It was indeed as a messenger of peace that Myron Taylor was welcomed at the Vatican on 27 February 1940. He was first received with his retinue in a public audience during which he presented Pius XII with his credentials, a handwritten letter from Roosevelt signed "Cordially, your friend." He then spent three quarters of an hour alone with the pope, their conversation revolving around the topic of peace. Since the Allies simply did not trust Hitler's government, they were not disposed to deal with this dictator. The German people were dissatisfied, but being closely watched by the secret police, they could do nothing. The same was true for the army. The Allies believed that Germany was incapable of sustaining an extended war but that it could fight on for a year or more. In Italy the pope had no direct contacts with Mussolini, but he knew that Ciano was opposed to war.

Myron Taylor's mission in the Vatican was part of President Roosevelt's plan aimed at restoring peace in Europe. At the time when the president's personal representative was arriving in Rome, Sumner Welles, who was the undersecretary of state in the United States, was on a mission as the extraordinary envoy to the governments that were at war or were threatened by war. Having disembarked at Naples, as did Myron Taylor, the undersecretary started his tour of the European capitals with Rome. His mission was one of fact finding, listening to various viewpoints, and determining whether present conditions were favorable for peace.

On 25 February he had lengthy talks with Ciano and then, the next day, with Mussolini. At the beginning of March Welles was in Berlin, where he met with Ribbentrop, Weizsäcker, Hitler, and Goering. On the 7th, 8th, and 9th of March he was in Paris, where he met with Lebrun, the president of the republic; with Daladier, the head of the government; and with Paul Reynaud. From Paris Welles went to London, where Halifax, Chamberlain, and Churchill received him after his audience with the king. On 16 March he was again back in Rome.

Except for Ribbentrop, who gave him a cold welcome before subjecting him to a two-hour monologue, Welles was received in a courteous, even warm, manner. On the other hand, the viewpoints expressed proved to be quite diverse, even among members of the same government. But in the midst of all these divergences Welles came to an unavoidable conclusion: In the present situation no peaceful compromise was in sight, and the road seemed to be leading toward an escalation of violence. All that could now be done on behalf of peace was to keep the war from spreading and, primarily, to stop Mussolini from entering the conflict on Germany's side, a viewpoint shared by the Vatican.

While the American undersecretary was traveling from capital to capital, Ribbentrop brusquely announced his arrival in Rome under the pretext of bringing a response to Mussolini's letter of 5 January. On 8 March Ambassador von Bergen, who had not been seen in the Vatican for months personally came to request an audience for the Reich's foreign minister. Such a request was not especially pleasing to the Vatican, but it was impossible to evade him, as Pius XII somewhat later explained to the archbishop of Breslau. In light of the official relations existing between the Holy See and the Reich, a refusal could have been interpreted to be an unfriendly act, especially under present circumstances.

> To avoid the danger of any policy being misunderstood and despite the perplexities existing in many respects, We granted a private audience, allowing Ourselves to be guided here by the consideration that a personal conversation with one of the Führer's closest collaborators might offer us the possibility of establishing a useful contact for restoring the best living conditions for the Catholic Church in Germany and also for the future of the war and of peace.

On 11 March Ribbentrop was received by Pius XII. The conversation, lasting from 11 A.M. to 12:10 P.M., essentially concerned the situation of the Catholic Church in Germany and the church's relationship with the national-socialist state. As had been his intention, Pius XII wanted to touch upon the problem of war and of peace. But Ribbentrop immediately cut short any suggestion of negotiated peace by repeating what he had said to Attolico, to Orsenigo, and to Sumner Welles: Germany was on the point of gaining a decisive victory. Shortly after the audience Pius XII told Monsignor Tardini that Ribbentrop "was adamant in telling the pope that Germany is very strong, and that half the world lies open before it, that Germany can take from Romania all the oil it wants, and that it will undoubtedly win the war sometime during 1940. He gave this assurance as if there were no doubt, not even the smallest. He repeated it several times, raising his voice and gesturing." Ribbentrop's visit only confirmed at the Vatican the information coming from elsewhere, namely, that an offensive was being prepared on the western front. Consequently the Holy See's objective did not change: Unable to stop the German offensive, it could at least increase efforts to keep Italy out of the conflict.

The Vatican's initiatives in this regard appeared even more urgent once Ribbentrop brought Mussolini an invitation to meet with the Führer at Brenner. Was Hitler's intention to drag Mussolini into the war at a time when the German leader would launch the decisive offensive? To Ciano's great displeasure, the Duce accepted the invitation, but although he reassured his son-in-law by promising to tell Hitler that Italy had decided to intervene as an ally, he would refrain from specifying a date, a date that would never arrive.

On 16 March Sumner Welles returned to Rome. He immediately went to the Quirinal and then went once again to confer with Ciano and Mussolini. On 17 March, the very day Mussolini was on the train to Brenner, the Italian ambassador told Cardinal Maglione that the meeting had been requested by Hitler. The presumption was that the Führer would insist on bringing Italy into the war, but that Mussolini would persist in his attitude of waiting. Yet the ambassador said that in the end Italy would find it quite difficult to preserve its neutrality.

It was in this context that, on 18 March, the cardinal secretary of state received Sumner Welles and Myron Taylor together. Welles began by reporting on the conclusions of his fact-finding mission. Officials in

Germany were convinced that the Allies wanted the Reich to be destroyed. The Allies themselves wanted guarantees that a war would not begin again every twenty years. Finally, the Germans were convinced that they would obtain a crushing victory within a year, and Mussolini had confirmed that Hitler was preparing an offensive to take place in the weeks ahead. Welles asked the cardinal what he thought about an attempt to mediate. Maglione replied that, with each camp believing that it would obtain complete victory, any attempt at mediation would be condemned to failure and would only compromise any steps that might be taken in the future.

Welles, indicating his complete agreement, then asked what Maglione thought of the Italian situation. The cardinal replied that the Italian people were strongly opposed to the war but that Mussolini's thinking was not clear. Certainly the Duce was leaning toward Germany and yet, on the other hand, he was a realist, and there was hope that Mussolini would consider public opinion before rushing into an adventure where the country's interests might risk mortal danger. But the Allies had to be careful not to offend him. Again on this point Sumner Welles shared the cardinal's opinion. The conversation concluded by considering the prospects and chances of a joint action.

At the conclusion of his travels in Europe, Welles devoted a special report to the Italian situation, for it was here that action by the United States was still possible. He stressed that everything depended on Mussolini. Now Mussolini was a man of genius, vindictive, and always mindful of the sanctions of 1935. Germany, the Duce believed, was invincible; furthermore, he detested France and England. A stunning victory on the part of the Allies was necessary to change all this. Regarding the possibility that the Germans might achieve substantial success, such as the occupation of Holland and Belgium, Welles wrote, "I greatly fear that Mussolini will force Italy to join the war." Except for Mussolini, explained Welles, no one in Italy wants war: Ciano, the ministers, the royal family, the church do not desire war; popular sentiment, though not with the Allies, is anti-German. Finally, the main request made to Welles by the pope, the secretary of state, and Count Ciano was that he urge Roosevelt to use all his influence on Mussolini to keep Italy out of the conflict.

While Welles was in Rome, Mussolini was meeting with Hitler at Brenner. According to the official record of the conversation, the Führer began by extolling the power of the German forces and the resolute confidence of both people and army that they would see a crushing victory. But he did not insist on Italy's immediate entry into the war; he simply wanted to present an overall picture of the situation. The Duce could then make his own decision. Mussolini replied that his country's entrance into the war was inevitable; only Italy's limited resources prevented a date from now being determined. Two days later Ambassador Alfieri brought some reassuring news to Cardinal Maglione: The meeting at Brenner brought no change of position on either side, and Count Ciano was pursuing his policy of peace.

But the horizon darkened toward the end of the month, when Ciano received the nuncio to Italy; the count's personal feelings remained the same, but he no longer was as confident: "I cannot tell you whether there will or will not be war, but I am working and you have no idea of what I have done and of what I am doing." The nuncio did not doubt Ciano's sincerity, even urging him to be on guard as to his own personal safety.

In Paris on 12 April Valeri, the nuncio, was received by Paul Reynaud, the new president of the council, who said that at Brenner Hitler had urged Mussolini to enter the war on the German side if he, Mussolini, wanted to gain anything from what was taking place. Reynaud did not conceal his concerns as to what might follow from this. Valeri asked if an agreement between Italy and France was still possible. Reynaud replied that it was impossible to come to terms with anyone who did not wish to do so. François-Poncet had spoken to Ciano about making Djibouti a free port, about allowing Italy to operate the Suez Canal, of keeping the status quo in Tunisia, and about internationalizing Gibraltar. Ciano kept his silence. In relating this conversation to Cardinal Maglione, Archbishop Valeri wondered whether these concessions had not arrived too late. He could only assure Paul Reynaud that the Holy See was doing everything possible to ensure Italy's neutrality, and the minister acknowledged the influence exerted in this direction by *l'Osservatore Romano,* the Vatican newspaper.

Archbishop Valeri's report, dated 12 April, must have been in Rome when, on 18 April, a cable arrived from Washington. The apostolic delegate, Archbishop Cicognani, notified the Vatican: "I have learned, in confidence, that the highest officials of this government believe that Italy will enter the war as Germany's ally within a few days."

Myron Taylor, who usually resided in Florence, was called to the Vatican, and the next day, 19 April, he had with Cardinal Maglione a meeting that he himself characterized as "long and very serious." The cardinal secretary of state, as well as the ambassadors from Great Britain, Belgium, Romania, Poland, Spain, and the ambassador of the United States at the Quirinal, believed that, as to Italy, the situation was very critical. Cardinal Maglione thought that President Roosevelt should write to Mussolini, dissuading him from joining the war. Taylor pointed out that the king of Italy and the pope could intervene along the same lines, and he asked whether Pius XII was inclined to move in this direction. Maglione requested Taylor to stay in Rome till the pope replied and insisted that Roosevelt take quick, if possible immediate, action. The following day, at three in the afternoon, Taylor cabled to his government the pope's response to the following two questions:

(1) Is it necessary to send at this moment a message from the president to Mussolini?

—The reply was that such a message should be sent immediately.

(2) Should a parallel endeavor be undertaken by His Holiness?

—The reply is Yes. But that the two steps, one taken by the pope and the other by the president, should remain independent and not appear linked.

PIUS XII'S LETTERS TO MUSSOLINI

Pius XII did not wait. Formerly when circumstances were the most critical, the pope sent Father Tacchi Venturi to the Duce. But this time Pius XII sent Mussolini a handwritten letter. Dated 24 April, the pope's letter basically recalled the confidential messages previously entrusted to the Jesuit. Pius XII first congratulated Mussolini for his efforts in regard to peace and for having kept the calamity within restricted boundaries. But, continued the pope, the fire is now spreading and the specter of war seems to approach.

> Not doubting the resolute work in the direction you have chosen for yourself, We ask the Lord to help you at this hour which is so serious for the people and which is filled with such great responsibility for those holding the reins of power. And by the universal paternity proper to Our office, Our most ardent and heartfelt desire is that Europe, thanks to your initiatives, your firmness, and your Italian disposition, be spared from the most widespread destruc-

tion and the most numerous sorrows. We especially desire that such a calamity be avoided by Our and your cherished country.

The following day, 27 April, at six in the evening the counselor at the nunciature in Italy, Monsignor Misuraca, gave the letter to Secretary Sebastiani, who promised that within half an hour it would be in Mussolini's hands. Mussolini received it and promised a response, but he did not hide the fact that the letter would have little influence on his decisions.

In his response, dated 30 April, the Duce thanked the sovereign pontiff for the message. He then went on to attack the western powers who in August 1939 had made impossible the proposed conference by "the absurd Franco-English requirement that the advancing German armies retreat to their staging points."

> I understand, Most Holy Father, your desire that Italy avoid war. Till the present it has been able to do so, but in no way can I guarantee that it will continue to do so. What third parties desire and intend must also be taken into account.

> ...I wish to assure you of one thing, Most Holy Father. If Italy must enter the field of battle tomorrow, it will mean that national honor, interests, and the future absolutely require it to do so.

ROOSEVELT'S MESSAGE TO MUSSOLINI

Pius XII's letter did nothing to change Mussolini's plans. Yet Roosevelt also intervened, although he had no knowledge of Mussolini's reply to the pope. On 29 April Roosevelt sent a cable to his ambassador, William Phillips, containing a message to be passed on immediately to the head of the Italian government. Phillips thereupon requested an audience and was received at half past nine the morning of 1 May. Like Pius XII, Roosevelt praised Mussolini's previous efforts to avoid war or at least to restrict it. The president admitted, as the Duce already told Sumner Welles, that thanks to the Italian leader two hundred million people were still at peace since the onset of hostilities. But Roosevelt warned that the extension of the current conflict might have repercussions that were difficult to foresee and that also the three Americas would have to reconsider their positions. It fell to Italy and to the United States to maintain their neutrality, which was their strength, and to work together for peace. Mussolini attentively read Roosevelt's message and, according to Phillips, "he understood each of its points." He expressed surprise that any extension of the war in Europe might involve a change in the position of the Americas. Then he insisted on the necessity of a realignment of the 1939 boundaries, and on Italy's need for free access to the Atlantic. He also promised that he would reply to the president.

The Duce's letter to the president was accurate but not any more assuring than his reply to Pius XII. Mussolini declared that he did not want a broadening of the war, but he also had to say that Italy never became entangled in American wars, and he did not see why the Americas would have to intervene because of differences among the European powers.

On 2 May Cardinal Maglione again met with Myron Taylor, who told him what Roosevelt had done and of Mussolini's response. Despite all, Maglione believed that Mussolini's reply to Roosevelt still left the door open. First, the blockade of Italy would have to be reduced; concrete proposals were hardly necessary; and the Allies were disposed to make some concessions. Myron Taylor said he agreed and promised to intervene along these lines with Lord Halifax.

On this date the cardinal secretary of state knew that serious events were being prepared for the next day, 3 May, and so he sent out two identical telegrams, one to the nuncio at Brussels and another to the internuncio at The Hague.

> To be decoded by the nuncio only. From a source that can be considered trustworthy we have learned that, unless something prevents it or happens in the meantime, an offensive will shortly occur on the western front; it will also affect Holland, Belgium, and perhaps Switzerland. Your Excellency, it is up to you to use this confidential information as you consider opportune.

Archbishop Micara hurried to inform King Leopold.

Three days later Pius XII received Charles-Roux, the French ambassador, who, after the audience, telegraphed his government:

> Once again the pope and Monsignor Montini informed me and my counselor that, according to information coming to them from a foreign country, the Germans will unleash an offensive on the western

front within a very short period of time (a week). In tomorrow's mail I will give you other details relating to the conversation I had. It is self-understood that I am restricted to imparting information without being able to relate my thoughts as to its value.

In his letter of the same date the ambassador specified that the offensive would be simultaneously launched against France, Belgium, and Holland; he also said that the Germans were placing a good deal of confidence in their bombers. Again on the same day Osborne sent a similar message to the Foreign Office, adding that he gave little credence to this warning.

GERMAN OFFENSIVE AND TELEGRAMS OF 10 MAY

On 10 May at three in the morning Hitler launched his offensive against France, Belgium, Holland, and Luxembourg. Without any ultimatum, without any declaration of war, the Wehrmacht invaded the territory of these three neutral countries.

Before half past nine in the morning the French ambassador telephoned the Secretariat of State and insisted that he be received that very morning, for he was awaiting from his government a telegram which he was to bring personally to the pope's attention. Pius XII immediately granted him an audience, and Charles-Roux presented the pope with the message that had just arrived from Paris. The ambassador's instructions were to point out "respectfully and urgently" to Pius XII that, faced with the violation of the neutrality of three neutral nations, the whole world was waiting for the pope to "formulate with his high authority the solemn condemnation that should stigmatize this hateful attack." For such a condemnation to be most effective, it was necessary that "the Holy Father's action be immediate and that there be no delay between this abominable violation of law and morality and the pope's protest denouncing it." The French government did not conceal the reason for its request.

On the other hand, it is essential that it [the condemnation] be expressed in sufficiently strong and explicit terms in order to guide Italian public opinion along lines where moral and political reasons, like the dynastic bonds linking together Belgium and Italy, should come together in keeping it.

42

During the same morning of 10 May Roosevelt's special envoy, together with the Belgian ambassador and the minister from England, requested that they might meet with the pope on the next day, and the Vatican understood that they, following the example of Charles-Roux, would ask him to take some action against the invasion of the neutral countries. That evening the English minister brought to the Secretariat of State a note similar to that of his French colleague. Lord Halifax counted on the Holy See to use all its influence to restrain Italy from joining Germany in the war.

Pius XII had already resolved to grant these requests. He instructed the cardinal secretary of state to prepare a document, and the pope himself sat down to work so that on the evening of 10 May he had to choose among three texts. Cardinal Maglione had prepared an official statement to be published in *l'Osservatore Romano*; Monsignor Tardini had drawn up a letter from the pope to the cardinal secretary of state. And Pius XII himself had typed out the texts of three telegrams, one addressed to the Belgian king, one to the queen of Holland, and another to the grand duchess of Luxembourg. These telegrams, not containing the strong words found in the letter prepared by Monsignor Tardini, which "deplored the injustice and the evil," fundamentally consisted of expressing condolences to the people who were suffering the miseries of the war. Yet it would be necessary to close one's eyes not to see there, especially in the message sent to King Leopold, a formal condemnation of the violation of Belgium's neutrality.

> At a time when the Belgian people, for the second time and contrary to its will and its law, see its territory exposed to the war's cruelties, We, profoundly moved, send to Your Majesty and to your whole beloved country assurances of Our paternal affection; in asking God that this difficult trial come to an end through the reestablishment of Belgium's full liberty and independence. From the bottom of our heart We grant Your Majesty and your people Our apostolic blessing.

The telegram to Queen Wilhelmina spoke of Holland—"contrary to its will and its law"—becoming a theater of war; and it concluded by asking God, "the supreme arbiter of the destiny of nations, to hasten with his all-powerful help the reestablishment of justice and liberty." Only the third telegram, to the grand duchess of Luxembourg, restricted itself to expressions of sympathy and to a desire that Luxembourg "be able to live in freedom and independence."

The meaning of these telegrams was quite clear. As Charles-Roux wrote later: "It was, therefore, a public affirmation of the guilt and the responsibility of the German government." In seeing the pope's texts both "Cardinal Maglione as well as Monsignor Tardin, finding the texts to be perfectly written, believed it opportune to send the telegrams to the sovereigns of the three countries attacked by the Germans." They were sent out at nine that very evening. And the next day, in the evening, they appeared in large print on the first page of *l'Osservatore Romano*.

The governing party and Mussolini himself, who wanted the Italian army to march alongside the Wehrmacht, saw these three telegrams as a direct attack on their policy. The vendors of the Vatican paper and even those buying it were molested and beaten, with copies of the journal forcibly taken from the kiosks and burned. Cardinal Maglione protested to Italy's ambassador to the Vatican, and a memorandum from the Secretariat of State informed the Holy See's representatives throughout the world of the incident. But this did not prevent the journalist Roberto Farinacci, director of the party's journal *Regime fascista*, from writing shortly after, in the 25 August edition, "that a telegram from the pope goaded Belgium's Catholic king to have his people shed their blood for the sake of the Jews, the Freemasons, and the bankers of the City."

But sending these telegrams did not stop the French ambassador from insisting, as early as Monday morning, to Monsignor Tardini that Pius XII explicitly condemn the invasion of the neutral countries: It was one thing to express sympathy to the victims; it was another thing altogether to condemn the crime. Tardini did not conceal his astonishment: Anyone who knew how to read would easily understand that the telegrams contained everything the ambassador wanted. The latter, somewhat confounded, nonetheless insisted that his request be brought to the pope's attention.

This same morning of 13 May the Italian ambassador, Dino Alfieri, was presented to the pope in a farewell audience, because the diplomat was to go to Berlin as Italy's representative to Germany. Despite the formal character of this act of courtesy, Mussolini had instructed Alfieri to protest the pope's telegrams of 10 May. The farewell audience quickly took on an "especially serious" direction, so much so that the ambassador's wife, who was accompanying him, withdrew. Alfieri noted that the messages addressed to the sovereigns of Belgium, Holland, and Luxembourg had angered the head of the Italian government, who saw them as a move against his policy. The ambassador stressed that a state of tension reigned among the Fascists, and he made it plain that serious events could follow. The pope calmly replied that he did not fear being shipped off to a concentration camp. Alluding to the most critical moments during his stay in Munich, Pius XII added: "We did not fear the revolvers that were aimed at us the first time around; We will have even less fear the second time." Furthermore:

> The Italians are certainly well aware of the terrible things taking place in Poland. We might have an obligation to utter fiery words against such things; yet all that is holding Us back from doing so is the knowledge that if We should speak, we would simply worsen the predicament of these unfortunate people.

Whereas Mussolini feared the effect of the pope's words on the Italian people, the Allies, placed in an extremely critical military situation and apprehensive of a second front being opened, sought all possible means for averting this danger. The next day, 14 May, the French ambassador returned to the Vatican and insisted that the secretary of state inform the pope that his government was demanding a forceful condemnation of Germany. Cardinal Maglione replied that he could not pass on the request since the pope had already done all that was right and opportune.

ITALY ENTERS THE WAR

In Paris on 15 May the nuncio received a visit from the ambassador from the United States who informed him that, according to the most reliable sources, Italy's entry into the war was no more than a question of hours. "The only way to prevent this would be for the pope to threaten Mussolini with excommunication if he took action and dragged Italy into the war." Archbishop Valeri's answer was that the pope had already done everything to keep Italy in peace; that it was not necessary to ask the pope to do the impossible, and especially to use the weapon of excommunication, whose effect at the present time would be highly doubtful.

On 17 May the French ambassador, preceded by a phone call, arrived at the Vatican at quarter past eleven in the evening; he was carrying an urgent document, which he handed over to Monsignor Montini. It was a letter to Pius XII from Cardinal Suhard, the archbishop of Paris. Knowing that Italy from one hour to the next might declare war on France, Cardinal Suhard, in the name of all the French bishops and Catholics and on behalf of the higher interests of religion, petitioned the pope to use all possible means to avoid this calamity. The archbishop specified that the president of the council and the foreign minister were aware of what he was doing. Immediately Monsignor Montini took the letter to Cardinal Maglione. He, in turn, phoned Pius XII, who also was still at work. The pope replied that he would certainly try anything, but that he could not exert too much pressure in light of the responses he had received on this subject. It was, in fact, on 25 May that Cardinal Maglione answered Cardinal Suhard: "The Holy Father has already done all in his power to intervene in the way you desire. Nonetheless, he has taken a new step although, and sadly so, he is not very hopeful as to its favorable outcome."

In fact, what were the pope's chances of having Mussolini listen to him at a time when the dictator scornfully spurned Churchill's proposals and Roosevelt's previous message? Up to the final moment, however, Pius XII continued to consider all possible methods to prevent Italy from entering the war. Charles-Roux had been called back to the Quai d'Orsay. On 26 May the pope received François-Poncet, the French ambassador in Rome, who talked about concessions the French government could make to Italy. Thought was given to a new letter from the Holy Father to Mussolini. The same day, the pope discussed the question with the minister from Great Britain. Pius XII said that he had in mind a new initiative in regard to Mussolini, namely, stating that France was open to some concessions on Italy's behalf. Might the same be said for England? Osborne appeared rather cool to the idea, and several days later the British government bore out its representative's reserve. In fact, the matter was no longer of consequence. On 28 May Ciano was quite clear when he told the nuncio: "The French now come with proposals. They should have done so four years ago. At present it is just a waste of time."

On 2 June, the feast of St. Eugene, Pope Eugenio Pacelli responded to the good wishes of the Sacred College. He spoke of his efforts on behalf of peace, although he had to admit that they were to no avail. Focusing attention on the countries at war and under occupation, he recalled that the occupying powers were to treat the people under their power as they themselves would wish to be treated in similar circumstances. The time for diplomacy seemed to be over for the Holy See until new events would make the situation more favorable. From England Archbishop Godfrey, the apostolic delegate, described the fierce determination of that country as it faced growing danger. His report was dated 10 June, the same day Mussolini, in turn, entered a war that he feared would end without him.

Having done everything possible to prevent Italy from joining the war, Pius XII now devoted his attention to keeping the city of Rome free from combat and to saving it from bombing, whether by naval or air strikes. On 10 June 1940 Cardinal Maglione called in the minister from England; the following day he summoned the ambassador from France. Two days later he telegraphed the nuncio in Paris and the delegate in London, requesting them to ask the French and English governments to refrain from bombing Rome. France immediately gave its assurances that Rome would not be bombed. But as the war progressed, much more importance came to be given to the English response, a reply that was constantly repeated throughout the years to come. Under no circumstances would the English government, wrote the apostolic delegate in London on 17 June, attack the Vatican City; as to the city of Rome, on the other hand, it kept all options open; everything depended on how the Italian government observed the rules of war.

The state of war existing between Italy and the French and the English also raised for the Vatican an immediate question regarding the diplomatic representatives of France and Great Britain accredited by the Holy See. Till the time of the war they resided in Italian territory. Thought was given to having them withdraw to Switzerland, but it was decided that they should live in the Vatican City. On 13 June the French and English representatives, as well as Casimir Papée, the Polish ambassador, were welcomed into the convent of St. Martha. The French ambassador, Wladimir d'Ormesson, recalled by Laval, left the Vatican on 30 October, but for Sir d'Arcy Osborne the compulsory stay within the limited quarters of Vatican City would last four long years, till June 1944.

FRANCE AND ENGLAND

Meanwhile, Pius XII believed for a while that Italy's entry into the war, which he had done everything to avert, would allow him to intervene once again on behalf of peace.

The cabinet formed in France on 16 June by Marshal Pétain immediately entrusted Baudouin, the foreign minister, with opening negotiations for an armistice and with establishing contact with the Germans by means of Spain and with the Italians through the Vatican. A little after midnight the request for an armistice was sent to Lequerica, the Spanish ambassador, whereas it was only the next day at nine in the morning that Archbishop Valeri received what he was to send to Rome. The message arrived in the Vatican as Mussolini was traveling to Munich, where Hitler had invited him for a conference concerning the French request for an armistice. Mussolini was to have been informed of the request before meeting with Hitler. The French request arrived too early for the Duce, whose armies had not yet begun combat. Mussolini ordered his troops to advance to the Alps, and Weizsäcker gave the Reich's ambassador in Madrid the task of informing the French that an armistice with Germany could take effect only at the same time as an armistice with Italy. In addition, he advised making contact with Italy and using Spain as an intermediary. Baudouin had to mention the fact that he had already sent Rome a request for an armistice, doing so through the good offices of the Vatican. Finally, the government of Bordeaux repeated its request to Italy for an armistice through the intermediary of the Spanish ambassador, and a press agency published news of this. Pius XII understood that he was to be excluded from any negotiations leading to an armistice.

After the double armistice of 25 June, Monsignor Tardini, together with Cardinal Maglione, envisioned a new papal initiative on behalf of peace, considering it to be a function of the apostolic office to take action so as to avoid the spilling of blood and the total destruction that Germany's assault on England would produce. Hitler, already anxious in regard to Russia, would surely be disposed to negotiate. From its side, England, with its army, its territory, and its fleet intact, remained in a good position to enter into discussions. On the following day Monsignor Tardini presented the idea to Pius XII, who replied that this was a delicate issue, one calling for reflection. Finally he decided to sound out the matter.

Notes were sent to the German and Italian ambassadors by Cardinal Maglione on 28 June at ten thirty and at twenty before eleven respectively, and a cable was sent to Archbishop Godfrey, the papal delegate to England. Ciano spoke about it to Mussolini, who immediately showed himself hostile. And on 5 July the Italian ambassador brought the official response of his government: The pope's initiative left one puzzled since it was not known what Hitler's reaction would be. Perhaps the leader of the Reich might make some proposals before launching his offensive against England, but these would probably take the form of an ultimatum.

The British government's response, although more courteous, was firmer, and it was negative. England decided not to allow itself and Europe to fall under Nazi domination; it would fight to the end.

On 19 July, in a solemn speech given before the Reichstag, Hitler issued an appeal to England in which he called for an end to hostilities. Immediate and unequivocal was the reply given by Lord Halifax. Nonetheless, the U.S. representative to Belgium, whom Pius XII received in an audience on 25 July, asked the pope to do something to persuade the British government at least not to give the impression of purely and simply rejecting what Hitler proposed: for example, would it not be possible to request that the German government be more specific in regard to conditions for peace? The American diplomat let it be understood that he did not believe that England was capable of withstanding an attack by the Reich.

A cable to be sent to the apostolic delegate in London was prepared by Cardinal Maglione, and the pope himself corrected its text. Mentioning the intervention of people "who were in favor of a just peace," the Holy See instructed Archbishop Godfrey to act together with the archbishop of Westminster in approaching the English government so that it "not allow the German chancellor's peace offer to sink without ado, but, on the contrary, that it request the German government to specify the concrete foundations on which to begin eventual negotiations." The telegram was sent at two in the afternoon on 26 July.

The reply arrived the morning of 29 July. Both the cardinal archbishop and the apostolic delegate believed that the action suggested by the pope might easily be misinterpreted, as if the Holy See were associating itself with Hitler in order to press England to capitulate. What the English government saw in Hitler's speech was not a peace offer but a ploy. The cardinal added that, furthermore, this speech was only a web of insults, challenges, and threats, containing no guarantee for the countries that had been invaded, no guarantee similar to that requested by the pope's Christmas message.

Osborne's position was less intransigent than the archbishop's. He approved the Holy See's initiative, and yet when Cardinal Maglione showed him the delegate's telegram, Osborne said he was unhappy with it since, in his understanding, the Holy See did not want to press England to capitulate. In Germany, Weizsäcker told the nuncio that Hitler had very clearly expressed his desire for peace but that Halifax categorically opposed it. Consequently it was evident who was responsible for the last phase of the struggle, which would be very bloody.

All diplomatic resources were now exhausted. The pope had not worked alone on behalf of peace: He was supported by the U.S. president, who joined his moral action to the prestige of a political and military force that one day would upset the equilibrium of forces. But Roosevelt's messages, no more than the pope's handwritten letter of 24 April, did not restrain Mussolini from going down the path of war. President Roosevelt's representative, who was seriously ill, returned to the United States, where, through the apostolic delegate, he continued to act as an intermediary between the Vatican and the White House. He brought back with him a letter from the pope to the president dated 22 August 1940. Previous failures notwithstanding and in spite of the darkness of the hour, Pius XII did not want to lose hope. "We redouble our prayers and our efforts," he wrote, "to find a practical way that will lead to peace, a way that will carry in itself enduring promises, a way that will free people from the heavy burden of insecurity and perpetual fear."

CHAPTER 3

The Pope and the Church in Germany*

~·~

O NCE WAR BROKE OUT, the thorny problems that had been facing the Holy See for quite some time became even more acute. First among these was the status of the church in Germany. When in March 1939 Cardinal Pacelli succeeded Pius XI, the national-socialist regime had already spent several years in an all-out struggle against the Catholic Church and other Christian communities. In territories recently annexed from Austria and Sudeten, Germany immediately reinforced measures that were already taken against the church in the old Reich, where the government less and less respected the guarantees of the Concordat of 1933. And so certain sinister forebodings seemed to accumulate as to the future of the church in Germany.

Two years earlier the Holy See used the most powerful means at its disposal against the Nazi regime, namely, the encyclical *Mit brennender Sorge* of 19 March 1937. Prepared with the agreement of the German episcopacy, it disclosed to the world the reality of national-socialism, its "arrogant apostasy from Jesus Christ, the denial of Christ's teaching and redemptive work, the worship of force, the idolatry of race and blood, the oppression of liberty and human dignity." The papal document opened the eyes of many people but not of all, as the pope lamented, and even some of the faithful remained victims of their own prejudices and their own hope for political advantage.

*Documentation for chapter 3 (including the minutes of the pope's meetings with the German cardinals during March 1939): See *ADSS,* vol. 2. Quotations from Pius XII's letters were originally in German except for the letter of 25 September, whose original was in Latin. The drafts of these letters sent by Pius XII to the German bishops were redacted by a German secretary, Leiber or Kaas, but the pope then carefully reviewed and personally corrected them. A long letter to the meeting of the bishops of Fulda in 1940 has more than a hundred handwritten corrections of Pius XII. See also the speech Pius XII gave to the cardinals on 2 June 1945 (*Documents pontificaux de Sa Sainteté Pie XII*) and Maccarrone, *Il nazionalsocialismo e la Santa Sede*, 1945.

Nonetheless, the encyclical "brought light, direction, consolation, and comfort to all who took seriously, and consistently practiced, the religion of Christ." Persecution did not abate; it even became more oppressive during the following two years. The church carried out its pastoral activity while undergoing increasingly harsh difficulties and restrictions, and the faithful suffered the consequences in regard to their personal goods and their own persons. Episcopal residences were searched in Cologne, Trier, and Aix-la-Chapelle, where files pertaining to the most confidential matters regarding the care of souls were seized.

In September of the same year the Congress of Nuremberg, at which the French and English ambassadors were present for the first time, awarded Alfred Rosenberg the "National Prize," appearing to make his *Myth of the Twentieth Century* the official catechism of the new Germanic religion. Christian teaching was repeatedly attacked, first at the local level and then progressively throughout the whole Reich. A decree of 29 December 1937 shut down eighty-two Catholic schools, embracing a total of fifteen thousand students. Parallel to this was the government's attack on religious instruction in public schools. On 10 March 1938 the Bavarian government enacted a law pertaining to the examination of academic standards, and one article of the law stated that priests entrusted with this instruction had to be given special authorization, which would be refused to non-Aryans and to those who were not "politically safe." On 2 April of the same year the Berlin government informed the directors of schools that they did not have to pay attention to any objections that ecclesiastical authorities might bring against lay professors who were teaching religion.

Austria, on the very day after its annexation, underwent a persecution that was not even curbed, as was true in the old Reich, by the terms of the Concordat. The Berlin government declared that the annexation voided the Austrian Concordat of 1934, and it refused to extend to Austria the concordat that the Vatican had concluded with the Reich in 1933. The closing of Catholic faculties in Salzburg, the dissolution of the faculty of theology in Innsbruck, the expulsion of the Christian Brothers from their institutions, the expulsion of sisters from numerous educational institutions and even from many hospitals—all were among the first fruits Austrian Catholics received from their union with the Reich. Even the cardinal archbishop in Vienna was insulted as he was leaving the cathedral, and the next day his episcopal palace was invaded and plundered. The persecution did not even stop with matters of conscience. Civil servants were forbidden to send their children to religious schools. Attempts were made to have them sign forms saying that they adhered to Rosenberg's neopaganism. In short, at the time that Cardinal Pacelli was becoming Pope Pius XII, one could restate what Pius XI had said in his Christmas address of 1937:

> To call things by their real name: in Germany it is religious persecution....It is a persecution lacking neither force nor violence, neither oppression nor threats, neither sly craftiness nor lying.

In 1939 a solemn protest, as the encyclical of 1937 had been, was no longer possible, if only for practical reasons, since it was impossible to restore the secret distribution network that allowed Pius XI's document to be sent to the farthest corners of Germany in the face of the most effective police force of the time. Besides, the Munich accords had just consolidated the regime, and the German people could not but compare the state of political humiliation and of economic distress that overwhelmed them when Hitler seized power with the new situation, relatively prosperous economically and dominating politically. It seemed that all the church could do was to try everything possible to put up with the situation and, yes, even attempt to change the Reich's religious policy.

DELIBERATIONS AND REPORTS ON THE RELIGIOUS SITUATION IN THE REICH

After the election of 2 March 1939, which made the former nuncio to Germany the successor of Pius XI, the Reich's ambassador, Diego von Bergen, requested an audience to extend the best wishes of his country's chancellor to the new pope. On 5 March Pius XII received the diplomat in a courtesy visit; perhaps the meeting was considered as a first step toward detente. The pope's exceptional knowledge of what was happening in Germany proved advantageous. Eugenio Pacelli was in Germany as nuncio, first in Munich from May 1917 till the summer of 1925, and then in Berlin till 1929. The concordats with Bavaria (1925) and with Prussia (1929) endured as a tangible result of his terms as nuncio. In his first letter, dated 20 July 1939, to the German bishops, Pius XII took delight in recalling the years he spent in Germany and the continuing relationships he had established there:

> We recall those many years when divine Providence allowed Us to live and work among your people. It is with emotion that We thank the Lord for what he has graciously done. And so We are very happy today that We have gained a broad knowledge concerning the situation and sufferings, the works and needs of German Catholics, a knowledge that can come only from direct experience, one prolonged over many years.

A year later, in a letter dated 6 August 1940 and also addressed to the German bishops, the pope spoke about the intimate contact he had not only with the church but with the German people throughout the years after the war and Germany's defeat. This message contains a long sentence within which Pius XII personally inserted four corrections; surely it allows us to understand his position during the Second World War.

> After seeing and experiencing during the years of our work in Germany how harshly the German people had to suffer the continuing and humiliating effects of their defeat, and after Ourselves witnessing the way in which the previous peace treaty's lack of proper balance has brought forth as a fatal consequence the contrasts whose elimination by violent means has the earth tremble today, We can only express our ardent hope that when the war ends, at a time known only by Providence, the eyes of the victorious will be opened to the voice of justice, equity, wisdom, and moderation, without which no peace treaty, no matter how solemn its ratification may be, can last and can have the happy consequences desired by all people.

Pacelli's activity as nuncio had been appreciated by Pius XI, who rewarded him at the end of 1929 by making him a cardinal and then by immediately appointing him secretary of state. In this new office Cardinal Pacelli himself handled affairs with Germany. He personally led the decisive negotiations with Baden (1932) and with the Reich (1933), as well as the discussions with the German government on implementing the concordat. From 1933 on, the German ambassador to the Holy See received a series of diplomatic notes that came directly from the office of the secretary of state, a practice that continued till the day the secretary of state became Pope Pius XII.

On the day after the pope's election, the four German cardinals who had come for the conclave remained in Rome till the day of the pope's coronation: Bertram from Breslau, Faulhaber from Munich, Schulte from Cologne, and Innitzer from Vienna. The new pope decided to bring them together so that he might discuss the church's situation in Germany and surface some ideas for alleviating it. The meetings began on Monday, 6 March; a further consultation followed on Thursday, 9 June. As early as the first session Pius XII declared: "For me the German problem is the most important. I reserve its treatment to myself."

In these two meetings, whose detailed minutes have been preserved, the pope, with the agreement of the German cardinals, drew up the broad outlines of the policy that the Holy See would adopt in face of national-socialism. Of the group that prepared in January 1937 the encyclical *Mit brennender Sorge,* three cardinals were once again gathered around the former secretary of state: Adolf Bertram, Michael Faulhaber, and Josef Schulte. Bertram and Faulhaber played a major role here, since before the first session they had sent the pope some memoranda, which served as the basis for the discussion.

The pope and the three cardinals were unanimous in believing that it was necessary to profit from the opportunity offered by the beginning of a new pontificate to try to ease relations between the church and the German government. Kept in mind was the precedent of 1878, when Leo XIII, succeeding Pius IX, had immediately adopted a favorable attitude toward the Prussian government and thus initiated a progressive abandonment of the Kulturkampf. During these two sessions a letter was redacted by which Pius XII would notify the head of the German state as to his election. This could be the first step toward detente. However, all were completely aware of existing difficulties and uncertainties. During the first discussion, which took place on 6 March, Cardinal Faulhaber said:

> There are times when we doubt that the upper echelons of the party in general desire peace. The [leaders] want to be combatants to such an extent that they would love nothing more than to be given a reason for fighting, especially when it concerns the church. But I likewise believe that we, the bishops, should act as

if we see nothing. This is why we are respectfully grateful to Your Holiness for the steps which will be taken on behalf of peace.

Pius XII responded:

We wish to see, to try an experiment. If they want combat, we do not fear it. But we want to determine whether there is any possibility of establishing peace. [After a digression describing the broad outlines of an encyclical for the beginning of his pontificate, the pope continued:] We cannot sacrifice principles. Once We have tried everything and if they still persist in their desire for war, then We will defend Ourselves. But the world should note that we have done everything to live in peace with Germany.

It was in a similar vein that Pius XII, during the second session, explained the reasons for trying to reach an understanding: "It is easy to destroy. Yet when it is necessary to rebuild, God knows how many concessions have to be made. The government will not renew relations without concessions on Our part. If the government severs relations, then...God knows what...!"

Pius XII invited the four cardinals, and through them the German episcopacy, to write to him directly, as they did in the past. Soon the war would make these communications with the German bishops even more valuable, when relations with German Catholics were reduced or broken. By inviting the bishops to write to him, the pope indicated to the cardinals that the nunciature in Berlin was a sure means for corresponding with Rome. The German bishops made full use of this opportunity to correspond directly with the head of the church, and they regularly sent him all possible information together with copies of the most important documents. It was in this way that contact was established between Pius XII and the German episcopacy; it continued till the last year of the war and allowed the pope to know what was happening to the church in Germany. On the other hand, the pope's letters, prepared by German secretaries but reviewed and corrected word for word by Pius XII, are an extraordinary record of his thoughts and intentions.

On 13 July, three months after the beginning of the pontificate, a detailed memorandum was sent by the secretary of state, Cardinal Maglione, to Ambassador von Bergen. The note, drafted in Italian, contained numerous alterations, words or sentences erased or added by the pope himself. The measures that the German government had recently taken against the Catholic Church were classified into two major sections. The first of these enumerates under eight headings and an appendix various general points that especially concern the suppression of religious schools, the obstacles placed in the way of religious instruction or even its suppression, the de-Christianization of schools, and the partial withdrawal of the church's means of subsistence. The second section, with eleven headings and an appendix, lists specific measures. Concluding the letter is an appendix, almost completely from the pope's hand, on the regime's propaganda:

> As to the national-socialist press, we must observe that, even though the daily press has generally observed over these past months a less hostile attitude toward the church, nonetheless the national-socialist party has demonstrated a broad anti-Catholic propaganda in the weekly newspapers that are diffused in the organizations and sectors of the party, as well as in books issued by certain publishing houses, Ludendorff-Verlag among others, whose advertising is done through the use of billboards. These books show no respect to the sovereign pontiffs, and the accusations they make are contrary to simple historical truth. On the other hand, the most strict and most severe censorship is placed on Catholic publications, which consequently cannot defend the church and refute these calumnious and injurious attacks. Furthermore, it is even forbidden to write about the conditions favoring the Catholic Church in countries that are politically friendly to Germany (see Instructions from the Reich's Office of Propaganda, 9 June 1939).

Somewhat later a detailed report, dated 17 January 1940, from the president of the episcopal conference of Fulda listed the measures taken against the church during 1939. In addition to associations dissolved, houses taken over, and religious communities expelled, educational institutions were especially affected by the progressive closing of private religious schools, especially those directed by congregations of female religious. The same was true for primary religious schools, especially in the regions of the west and finally also in Silesia. In western Germany many boarding schools were closed.

Added to this were the measures taken against the people's participation in religious ceremonies; forbidding priests to speak; threatening to suppress the Catholic Sunday papers (*Sonntagsblätter*); intimidating people from belonging to Catholic organizations; indirectly hindering the youth from attending divine services; and introducing school books that attack the church. Once war began, there was hope that at least during the time of conflict Catholic interests would not be attacked. Yet just the opposite took place: The Nazi party used the war to accomplish what it had been nourishing for a long time.

CONCERNS AND POLICY OF PIUS XII

Without being deceived as to anticipated results, it was Pius XII's intention to make the most of all opportunities that could lead to detente. He explained this in a letter of 8 December 1940 to Cardinal Bertram, president of the Fulda episcopal conference.

> Now as before, We consider it Our pressing and conscientious duty not to let pass by any opportunity capable of bringing about an acceptable peace between the church and the state. It is with insistence that we declare it: We speak of a peace that is acceptable before God and before the future of the Catholic Church, of a peace that will ensure the life of the church, even if some of its activities might significantly differ from those of the past. But We are not speaking about "peace at any price"; such a formula as expressing the church's hopes for peace would be incompatible with the principles of the faith and with the very nature of the Catholic Church.

On 11 March 1940 Ribbentrop, the German foreign minister, visited the Vatican. This gave rise to several hopes. The nuncio in Berlin, in an initial report sent shortly after the minister's return to Germany, believed he could promise a positive result. The apostolic administrator in Innsbruck had written to the nuncio that "a highly placed minister reported to him that Ribbentrop, after visiting the Holy Father, could have invited various ministers to suspend their attacks on the Catholic Church." But he had to admit that the effects of this recommendation were not visible everywhere. In fact, attacks on the church continued in the same manner as before despite the audience the pope gave Ribbentrop.

The principle followed by the Holy See was always the same: to seize every acceptable opportunity that might lead to detente and to give practical assistance to German Catholics who were being persecuted, but at the same time, perfectly aware of concrete situations, to refrain from any action that was excessive or idealistic. The most explicit expression of the causes persuading the pope to renew attempts for peace is found in his letter of 5 June 1942 to the bishop of Mainz:

> None of those who pretend to pass an objective judgment can still have doubts today: for in spite of the efforts of Our great predecessor, Pius XI, and Our own efforts to smooth relationships between the church and the state, the result that has been sincerely hoped for and seriously desired has remained null, and the responsibility for this failure should not be placed on the church. The rougher the road of suffering Catholics have to travel during this time, the more important it is, for their strength of interior resistance and for their unity before their adversaries, that they perfectly know that their struggle has not been sought gratuitously but has been imposed on them. The only purpose of such a struggle is the just defense of their most holy rights.

LETTERS TO THE BISHOPS

When listing the dangers brought about by the persecution, Pius XII insisted less on the material sacrifices imposed on Catholics than on the dangers to their faith and their loyalty to the church. On 6 August 1940 he wrote to the Fulda episcopal conference:

> A thousand influences opposed to the church and to Christ, in speech, in writing, and in attitude, constantly flow from a more or less de-Christianized society upon the souls of believers. It subjects them to a moral pressure which, accompanied by coercion and harassment, often forces them to undergo trials that demand heroic fidelity to their faith.

Those succumbing to propaganda held the church responsible for the fact that religious peace had not come to Germany. According to the church's adversaries, the struggle between the church and the state continued because it refused the legitimate demands of the state or was clinging to outdated political forms.

In his struggle against Nazi ideology the pope attributed great importance to the instruction and direction that priests and bishops were able to give on the local level, and he considered it essential that the bishops be of one mind among themselves. Pius XII had already begun the first part of his letter, dated 20 July 1939, to the episcopal conference by urging the bishops to carry out the struggle in the most perfect unity of thought and action. It was known that the German episcopacy was divided regarding the approach to be taken when dealing with the Nazi regime. As Pius XII saw it, the reason for these differences was continuing uncertainty about the real intentions of those in power.

> The doubts and confusion surrounding the real intentions of the most influential forces concerning religion and the church have as their consequence that among some people, whose fidelity to the church can in no way be questioned, there are various ideas regarding what course of action is to be followed.

It was Cardinal Bertram who precipitated a crisis within the German episcopacy. By reason of his position as president of the Fulda episcopal conference, he sent a letter to Hitler in which good wishes were extended to the German leader on the occasion of his anniversary in April 1940. This letter was supposed to have been written in the name of all the German bishops. The bishop of Berlin who, like his colleagues, was only later informed of this, saw the letter as an excessive concession to the Nazi regime, a completely unjustifiable concession. In May 1940 he sent three letters to inform Pius XII of this incident, and he requested permission to retire from his diocese. Pius XII took care not to approve an action that might have completely exposed the difference of opinion and perhaps might have even aggravated it. On the contrary, the pope used his influence to reestablish the threatened unity by writing on 6 August 1940 to the Fulda conference. His hope was that the tension created by different understandings would bring about a deep examination "so that what your strength—and indeed it has been admired over the years—has achieved, namely, your episcopate's unity of spirit and its consensus in making decisions and taking action, will in the end be purified and affirmed."

If the dominant tendencies within the German episcopacy could be classified under the names of the two leading men, on the one hand,

Cardinal Bertram of Breslau and, on the other hand, Bishop von Preysing of Berlin, it is evident that Pius XII adopted the latter's views, for the most part making his own Preysing's understanding of Germany's internal situation. The correspondence between the pope and the Berlin bishop during these years is most rich, not only by the number of letters but also by their content. The pope's basic outlook was in total conformity with that of Preysing. A passage from one of these early letters, that of 7 May 1939 and containing a whole agenda, is one of the most explicit:

> In the first of your two letters you summarize as follows what is presently being done by the venerable German episcopate: continuing to do what has been done up to the present (since the encyclical *Mit Brennender Sorge,* etc.), without inciting useless conflicts; strongly and resolutely defending the faith and the rights of the church; and strengthening the clergy and the faithful in their perseverance. We must emphasize that this expresses Our own intent regarding the religious situation in Germany, and We can only encourage the episcopate to firmly hold fast to this line of action for as long as certain and true signs fail to show an improvement in behavior against the Catholic Church.

Reciprocally, no German bishop taught Pius XII more on the German situation than did Preysing, whose information obviously influenced the pope's decisions, as can be seen from the many instances when the pope expressly requested his opinion. Thus in the pope's letter of 22 April 1940:

> Today, venerable brother, We have two questions. The first concerns the information (which by the way is not usually considered official) given by Vatican Radio on the status of the church in Germany. The news was broadcast since it was thought that complete silence on the part of the Holy See before the public might have resulted in German Catholics loosing courage. And outside Germany such a silence would have led to a misunderstanding, with people believing that everything was normal with the church in Germany, or in any case that things would improve. It is such camouflage, usually well arranged and always with success, that those in charge of the broadcast wanted to unmask. On the other hand, We receive, and also from bishops, complaints and even genuine appeals for help as people face reprisals from those who

threaten them because of the news being broadcast by Vatican Radio. To be sure, We do not want to impose useless sacrifices on German Catholics, who already are so oppressed for the sake of their faith. And so We have suspended these broadcasts till We can safely evaluate their pros and cons. We would be very appreciative if you would communicate to Us your judgment, so valued, and your experience concerning this matter.

Pius XII also consulted with Preysing on the stance the Holy See should take in case Franz von Papen would be reappointed as ambassador to the Vatican. The bishop's reply was clearly negative. Finally, the pope asked what he thought about the appointment of a candidate, whom perhaps Preysing was acquainted with, to a vacant episcopal see. Preysing responded that the candidate was too weak in regard to the government. So Pius XII scratched this cleric from the list of the three names from which the cathedral chapter was to choose a new bishop.

Surely Pius XII did not move people around: In particular, he did not replace Archbishop Orsenigo, the nuncio in Berlin, who somewhat favored Bertram's views and whose official behavior the bishop of Berlin frequently criticized to the pope. It was a question of conserving what was still existing, and it was unthinkable that the government would agree to the appointment of a new nuncio. On the other hand, continuing to have a nunciature in Berlin was of the highest importance both for the Vatican and for the church in Germany since the Holy See's diplomatic representation was the means of communication between the church in Germany and the Vatican. If this nunciature had been throughout the years of international peace a sure way of sending information between Catholic Germany and Rome, it was made even more indispensable by the war.

The frequent references to papal addresses, including the Christmas radio messages, that continually appear in Pius XII's letters to the German bishops, clearly indicate that the pope wanted to repeat in his correspondence the teaching he had developed in his addresses. He had learned that the German episcopate was increasingly being cut off from him and that often enough His messages were not reaching it. The longer the war, he explained to Cardinal Faulhaber on 2 February 1942, the more urgent it was that the episcopates of warring countries remain in touch with him so that they might be able both to hear each other's voices on essential moral problems as well as to avoid isolating any national episcopacy. In a letter dated 1 March 1942 he said:

> Whereas Our Christmas radio message found a strong echo in the world, indeed beyond the circle of Christianity, We learn with sadness that it was almost completely hidden from the hearing of German Catholics.

The pope's letters had to ward off the isolation of the German bishops. The principal elements for a program of peace as enunciated by Pius XII in his Christmas messages are again found in his letters to the bishops. Pius XII always spoke out in favor of a peace "with justice for all and for each of the belligerents, [a peace] that need not be ashamed when measured by Christian principles and, for this reason, a peace carrying in itself the guarantee of security and of time," as he wrote on 17 January 1940. And on 22 February 1942 Pius XII explained to Cardinal Faulhaber the way that would lead to what the pope called a "peace of understanding":

> It should rest neither on the question of war debts nor on that of claiming indemnities; it should call for the restoration of all territory that has been conquered and occupied by force; finally, it should not obligate any people to renounce essential or juridical necessities, a repudiation that each person would consider intolerable for his own country.

Pius XII did not change his position when Germany began its war with Russia, and he never spoke, even by means of allusion, about a "crusade" against Bolshevism or of a "holy war." His work on behalf of peace after June 1941 was in no way different from what he did previously; at the very least, it increased in intensity and extension. He never gave up his efforts "for a merciful peace which protects against violence and injustice, which brings together and reconciles, which establishes for all former belligerents without exception supportable relations and the possibility of a prosperous development" since "there can be no question of any other kind of peace for a Christian conscience" (24 February 1942).

In the principles he proposed for reestablishing peace, Pius XII was setting out from the presupposition, which at the time was anything but evident, that there was no collective fault and consequently no collective responsibility: "For Our part," he wrote on 15 October 1942, "We do whatever is in Our power to spare the German people from reprisals for things for which they, for the most part, are not responsible, and of which most of them perhaps know nothing at all."

In the midst of people at war, the Holy See's position each day became more delicate. Pius XII always returned to this more at length in his letters. On 20 February 1941 he wrote "that times are hard, and especially for the vicar of Christ, and that the papacy and the church are slowly being placed into a complex and perilous situation, such as they have but little seen throughout their long and sorrowful history." The vicar of Christ found himself confronted with some very painful choices, as he wrote on 20 February 1941, and was placed between contradictory demands of his pastoral office: "Where the pope wants to cry out loud and strong, it is expectation and silence that are unhappily often imposed on him; where he would act and give assistance, it is patience and waiting [that are imposed]."

Nonetheless, Pius XII believed it urgent frequently and insistently to warn believers, both priests and faithful, against the temptation to yield to the excitement of hatred and to blind violence, presented under the pretext of vigorous working for one's native country. If what he said remained fruitless as far as the leaders of the German regime and the belligerent powers were concerned, he at least wanted to safeguard the values of the Christian ideal among the faithful. What he feared was an insidious contagion of hatred and violence in the thinking of certain Catholics, especially the youth, and he strove by means of the bishops to immunize the faithful against this danger. As he wrote on 1 March to the archbishop of Freiburg:

> It is too painful to see those who till now have remained good Catholics being afflicted with a contagious way of acting and thinking, one that is opposed to God. This is especially true for the young. Do everything possible to spare the German people the unhappiness of having a youth that understands only force and violence, a youth that has lost respect for life, for the dignity and rights of all including those from other countries, a youth that no longer venerates the spiritual, the moral, and the religious.

And Pius XII congratulated the archbishop who, in his episcopal letter, considered not "only exclusively Christian and Catholic values, but also the highest moral principles of human existence and dignity."

Only the official German press, which formerly was obstinate in its opposition to Cardinal Pacelli, now attempted to represent Pope Pius XII as an enemy of Germany. Not only could each of his talks unleash a wave of reprisals, but, when they were cunningly presented by Nazi propaganda, there was the danger of alienating him from Catholic hearts and souls.

PIUS XII AND THE EPISCOPACY

It was for this reason that Pius XII in his 6 August 1940 letter to the Fulda episcopal conference reaffirmed his neutrality, or rather his impartiality, which did not mean any lack of interest. In regard to the telegrams he sent to the sovereigns of Belgium, Holland, and Luxembourg following the invasion of their countries, he explained that he could not remain silent in the face of the injustice, and yet he did not want to cast blame on the German people. If in 1914 Bethmann-Hollweg, the German chancellor, could say that the invasion of Belgium was contrary to international law without his patriotism being called into question, could the father of Christianity, when confronted with the repetition of this event on a much larger scale, be reproached for having expressed his compassion and his hope that the wrongs that caused the conflict would be rectified?

Throughout the war Pius XII returned to the same argument. He told the bishop of Limbourg not to allow faithful of his diocese to believe those who were presenting the pope as Germany's enemy. And the pope explained to Cardinal Faulhaber that he had always characterized his position concerning the war by using the word *impartiality* and not *neutrality. Neutrality* could be understood as indicating passive indifference, something not fitting for the head of the church when faced with such events:

> For Us impartiality means judging things according to truth and justice. But when it concerns Our public statements, We have closely considered the situation of the church in the various countries in order to spare the Catholics living there from unnecessary difficulties.

The conflict raging on two levels, that of the military between Germany and the western powers and that of the ideological and spiritual between Christianity and Nazi neopaganism, made the pope's task uniquely delicate. Among the things disturbing him, as he wrote on 3 March 1944 to the archbishop of Cologne, were "the superhuman effort necessary to keep the Holy See above the quarrels of the parties, and the confusion, almost impossible to unravel, between political and ideological currents, between violence and law (incomparably more so in the present conflict than in the last war) to the extent that it is extremely difficult to decide what must be done: reserve and prudent silence, or resolutely speaking out and vigorous action." In many cases an intervention by the pope might be understood as taking a stand against Germany and thus might provoke either reprisals against the church or misunderstandings among Catholics. Such confusion would risk not only nullifying everything he said but also placing too heavy a burden on believers and of disturbing their loyalty to the church and its leader. And so Pius XII's intention was to allow pastors to determine their responsibilities on a local level, as he very clearly explained in a 30 April 1943 letter to Cardinal Preysing:

> We give to the pastors who are working on the local level the duty of determining if and to what degree the danger of reprisals and of various forms of oppression occasioned by episcopal declarations—as well as perhaps other circumstances caused by the length and mentality of the war—seem to advise caution, *ad majora mala vitanda* [to avoid greater evil] despite alleged reasons urging the contrary.

It appears clear that these *majora mala vitanda,* which imposed on Pius XII the prudence of which he was a witness and to which he here alludes, were not only possible reprisals but even more misunderstandings capable of disturbing loyalties. Having congratulated the bishop of Trier for a courageous statement, the pope added: "We believe that reprisals, even if they are violent and even if they extend not only to the bishop but perhaps to others as well, cannot cancel out the good that the bishop's words, like your own, bring about among Catholics and certainly among others as well."

On the contrary, the pope himself felt that he had to observe great reserve. He gave proof of this in 1940 when euthanasia, practiced in the Reich upon the mentally ill, was condemned; a short decree from the Holy Office recalled the deep-seated immorality of the procedure: "We," said the pope, "had the highest court of the Curia speak as briefly and also as soberly as possible." But after the decree was issued, he waited for the bishops to draw conclusions. And when a bishop, like the bishop of Münster, spoke out against the condemned practice, the pope did not conceal his satisfaction. Clemens August Graf von Galen, the bishop of Münster in Westphalia, did not feel that he was bound to the same discretion as was the pope. The bishop's personal safety might well have been endangered, but no one could question his patriotism or accuse him of being an enemy of the German people. Furthermore, when in July 1941 the Gestapo expelled from Münster the Jesuits and the women religious of the Immaculata, and when eight hundred mentally ill people were moved out of the city's hospitals only to be returned to their families in cinerary urns, Bishop von Galen ascended the pulpit and called things by their real names: expelling innocent religious is a crime against justice; euthanasia is murder, punishable by death according to the code of criminal law; it is the gravest violation of the fifth commandment and it brings down the anger of an outraged God upon the guilty and their accomplices.

When Pius XII was made aware of these sermons, he wrote on 30 September 1941 to the bishop of Berlin, who had expressed his joy because of them:

> They brought about in Us also a consolation and a satisfaction which We have not experienced for a long time as We walk down a sorrowful path with the Catholics of Germany.

And on the following 2 February the pope showed that he was pleased with two sermons preached by the cardinal of Munich, one given on 2 November and the other on 31 December 1941

> We have read them with deep edification. And We also often know that the enlightened and courageous words of the bishop reverberate among his people. We know that such words are extremely effective, not to say necessary, in strengthening the faithful's moral resistance.

What the pope could not say without the risk of appearing as an enemy of Germany and of driving from the church Christians who were weak in their faith and enthused by German victories, a Bishop von Gallen or a Cardinal Faulhaber could declaim from the pulpit in Münster or in Munich.

And so at the beginning of 1942 Cardinal Faulhaber, addressing the priests and theology students who were called to military service, expressed the pope's views and exhorted them to "shun all ideas that are contrary to justice and Christian charity, to profess by action and when necessary also by word their Catholic convictions." He expressed his belief "that the Catholic Church in Germany and the German population will perhaps see a day when they can be pleased with themselves since the world will know that German Catholic priests, military chaplains, and soldiers are showing themselves, despite all, as representatives of the Redeemer's *benignitas et humanitas.*"

When Pius XII mentioned the millions of Catholics living in the Reich, he not only had in mind any reprisals that an address from him might unleash against them, but he was worried that he not place too great a burden on the faith and on the loyalty to the church of those who were sympathetic to the seductions and successes of the Nazi party. Pius XI's encyclical had explained at an opportune time the opposition between the national-socialist ideology and the doctrine of the church, which the party's propaganda was representing as being an enemy of the German nation. During this time of war such propaganda was bound to find some hearts and spirits more easily open to its arguments.

In order to foil such devices, Pius XII considered it to be of the highest importance that he stay in close contact with the episcopate so that his teaching might reach the faithful. And it was indeed to guarantee communications with the bishops, and through them with the priests and faithful of Germany, that the pope, contrary to the advice of the prelate in whom he placed the greatest confidence, kept open the nunciature in Berlin. Policy and diplomacy were serving the mission of the supreme pastor.

CHAPTER 4

The Church in
Occupied Poland*

~.~

A LREADY, several years before the war, the church's situation in
Germany had been of the utmost concern to the pope. In
Poland, it was the political and military events of September
1939 that presented the church in Poland and the Holy See with very
serious problems. Within a few weeks the country was divided by the
occupying forces of two foreign powers, each professing and practic-
ing, although under different forms, an antireligious doctrine and striv-
ing to have this become a daily reality with no regard for the norms of
international law and of human dignity.

On 11 September, when the German offensive was running wild
with no desire to spare civilian and military populations, the French
ambassador told the Secretariat of State that public opinion was "waiting for the Holy Father to say something to the effect that he was passing judgment on, and that he resented (?), this explosion of violence
and cruelty." Although the pope did not issue this condemnation, he
wanted to bring a word of comfort to the victims. On 30 September
1939 and in the presence of Cardinal Hlond, the primate of Poland,
Pius XII addressed the Polish colony in Rome and gave a message of
consolation and hope.

> You shall have like a bright cloud during this present night all the
> wonderful memories of your nation's history, ten centuries of
> which will soon have elapsed. These centuries have been conse-
> crated to the service of Christ and often to the noble defense of
> Christian Europe. You shall have your faith, especially a consistent

*Documentation for chapter 4: See *ADSS*, vols. 3 * and 3 * *; and the papers relative
to the letter of 2 March 1943, *ADSS*, vol. 7; and in Albrecht, *Der Notenwechsel;* and
ADSS, vol. 8 for references to the camp at Miranda del Ebro. Add: Gabriel Adriányi, *Dir
Kirche in Nord-Ost und Südosteuropa*, in *Handbuch der Kirchengeschichte* 7, pp. 508–36.

faith, still today worthy of what it was formerly, of what it was even yesterday....In its eventful life this people has known hours of pain and periods of apparent death; but it has also seen days of recovery and resurrection. Yet there is one thing your history has not seen, and your presence here today assures Us that it will never see, namely, an unfaithful Poland, a country separated from Jesus Christ and his church.

A week later, when Pius XII was working on the inaugural encyclical of his pontificate, the primate of Poland suggested that he insert several allusions to what was happening in Poland, for example, an affirmation of Poland's future resurrection and an invocation of the Virgin Mary under the title of "Help of Christians." The Poles would see this as a message of hope and faith. The pope adopted these suggestions in his encyclical *Summi Pontificatus:*

> The blood of countless people, even noncombatants, gives rise to a harrowing funereal lament, especially over Poland, a dearly beloved country. Because of its glorious attainments on behalf of Christian civilization, attainments indelibly inscribed in the annals of history, Poland has a right to the world's human and fraternal sympathy, and confident in the powerful intercession of Mary who is the *auxilium christianorum,* it awaits the hour of its resurrection in justice and peace.

In a letter of appreciation sent several days later Cardinal Hlond wrote: "These official and solemn expressions together with the unforgettable fatherly address of 3 September, first appreciated by the Poles, will greatly comfort future generations in their faith and in their traditional loyalty to the Holy See."

Meanwhile, all Poland had fallen to the power of national-socialist Germany and to Soviet Russia. Its western territories were for the most part annexed to the Reich; its middle section and the rest of the country were established as a type of colony, the *General Government,* whereas the Soviet Union annexed the eastern territories. And so Poland found itself between the hands of two powers, both intent upon eliminating Christianity. What the Nazi powers were still unable to do in Germany, where they faced a very solid ecclesiastical structure, they felt they were powerful enough to bring about in a country now in the hands of its army and police. To include here all the war years, it is estimated that 4 bishops, 1,996 priests, 113 clerics, and 238 female religious were murdered; sent to concentration camps were 3,642 priests, 389 clerics, 341 lay brothers, and 1,117 female religious.

PASTORAL ADMINISTRATION OF DIOCESES

One of the first questions the Holy See had to face was the government of dioceses. Many episcopal sees were already vacant when war broke out, including that of Warsaw, the capital, where negotiations regarding the successor of Cardinal Aleksander Kakowski, who died in December 1938, were constantly in progress. Archbishop Adam Stefan Sapieha, from Cracow, was elderly and in poor health, and he had already sent the newly elected pope his letter of resignation. Cardinal August Hlond, primate of Poland, was unable to return to his Diocese of Gniezno. He had gone to Warsaw at the request of the civil and military authorities; then he accompanied the Polish government to Romania; and from there he continued on to Rome. Stanislaw Okoniewski, the bishop of Chełmno-Pelplin, and Karol Mieczysław Radoński, the bishop of Włocławek, also had to leave their dioceses during the first days of the war. Bishop Radoński's auxiliary, Michał Kozal, was arrested at the end of 1939 and despite repeated entreaties by the Holy See for his freedom he remained in German hands till his death in Dachau. In this he shared in the fate of Bishop Władysław Goral, the auxiliary of Lublin, who died in the prison at Oranienburg-Sachsenhausen, close to Berlin, and of Bishop Leon Wetmański, the auxiliary of Płock and who died in Auschwitz. In the course of the following years other bishops were forced from their dioceses and were interned or arrested.

From the very first month of the occupation, hundreds of priests were arrested and executed; Catholic intellectuals, both clerics and laics, were sent to the concentration camp at Oranienburg. Beneath these measures was a scheme to eliminate the intellectual elite and the traditional influence of the clergy. Under such circumstances it was not allowed to appoint bishops. In the dioceses that were divided by the German-Soviet border, the bishops of neighboring dioceses, as apostolic administrators, assumed jurisdiction over those sections of a diocese that were separated from the episcopal see. Apostolic administrators (temporary and provisional diocesan heads who were given the powers of residential bishops) were appointed in other dioceses whose incumbents had been removed, whether interned or imprisoned. Faced with the prospect of further arrests, the bishop or apostolic administrator received instructions to designate two priests who might succeed him in case he should die or be interned.

On 9 October, when the Wehrmacht and the Red Army had taken over those territories laid out by the treaty signed in August, the Reich's ambassador to the Holy See, Diego von Bergen, told the pope "that no one envisioned any interference in the religious life of the people living in occupied territories." If, later on, pledged Bergen, any changes were anticipated, the government of the Reich would consult the Vatican. Meanwhile, the Holy See was attempting to obtain permission for Cardinal Hlond to return to his see of Poznań. But on 17 October the German ambassador sent the cardinal secretary of state a note saying that Cardinal Hlond was an enemy of Germany and could not receive permission to reenter his diocese. A similar decision was taken against the bishop of Chełmno-Pelplin and the bishop of Katowice.

The ambassador's note also said that the government of the Reich would not object if the temporary administration of these three sees were confided to three German prelates. Bishop Franz Hartz, from the *prelatura nullius* of Schneidemühl, could be administrator of the Archdiocese of Gniezno-Poznań; and it would be appreciated if Karl Maria Splett, bishop of Danzig, were entrusted with the Chełmno-Pelplin Diocese, and if Cardinal Bertram, archbishop of Breslau, be put in charge of the Katowice Diocese. On 20 October, following a meeting between the pope and the secretary of state, Monsignor Tardini noted: "His Eminence does not believe it opportune at this time to commit Polish dioceses to German prelates. His Holiness, acknowledging the soundness of this proposal, has decided to postpone it."

On the other hand, with the absence of a nuncio in Warsaw—he had escaped to Romania with the government—the Polish bishops began to address themselves to the nuncio in Berlin since this was the only recourse against the arbitrary actions of the German authorities and since it offered a more certain means of communicating with the Holy See. On 1 November Archbishop Orsenigo, the nuncio in Berlin, was authorized to exercise in Poland the same authority he had for Germany.

It was during these last months of 1939 that the pope made one of his most controversial decisions. A dispatch from Orsenigo on 25 November sketched a distressing picture of the church's situation in the Diocese of Chełmno-Pelplin in Poméranie. Stanislaw Okoniewski, the bishop, was in exile; his auxiliary was sick and unable to carry out his duties; the canons of the cathedral were scattered, with only one canon remaining there; the clergy were in hiding or in prison, or they had been murdered. Of the five hundred priests in the diocese, only twenty were still active.

Upon receiving Orsenigo's report, Pius XII changed his mind regarding his initial decision not to place, not even temporarily, German bishops as heads of Polish dioceses. Upon Orsenigo's letter the pope personally wrote on 29 November: "It seems opportune to appoint the bishop of Danzig as apostolic administrator *ad nutum Sanctae Sedis* for the diocese of Chełmno; eventually it should be explained to the Poles that this is a temporary arrangement since what we have here is a case of extreme necessity which, according to the nuncio's report, indeed seems to exist," and he named Karl Maria Splett, the bishop of Danzig, as apostolic administrator of Chełmno-Pelplin. The Polish government in London saw this appointment as violating a clause of the 1925 concordat, which stated that no part of Polish territory could be placed under the jurisdiction of a bishop whose see was located outside Poland. It was the Holy See's position that the temporary character of the appointment, and especially the extreme spiritual need of souls in this diocese, justified Splett's designation.

No less thorny was the question of Vilna, a city that now belonged to Lithuania by reason of an agreement made with the Soviet Union on 10 October. The Lithuanian government attempted to have the archbishop, Romuald Jałbrzykowski, removed from his see. On 4 January Cardinal Maglione replied to the minister of Lithuania: "The government of Kaunas should appreciate that the Holy See cannot run behind armies and change bishops as combatant troops occupy new territory belonging to countries other than their own." Archbishop Jałbrzykowski remained at his post till the Germans expelled him in 1942.

It was the government of the Reich itself that offered the Vatican an opportunity to make its position explicit. In a note of 29 August 1941 Ambassador von Bergen demanded that all ecclesiastical appointments to important posts in annexed or occupied regions be first communicated to Berlin. This applied to residential bishops, coadjutors with the right of succession, *prelati nullius,* apostolic administrators, capitular vicars, and all having equivalent functions in the governance of a diocese. The note expressly mentioned the General Government, Alsace, Lorraine, Luxembourg, lower Styria, Carinthia, and Carniole detached from Yugoslavia. Lastly, the note requested the same right of previous consultation for such ecclesiastical appointments made by the Holy See in the former Reich. German sovereignty, the note said, gave the government the right to make observations in matters of general policy concerning these appointments.

To this demand for the right of a quasi-veto on ecclesiastical appointments in regions under German control solely because of military occupation, the secretary of state replied on the following 18 January with a categorical refusal: it was the Holy See's custom not to initiate any change in the religious life of a country when that country was annexed or occupied following military operations. In addition, the appointment of religious leaders is the exclusive business of the church, and in this case the state's sovereignty cannot be invoked; finally, such matters can only be the object of concessions agreed upon in a concordat.

The reaction was not long in coming. On 10 June 1942 Hitler gave the following order: Since the Holy See had decided not to recognize the Reich's authority concerning ecclesiastical appointments in occupied territory, the Vatican would be denied any prerogative of mediating with the German authorities in regard to these territories. On 27 June Archbishop Orsenigo noted that responses to his requests and interventions were recently delayed longer than usual, and he reported that on the previous day Weizsäcker, the German secretary of state, told him that "the government had decided to no longer give consideration to initiatives and requests concerning territories that were not part of the former Reich."

Meanwhile, on 21 December 1939 Cardinal Hlond sent the Vatican a detailed report describing the waves of brutality and oppression surging over the church both in his two archdioceses and in other dioceses under German occupation. Two days later the pope ordered that a dossier be prepared that would be discussed in a special meeting of the cardinals belonging to the Congregation for Extraordinary Ecclesiastical Affairs: "What measures should be adopted?"

VATICAN RADIO

Following this meeting, the pope decided to make use of Vatican Radio. On 19 January 1940 Monsignor Montini wrote down the pope's

74

directive: "*Ex audientia Sanctissimi:* To give Vatican Radio, for its German broadcast, information regarding the conditions of the church in Poland." Consequently, on 21 January the radio station broadcast, not only in German but in other languages as well, a description and a denunciation of German policy in Poland. The announcer stated: "Conditions of religious, political, and economic life have thrown the Polish people, especially in those areas occupied by Germany, into a state of terror, of degradation, and, we dare say, of barbarism, much akin to what the communists imposed on Spain in 1936....The Germans employ the same methods, perhaps even worse, as those used by the Soviets." The English language broadcast declared that the outrages committed against the Polish people were not limited to Soviet territory. "Still more violent and constant are the attacks upon justice and the most elementary decency in sections of Poland that have fallen under German control."

The broadcasts of 21 January were well received by the Allies. For example, the *Manchester Guardian,* in an editorial of 24 January, mentioned the Vatican Radio broadcast devoted to Poland and concluded that it was "a warning to all who value our civilization that Europe is under a mortal danger." German reaction was soon to come. On 27 January Fritz Menshausen, the counselor of the German embassy, appeared at the Secretariat of State and told Monsignor Montini that his government had instructed him to inform the Holy See of the inopportuneness of the recent broadcast on Vatican Radio. The government deplored that the broadcast was provoking an anti-German attitude in the world press and in public opinion, and this could lead to "disagreeable repercussions" in the German newspapers as well as on the part of the German government. The Vatican was not mistaken as to the veiled threat of reprisals and, two days later, Monsignor Montini informed Menshausen that Cardinal Maglione had requested Vatican Radio to suspend any broadcasts about the sad conditions in Poland. On the same day as Menshausen's protest, 27 January, Cardinal Maglione sent a message to Archbishop Orsenigo; it appeared to be most innocent, authorizing Polish priests to offer mass during the week in private homes. In reality, this was a measure benefiting priests living in hiding, in the underground as people would soon say, and which Bishop Adamski from Katowice had requested through Orsenigo.

Somewhat later, in June, Germany's ambassador sent a note from his government declaring that, in view of the hostile and anti-German attitude of the Vatican's press and radio, priests and religious would not be allowed to leave Poland. This order further complicated the question of the pope's communications with Poland. The danger of having his letters intercepted by the Germans or by the Russians forced the pope, as it did the bishops, to be extremely cautious when drafting letters. Rarely mentioned were political questions and obvious allusions to the poor treatment of the population.

SOVIET OCCUPATION AND NAZI OCCUPATION

Relations between the Holy See and the bishops of Poland and the Baltic countries that for a time fell under the Soviet regime were still more difficult than relations with the bishops of areas occupied by the Germans. In addition to the nationalization of property and schools, a plan to impose atheism was set afoot, especially among the youth. Large-scale deportations were used to eliminate resistance, particularly among the intellectuals. In a letter of 30 August 1941 the metropolitan of Lwów, Andrzey Szeptyckyj, estimated that a half-million people had been deported from the Ukraine alone, where the vast majority were Greek Catholics.

The apostolic administrator of Estonia, E. Profittlich, a Jesuit, asked the Holy Father if, considering that he was a German citizen and in light of the Soviet occupation of Estonia, he should not return to Germany since he believed that under the Soviets he would not be able to carry out his office and would probably be deported to Siberia. The pope allowed the final decision to be made by Profittlich himself, who interpreted this reply as an invitation to remain at his post. As anticipated, he was deported to Siberia where he died. Mecisla Reinys, the apostolic administrator of Vilna, died in a Russian prison. Bishop Matulionis, from Kaišedorys, was often imprisoned by the Soviets and died in their hands. The Ukrainian bishops were hard hit. Bishop Kocyłowskyj from Przemyśl died in 1947 in a Kiev prison; his auxiliary, Bishop Lakota died at Vorkuta in 1950; Bishop Chomyszyn from Stanislawów also died, in 1945, as a prisoner in Kiev.

There can be no doubt that the occupying forces were determined to wipe out religion. On 29 December 1939 Andrzey Szeptyckyj wrote: "In all circumstances we see enmity, a hatred of religion, of the clergy, unbelievable; we might even say that there is enmity toward humanity in general." Further on he added: "This regime can only be explained by a universal diabolical possession." He suggested that the pope request the prayers of contemplative orders, the Carmelites, Trappists, Carthusians, and Camaldolese, for "the church's exorcisms are above space and can be done from a distance." In a letter of 6 August 1941, after the retreat of the Red Army, Bishop Chomyszyn expressed a similar judgment on the Soviet system: "They are fierce beasts animated by the spirit of the devil." Three weeks later, on 30 August 1941, the metropolitan of Lwów wrote: "It is indeed certain that under the Bolsheviks all of us came close to being killed; no attempt was made to hide their desire to destroy and suppress the last vestiges of Christianity." The substance of reports coming from the Baltic states was similar, like the one dated 10 October 1941 from Archbishop Skvireckas of Kaunas.

In 1941 occupation by the Germans replaced that by the Russians. Bishop Szeptyckyj, characterizing Nazi domination, repeated what he formerly said about Soviet control. In an August 1942 letter to Pius XII he wrote that he had experienced a certain measure of relief after the German army had liberated him from the Russians, but such a feeling was to last for only a short time:

> Today the whole country agrees that the German regime is evil, almost diabolical, and perhaps even more so than the Bolshevik regime. For at least a year no day has passed without the most horrible crimes being committed, assassinations, stealing, rapes, confiscations, and extortions. The Jews are the first victims, more than two hundred thousand of them having been killed in our small country.

A large part of the western Polish territories annexed to Germany after September 1939 formed an administrative unity called the Reichsgau Wartheland. From an ecclesiastical perspective, it included the Poznań Diocese, almost the whole Archdiocese of Gniezno, most of the Włocławek and of Łódź Dioceses, and small sections of the Warsaw and Częstochowa Dioceses, with several parishes belonging to the Diocese of Płock. Hitler appointed Arthur Greiser, the former president of the Danzig senate, as head of this region. Bearing the title of Reichsstatthalter, he was given exceptional powers. Under Greiser the policy was one of violent measures against priests and bishops, with an attempt by the Nazis to reorganize the church according to their own ideology. In the mind of the occupying forces, the ultimate objective was a Catholic Church independent of Rome, first in Warthegau and much later in the Reich and its dependent territories.

The number of priests from these areas who were arrested and then sent to Dachau or shot to death was exceptionally high. A report sent to Rome concluded that out of two thousand priests a third were dead and that seven hundred were in prison. Out of the six bishops who resided in this region when war was declared, there remained at the beginning of 1943 only the auxiliary and vicar general of the Archdiocese of Poznań, Walenty Dymek, who was kept under house arrest. Cardinal Hlond, Bishop Radoński, and Bishop Kozal were far away from their dioceses, and the Diocese of Łódź had lost its bishop and its auxiliary, both having been expelled by Germans in the General Government. In June 1941 Antoni Nowowiejski, the bishop of Płock, died in the concentration camp at Działdowo. His auxiliary, Bishop Leon Wetmański, died at Auschwitz. In October 1941 renewed harassment on the part of the authorities resulted in many hundreds of priests being sent to prison. Priests belonging to religious orders shared the same fate of expulsion, imprisonment, or execution. The seminaries in Gniezno, Poznań, Włocławek, and Łódź were closed, as were all the novitiates and houses of study belonging to religious communities. Four hundred religious were sent to a special internment camp.

As to the education of children, a decree from Greiser dated 19 August 1941 stated that religious instruction could only be given to children from ten to eighteen years, only in churches, and only for one hour each week, between three and five in the afternoon, and after previously notifying the police. Many churches were closed to worship, especially after October 1941. In churches that remained open, the liturgical offices were necessarily limited to specified hours, unless the lack of priests brought about the complete cessation of all religious services. Once the decree on religious associations establishing "the Roman Catholic Church of the German nation" was promulgated by Greiser on 13 September 1941, the vicars general of Gniezno and of Poznań had no doubts that Greiser's ultimate objective was a German Reich from which Christianity would be banned.

Consequently, these two prelates simultaneously decided to send an appeal to the pope, first alerting him as to the seriousness of what was happening because of the new legislation and then suggesting some possible solutions. This double petition was sent from Poznań on 26

September 1941. The two letters requested the pope to name one apostolic administrator for all the Germans within the whole district and another apostolic administrator for all the Poles. This was, as they saw it, the only solution capable of warding off, at least for the time being, the threat to religion brought about by the division, imposed by the occupation authorities, between Catholic Germans and Catholic Poles.

This appeal from the two interested parties did not fail to create a certain degree of perplexity in the Vatican. Nonetheless, the pope, taking into consideration the warning of the petition's authors that a quick decision was absolutely necessary, appointed Canon Paech from the cathedral in Poznań as apostolic administrator for the German Catholics in Warthegau. In March 1942, due to ill health, he was succeeded by Father Breitinger. But the apostolic administrator for the Poles, Walenty Dymek, who was the auxiliary and vicar general, was not appointed till April 1942, once he had given his consent. The new division of jurisdictions according to nationalities especially affected the Dioceses of Gniezno and of Poznań, whose ordinary, Cardinal Hlond, was in exile at Lourdes. On 26 May 1942 Cardinal Maglione instructed the nuncio at Vichy, Archbishop Valeri, to explain to Cardinal Hlond that the appointment of the two apostolic administrators was dictated by the "very grave religious situation" in Wartheland, where the crisis urgently required exceptional measures.

Meanwhile, requests continued to arrive at the Vatican asking the Holy See to do something about the extortions victimizing the Polish people. Archbishop Orsenigo in Berlin renewed his protests with Ribbentrop in letters of 28 August, 2 September, and 29 September. After the publication of Greiser's regulation of 13 September pertaining to religious associations, the nuncio sent another protest. Of all his messages, only the last two sent in August regarding ecclesiastical property received a reply.

COMPLAINTS FROM POLAND

These protests, sent through diplomatic channels, remained hidden within the recesses of chancellery walls. Polish Catholics, victims of the abuses against which the protests were raised, were completely unaware of them. As a consequence, people tended to surmise that the Holy See remained indifferent to their fate. In a letter of 2 August 1941

Cardinal Hlond gave a report describing the increasing discontent within certain Polish circles:

> We hear that the Poles are complaining that the pope does not protest against crimes when the Germans have three thousand Polish priests killed in concentration camps, that he does not speak out in condemnation when hundreds of priests and members of Catholic Action, including papal chamberlains, are shot to death, all exterminated without the slightest offense on their part.

The Vatican took seriously the warning given by the primate of Poland. On 3 September Cardinal Maglione sketched out the broad lines of a response and instructed Archbishop Valerio Valeri, the nuncio in Vichy who was vacationing in Rome, to personally clarify the matter to Cardinal Hlond.

First, Cardinal Maglione rejected the premise that the pope was silent as to the fate of the Polish Catholics. During the present year, 1941, the pope had spoken out three times: first, in an Easter message; then in a message to the United States on the occasion of a eucharistic congress in St. Paul, Minnesota; and finally in a message of 29 June, for the feast of Sts. Peter and Paul. Regarding a public declaration that more explicitly treated Poland, Cardinal Maglione said that the pope himself had to decide the opportune moment and the most advisable way of doing so.

It was not long before voices were heard from within Poland itself, voices requesting a forceful statement from the pope. On 3 November Archbishop Sapieha, after having explained that religious persecution was more intense than ever, most respectfully asked for an explicit condemnation or at least a message of comfort.

The response of the cardinal secretary of state, dated 29 November, was similar to the reply sent previously to Cardinal Hlond. Furthermore, Pius XII himself wrote to Archbishop Sapieha on 6 December, and through him to all the other bishops of Poland, encouraging them and praising their loyalty which, he said, was well-known to him. Nonetheless, he did not promise that in the near future he would issue more explicit words of condemnation, as Sapieha had suggested.

Archbishop Sapieha, not pressing the case, said that he believed he had done his duty by making the sovereign pontiff aware of the situation. Somewhat later, however, he wanted to the pope to know the exact tragic conditions being experienced by the Polish church. These hours of the nation's life, while Nazi power was at its height, are sadly disclosed in the letter he wrote to the pope on 28 February 1942. It describes all the horrors of the Nazi occupation of Poland:

> Our condition is indeed most tragic: deprived of almost all human rights, handed over to the cruelty of men who for the most part are bereft of all human feeling, we live in terrible horror, continually in danger of losing everything in case of escape or of deportation, óf incarceration in camps called concentration camps, from which but few leave alive. In these camps thousands and thousands of our best brothers are detained, and without legal proceedings or having committed any crimes. Among these are many priests, both secular and religious. According to the law, we are deprived of almost everything necessary for life, for what is legally assigned us is not sufficient for the minimal necessities of life. At this time a contagious typhus rages, spreading more and more since medicines and remedies are lacking, and the authorities satisfy themselves with promises or restrict themselves to a cruel segregation of the sick. In these conditions is it any surprise that people are irritated and exasperated, and that Communism and other such movements have so much room in which to agitate?

Under such conditions, continued the prelate, anti-Roman propaganda finds a well-prepared soil among those people who, "seeing the violence and atrocities that overwhelm us, wish to hear a condemnation of these crimes, and they make their own without reflecting the rash judgments of agitators."

The prelate sent this letter to an Italian chaplain, Pirro Scavizzi, but he then became fearful and dispatched a messenger to the chaplain asking him to burn the document "so that it not fall into the hands of the Germans who would shoot all bishops and perhaps even others." The chaplain in effect destroyed the letter, but only after he made a handwritten copy of it, a copy on which he certified the document's authenticity.

H. Breitinger, a Franciscan who was the apostolic administrator for the Germans in Warthegau, noted somewhat later, on 28 July 1942: "Polish Catholics can always be heard asking if there is a God when such injustices are possible, or indeed if the pope, concerning whom one has so often told stories and preached when things were going well for the Poles, has not completely forgotten the Poles now that they are in such great need." These complaints were not justified, believed Breitinger, but he thought it was his duty to point them out.

Later, two letters arrived in the Vatican from Karol Radoński, bishop of Włocławek, one of the three Polish prelates who were forced to pass the war in exile. He had just read the news, although it was not exact, published by the Catholic press in England that Father Breitinger had been appointed apostolic administrator for Warthegau, which included his own Diocese of Włocławek. Radoński, in a letter from London dated 14 September 1942, strongly protested to Cardinal Maglione:

> Here it is, say the Poles, that churches are being profaned or closed, that religion has been laid waste, that worship ceases, that bishops are expelled, that hundreds of priests have been killed or sent to prison, that holy virgins are handed over to the pleasures of depraved brigands, that almost every day innocent hostages are killed under the eyes of children who are forced to participate in this spectacle, that the people, deprived of everything, die from hunger, and the pope remains silent as if he did not care for his sheep.

He added that the Germans clamor that everything is being done in the sight of the pope, with his knowledge and consent. And since no denial has been made, the people, in the end, believe this to be true. Radoński finally added that according to recent information the Germans had allowed *l'Osservatore Romano* to enter Germany and even Poland. The price of such silence, it was said in Poland, stood in unfortunate contrast with Pius IX's conduct in 1864.

Breitinger, in a further letter to the pope dated 23 November, confirmed the warning that had come from London: "The Catholic population of Wartheland always asks the same question: the people want to know whether the pope is unable to assist them and why he keeps silent." Even if a public condemnation were not possible, the Catholics of Wartheland believed that a vigorous protest from the pope to the German government would not be without effect.

But a letter from Archbishop Sapieha on 28 October had already given the key to the situation: "We greatly deplore the fact that we are unable to communicate to our faithful the letters from Your Holiness, but doing so would merely be a pretext for new persecutions, and we already have victims who were suspected of communicating secretly with the Apostolic See."

Wladislas Raczkiewicz, the president of the republic, in turn sent a letter dated 2 January 1943 to Pius XII. Confronted with a situation that was always becoming more insufferable, the president stated that his people "were not thirsting for vengeance but for justice." He was asking less for diplomatic and material assistance than for words that would clearly and distinctly indicate where the evil was to be found, words that would stigmatize the authors of the evil.

Replying to the president, Pius XII recalled what he had said and done since the beginning of the war in his attempts to alleviate the terrible suffering. He did not fail

> to remind those leading the war and those responsible for it of the requirements of justice and of humanity, that no reason for war authorizes trampling anyone under foot. This is what Our ministry demands of Us as a defender of law, both divine as well as human. Unhappily, Our words have not been listened to all over, and at times they have not even been brought to the attention of those to whom they should have surely brought inner comfort.

By coincidence, the very day the pope's response was sent to President Raczkiewicz, namely, on 20 February 1943, Ambassador Papée informed the Vatican that his government had instructed him to thank the sovereign pontiff, who "in his last Christmas address had implicitly condemned all the injustices and cruelties suffered by the Polish people at the hands of the Germans. Poland acclaims this condemnation; it thanks the Holy Father for his words, as well as for everything he thinks fit to do so that the sufferings of the Polish nation may be alleviated." And yet the Polish government believed that an explicit denunciation of Nazi crimes would not only bring comfort to the Poles but would bring back most Germans to reason.

Nonetheless, the cardinal secretary of state responded to Bishop Radoński on 9 January 1943, and yet a certain trace of irritation was apparent. The bishop had taken Breitinger's appointment as an accomplished fact, and he gave the impression that he believed the accusations he reported, even the most outrageous ones, for example, seeing the pope's silence as a trade-off for the unhindered distribution of *l'Osservatore Romano*. It was deplorable to see such false news finding credence among those whose mission it was to defend the truth. Cardinal Maglione recalled the circumstances that led to the appointment of Bishop Splett as administrator of the Diocese of Chełmno-Pelplin and to the appointment of the two apostolic administrators in parts of Poland annexed by Germany. He stressed that the pope's conduct had been approved by those bishops who still remained in Poland, and he then went on to explain why the words of encouragement and consolation sent to the Polish bishops had not been made public:

> If you ask why the documents sent by the Pontiff to the Polish bishops have not as yet been made public, know that it is because it seems better in the Vatican to follow the same norms that the bishops themselves observe. As is known, they have not made these documents public so that the sheep confided to their care do not become victims of new and still more fierce persecutions. Isn't this what has to be done? Should the father of Christianity increase the misfortunes suffered by the Poles in their own country?

Bishop Radoński then replied in a letter of 15 February, in part to apologize because of the extraordinary and abnormal living conditions of the Poles, who were now approaching their fourth year of exile, and to return to the arguments he proffered as to the pope making a public statement. He questioned the so-called wisdom of those loudly clamoring for prudence and silence.

> I wonder just which bishops have asked the Holy Father to remain silent, and I do not venture to judge whether their advice has been well chosen. According to Your Eminence, they did so out of fear of aggravating the persecution. But the facts prove that with the pope being silent, each day sees the persecution becoming more cruel. Infants are now being snatched from their parents and deported as a group to Germany, and the mothers who try to defend them are immediately killed. When such crimes, which cry out to heaven for vengeance, are committed, the inexplicable silence of the supreme head of the church becomes for those who do not know its reason—and there are thousands of them—a cause for spiritual downfall.

The requests coming from London, despite their somewhat unrestrained tone, were given consideration. On 4 February 1943 Cardinal Maglione wrote to Archbishop Sapieha and suggested that perhaps it would be useful if some of the letters—or at least one or two of them—sent by the pope to the bishops of Poland be made public. The archbishop of Cracow came up with a different solution, namely, that the pope write another letter, one that would recapitulate the previous ones. New information would eventually be given on the relief efforts mentioned in the address given on 23 December 1940. This letter could be immediately printed in the *Acta Apostolicae Sedis* and sent to Poland in the usual way.

RESPONSES OF THE HOLY SEE TO THE BISHOPS

A letter conforming to what Archbishop Sapieha wanted was drawn up at the Secretariat of State and completed on 31 May 1943. At the last minute Pius XII took the matter in hand. On 2 June 1943, the feast of his patron St. Eugene, the pope himself spoke directly concerning the Polish situation, doing so in terms that had not been heard since the first year of the war. His allusions to Poland were brief but forceful, and this time they were not lost upon Polish Catholics. The pope said that he was not forgetful of any of the people victimized by the war, but at this time he wanted to call special attention

> to the tragic fate of the Polish people who, surrounded by strong countries, are being tossed about by the vicissitudes and the uncertainties of a dramatic cyclone of war. Our teaching and Our declarations, so often repeated, leave no room for doubt as to the principles with which the Christian conscience should judge such actions, no matter who is responsible for them. No one who knows the history of Christian Europe can be ignorant of, or allow to be forgotten, how so many of Poland's saints and heroes, its intellectuals and thinkers, have contributed to the formation of Europe's and the world's spiritual patrimony, and also how so many of the simple and faithful Polish people, being heroically silent about their sufferings down the centuries, have contributed to the development and preservation of Christian Europe.

On 11 June Cardinal Hlond wrote the cardinal secretary of state: "The Poles needed this, and they anxiously awaited this statement, which put an end to the fables of Hitler's propaganda that the Holy See had simply given up in regard to the situation in Poland." In warmer terms the cardinal addressed Pius XII, and he described the speech of 2 June as an especially valuable document for future generations, as were the unforgettable speech at Castelgandolfo and the encyclical *Summi Pontificatus.* An almost identical reaction was that of Archbishop Sapieha writing from Cracow on 18 June:

> I am convinced that the gratitude of the Polish people will never forget these noble and holy words, which will not only be the source of a new and even more faithful love toward the Holy Father, but will also be a new bond always more closely uniting this people with the Holy See; at the same time they will be a very effective antidote against the poisonous efforts of enemy propaganda.

The archbishop added that he would try to publicize the speech as much as possible by having copies printed, provided the authorities would give permission for this.

The German government could not mistake the implication of the pope's words. Three months earlier it had received a diplomatic note that represented the culmination in a series of questions addressed to it by the Holy See.

When Archbishop Sapieha's letter of 28 February 1942, which had been entrusted to Pirro Scavizzi, arrived at the Vatican—it was the copy made by the same priest who accompanied it with his own oral report—it produced a deep impression. An attempt was made to discover measures appropriate to the unheard-of circumstances described in the letter. A note from Monsignor Tardini on 18 May 1942 reports:

> I spoke with His Highest Eminence (Maglione) about the very sad situation in Poland where the unfortunate Poles are deprived of the most fundamental rights, where the bishops and the clergy are persecuted, beaten, and impeded from exercising their ministry. The archbishop of Cracow continues to be the support of the episcopate and of the faithful: his firm and courageous attitude has attracted the sympathy and admiration of all but, as is obvious, it has also invited the threats of the Germans whose Gestapo surround him, spy on him, set traps for him, steal from him, and imprison his associates: in a word, they are creating a repressive atmosphere around him.

Two things, noted Tardini, were necessary: first, to support the morale of the Polish bishops and especially that of the archbishop of Cracow; and then to offer encouragement to the Polish people by showing them that the Holy See is the defender of inviolable Christian and human rights. The first objective seemed rather easy to accomplish: the second much less so. Was it necessary to issue a solemn protest before the whole world? Tardini rejected a display of this kind, not that there was no basis for such a protest, nor that a public condemnation did not fall within the prerogatives of the Holy See, "which is likewise the protector of natural law." And yet,

> in present circumstances, a public condemnation by the Holy See would largely be exploited for political gain by the parties engaged in the conflict. Furthermore, the German government, feeling itself chastised by this, would undoubtedly do two things: it would increase its persecution of Catholicism in Poland, and it would use every means to hinder the Holy See from having contact with the Polish episcopacy and from performing its works of charity, which for the moment it can still carry out although in a limited way. And so a public statement from the Holy See would surely be perverted and exploited for purposes of persecution.

THE NOTE TO RIBBENTROP

A diplomatic note, in Tardini's opinion, would avoid the drawbacks of a public statement. What he had in mind was a "good report," one that would simultaneously be elevated, noble, delicate in form, and yet serious in substance, namely, in the arguments offered. He was under no illusion: the note would not put a halt to the persecutors, but it would be a document for the future. Perhaps it could be sent to the archbishop of Cracow and even to the bishops.

The task of composing the note was begun. While awaiting it, Archbishop Orsenigo, the nuncio in Berlin, received instructions that allow us to glimpse a hardening of the Holy See's attitude. Several letters from Cardinal Maglione, from the end of 1942 and the beginning of 1943, as well as those from 18 November 1942 and the following 13 January, might in retrospect appear as preparatory material for the note. Much time was spent preparing the document. This was done under Tardini's watchful eyes by the *minutante,* much later Cardinal Antonio Samoré, who began work on it seventeen times. Its final form was that of a letter dated 2 March 1943 and signed by the cardinal secretary of state. Notwithstanding its obvious diplomatic language, the substance of the note was a crushing indictment of the abuses and violations of the most elementary rights inflicted on the church in Poland.

The Holy See stated that it was "acutely disturbed by the serious and systematic difficulties which, in certain territories under the authority of the Reich, affect the free profession of religious faith and the exercise of Catholic worship." There followed a detailed report of the cruelties brought upon Poland by the Nazi powers. Of the six bishops who lived in the territory annexed from western Poland, only one remains, and he is hindered from exercising his pastoral mission; no satisfactory explanation has been given in regard to the arrests, expulsions, and internments suffered by the other bishops.

In the western provinces, the report continued, there were more than a thousand priests. Their number has been drastically reduced: many have been shot and others have been sent to prisons or concentration camps. At Dachau many hundreds of them were already found in October 1941, and the number has since increased by several hundred. Some areas are completely without priests; the city of Poznań, with its two hundred thousand inhabitants, has only four of them. There is a similar elimination of religious; female religious, about four hundred in number, have been interned in a camp, and even though it was said that this was only a temporary measure, these sisters are still detained there. In Warthegau Catholic schools have been closed, and a decree of the Reichstatthalter imposes the strictest limits on religious instruction, worship, and the religious participation of the faithful. It is forbidden to use the Polish language in religious functions and even in confession. Polish men are forbidden to marry before the age of twenty-eight; for women the age is twenty-five. The cathedrals in Gniezno, Poznań, Włocławek, and Łódź are being used for profane purposes. And abolished is the system providing financial aid to the clergy.

According to the report, the situation is hardly any better in other areas annexed to the Reich: the district of eastern Prussia, the district of Danzig-Prussia in the west, and the district of upper Silesia. The bishop of Chełmno has not been given permission to return to his see. The bishop of Płock, Antoni Nowowiejski, has been expelled, whereas his auxiliary, Bishop Wetmański has died in a "transit camp." As to the General Government, the few seminaries that are still functioning do so under difficult circumstances, and the recruitment of candidates has been made almost impossible. Two dioceses are completely without bishops: Pińsk whose ordinary, Kasimir Bukraba, is sick and whose auxiliary, Karol Niemira, has not been granted permission to return; and Lublin where the ordinary, M. Fulman, and his auxiliary, Wladyslaw Goral, are under arrest, the former having been sent to a far distant place of residence, and the latter being held in a concentration camp. The archbishop of Vilna, Romuald Jałbrzykowski, is under house arrest somewhere far removed from his diocese and is deprived of any possibility of directing the faithful.

Another area of complaint and protest was the government's refusal to allow religious assistance to be given to the Poles working in Germany. Among other restrictions, they were not allowed to contract legal marriage, and confessions in Polish were forbidden. And during all this time communications between the Polish hierarchy and the Holy See remained broken. The note recalls that in March 1940 the pope had in vain personally requested the foreign minister, Ribbentrop, that a papal representative be sent into Poland. Even humanitarian assistance was obstructed by the German authorities in the General Government.

In conclusion, the always diplomatically worded letter to Ribbentrop stresses that the Holy See observes the greatest reserve and only does what is required dictated by spiritual principles alone, namely, the good of souls. It might have been expected that this attitude would have been requited, thus leading the German authorities to modify their behavior toward Catholics and to grant them religious freedom. Yet even today the Holy See hopes

> that the present report because of the number of particular facts it recalls will, as it should, engage the attention of the government of the Reich and lead this same government to effect a cessation of such a painful situation created by measures opposed to both natural and divine law.

The document was sent to the nuncio in Berlin, who was instructed to present it to Ribbentrop, the foreign minister, since it was almost certain that the German ambassador to the Vatican would reject it. On 15 March Archbishop Orsenigo presented the note in an envelope with a seal to Weizsäcker, the secretary of state, and asked that it be delivered to the foreign minister. Weizsäcker promised to pass it on, but two days later he summoned the nuncio to tell him that he had opened the letter and that, viewing its contents, he was unable to forward it to the minister since the document concerned questions that, in the eyes of the Reich, fell beyond the nuncio's competence. To avoid very serious consequences and so as not to further undermine already strained relations between the Holy See and Germany, Weizsäcker did not send the letter to the minister, and he asked the nuncio to take it back and to consider it as not ever having been presented. Initially the nuncio insisted that the letter be sent to its intended recipient, but he soon realized that "the document had been brought to the attention of the foreign minister, and perhaps even to someone higher up." He believed he would do well by following Weizsäcker's advice and took the document back from him.

In the Vatican, after consulting with the Congregation for Extraordinary Ecclesiastical Affairs, Pius XII instructed Orsenigo to tell the minister that the Holy See regarded his refusal to accept the letter as an unfriendly act and that it considered the document "as having reached its destination." In fact, the letter had already been translated into German for use by higher authorities.

Although Pius XII did not judge it opportune, at least for the present, to issue a new public statement, he took an action that could not but displease Germany when he decided to appoint a chargé d'affaires to the Polish government in London; it was Archbishop Godfrey, the apostolic delegate to Great Britain. It had not been possible for the Holy See's chargé d'affaires to the Angers government, Monsignor Pacini, to join the Polish government on English soil since England refused to admit him because he was "an enemy by birth," namely, he was Italian. On 5 April Monsignor Tardini informed Casimir Papée, Poland's ambassador to the Holy See, of the pope's decision and requested that he inform his government. It was satisfied with the appointment, and on 14 May Cardinal Maglione officially notified the Polish foreign minister, Count Raczyński, as well as Archbishop Godfrey, both of whom gave their full consent. This action might seem to have been of minimal importance. And yet the English government sent a message to the Holy See saying that "it had given its consent to this solution, which was exceptional in every way."

MIRANDA DEL EBRO

It was about the same time that what the Holy See had been doing for more than a year on behalf of the Poles saw success. Some of them, fleeing the invasion of France by the German armies, were taking refuge in Spain, where they were arrested and detained under wretched conditions in the camp at Miranda del Ebro. For the most part they were former soldiers, always ready to bear arms and numbering about five hundred. On the one hand, they risked having the Germans demand their return; and yet, on the other hand, for the Vatican to request their freedom would appear as a hostile act against the Reich. Nonetheless, the nuncio in Spain was instructed to ask the Spanish government to allow them to leave the Iberian peninsula for a South American country. And when the foreign minister returned to Rome in 1942, Cardinal Maglione spoke to him about giving them their freedom. Serrano Suñer said that he personally favored doing so, but that he could do nothing without the agreement of the Germans—at the time, this was tantamount to a refusal. Finally, in March 1943 the refugees were allowed to leave Spain.

Meanwhile, during the second half of 1943 communications became more and more uncertain between the Poles in Poland and the Holy See, which was progressively losing all contact with the bishops. On 16 November 1943 Cardinal Maglione requested Archbishop Orsenigo to send him more information regarding Warthegau since news about Polish Catholics was becoming very infrequent. Contact with eastern Poland, which was already almost completely under the control of the Red Army, was even more difficult. On 11 February 1944 the auxiliary bishop of Przemyśl, who had been appointed apostolic administrator of the Diocese of Luck, informed the nuncio that it was physically impossible for him to reach this city. The situation was summarized in a pithy statement from the Secretariat of State on 12 February 1945: "The situation in Poland has to be most sad. For almost two years now there has been no news. In the beginning it was very infrequent; now there is absolutely nothing." As to the chapter vicar of Warsaw, Wladislas Szlagowski, nothing was known, not even whether he survived the battle of Warsaw. There was no news about Bishop Dymek, Archbishop Sapieha, and Bishop Twardowski. In the Vatican there was talk of asking the United States to help send a representative of the pope, perhaps an American of Polish origin, who could report to the Holy See on the situation in the country. Although a letter containing this proposal was sent on 17 February 1945 by Monsignor Tardini to Archbishop Cicognani in Washington, nothing came of it. In like manner nothing could be done when the Germans, in the middle of 1944, forcefully banished almost the whole Catholic hierarchy from the Baltic states.

The arrest of Cardinal Hlond at the beginning of 1944 brought about repeated yet useless attempts to secure his release. The imprisonment of Poland's primate was announced on 9 February 1944 by Archbishop Valeri, who somewhat later wrote that two members of the Gestapo arrived at the abbey of Hautecombe, located in Savoy, where the cardinal was then residing, and had him taken away under the pretense that he was to have a brief interview. In fact, he was escorted to Paris and much later to Bar-le-Duc. The reasons for the cardinal's arrest have never been made very clear. He was finally taken to Wiedenbrück in the Archdiocese of Paderborn; it was here that he was found and liberated by the American troops. He was flown to Paris, and from there he went to Rome. Even though the United States refused to intervene with the Polish authorities for his return, the primate was able to go back to his native land after an automobile trip through regions greatly devastated by the war. The Holy See, abandoning the idea of sending a special papal representative to Poland, granted Cardinal Hlond the broadest of powers to restore the church's life in that country.

CHAPTER 5

The Victorious Reich*

~·~

THE NOISE OF PANZERS roaring down the roads and of nose-diving stutkas dropping their bombs was followed by the silence of the June 1940 armistice. Continental Europe coming out of its torpor appeared to awaken under Nazi domination. Holland, Belgium, Luxembourg, the northern half of France, all had fallen under the Wehrmacht's control, with so-called free France being under strict surveillance; Mussolini's Italy had coupled its fate to that of Hitler's Germany; the Balkan states felt that the days of their freedom were numbered; Switzerland, entrenched in the Alps, feared what had happened to Austria and Czechoslovakia; Spain in its very weakness was able to avoid immediate submission. Facing the continent, Great Britain alone proclaimed through Churchill's voice the will to continue the struggle on land, on sea, and in the air till total victory be achieved. Yet a number of politicians were questioning the consequences of this resolve, and in June 1940 the question remained whether the western powers had lost only the battle or whether they had indeed lost the war. Mussolini in Italy, Serrano Suñer in Spain, and Laval in France believed the latter; Churchill and de Gaulle strongly believed the former; and many others, among whom appeared to be Pétain and Franco, were asking the same question and were awaiting decisive signs.

The identical question was also being asked in the Vatican. Nothing in the Third Reich's relations with the church would dispose the Holy See to hope for a German victory; such a hypothesis could not have been a priori discarded in light of the Wehrmacht's stunning victories. From early on Pius XII clearly defined the contours of his policy: impartiality between warring countries. But this impartiality required a constant effort to retain the clear-sightedness and the will power needed by the Vatican to resist the pressures that were renewed each day.

*Documentation for chapter 5: See *ADSS,* vol. 4; document of 15 July 1941, see *ADSS,* vol. 5. Add *FRUS,* 1941, vol. 2. See also Chadwick, *Britain and the Vatican.*

The German offensive of May 1940 led the German armies through all of Holland, Belgium, and Luxembourg. The sovereigns of the Low Countries and of Luxembourg had left their countries, and King Leopold was a prisoner in his own kingdom. The administration of these countries was in the hands of the authorities of the Reich. In a verbal note dated 29 June 1940 and given to Archbishop Orsenigo the Vatican was informed that the nunciatures in Brussels and The Hague no longer served any purpose, and if the Holy See had to discuss any questions concerning these countries, it should address Wilhelmstrasse by means of the nunciature in Berlin.

Archbishop Orsenigo responded by explaining to Ernst von Weizsäcker, the German secretary of state, the special position of the Holy See's representatives as compared to other diplomats: In addition to their political role as being ambassadors to a government, nuncios carried out a religious mission to the bishops and the faithful. Weizsäcker listened politely but without leaving much room for hope. In fact, further notes presented to Berlin upon instructions from Pius XII proved useless: The nuncio in Belgium, Archbishop Micara, had to depart Brussels, and Paolo Giobbe, the internuncio in Holland, was forced to take leave of The Hague.

Hardly had Micara and Giobbe returned to Rome deprived of their respective posts by the Nazi invasion when their colleagues in the Baltic States underwent the same fate after the Soviet invasion. The nuncios in Kaunas and Riga, Archbishops Arata and Centoz, were forced to leave, and similar difficulties soon appeared elsewhere on the horizon.

Italy's entrance into the war gave rise to military activity within the borders of certain English and Italian colonies. In the English colony of Kenya, the Catholic mission was under the direction of the apostolic delegate in Mombasa, Archbishop Riberi. The apostolic delegate in London, Archbishop Godfrey, informed the Secretariat of State that at a time of war, the presence of these Vatican envoys, belonging as they did to an enemy nation, could have unfortunate consequences and become a source of friction between the British government and the Holy See. To avoid such risks, London believed it desirable that members of apostolic delegations who were of enemy nationalities be transferred to other missions, at least for the duration of the war. In vain did Monsignor Tardini explain to Osborne, the British minister at the Vatican, that the Holy Father would be all the more offended by this since during the last war he was nuncio to Germany, where he enjoyed the greatest freedom of movement. But His Majesty's government remained intractable. Pius XII, personally receiving the British minister in an audience on 2 October, promised to recall Archbishop Riberi.

Somewhat later and seemingly with little resistance the Vatican resigned itself to the removal of the vicar apostolic in Egypt, Monsignor Igino Nuti, and the secretary of the apostolic delegation in London, Monsignor Umberto Mozzoni.

The British government had not reached the end of its demands. For almost a century and a half Malta had served as a base for the English Mediterranean fleet. After Italy entered the war, Mussolini conducted air and sea attacks against this island whose proximity seemed to promise easy victory. The very person of Malta's archbishop could not leave the English indifferent. The archbishop at the time was Mauro Caruana, seventy-three years old, and the condition of his health had caused the Holy See to consider appointing a coadjutor, namely, Bishop Gonzi. By virtue of an agreement signed in 1890, the British government had the right to present its observations on the appointment of Malta's archbishop. And so the Holy See sent London the name of Gonzi, who was the bishop of Gozo, a neighboring island that formed one ecclesiastical province together with Malta. Bishop Gonzi, however, had enemies among the local authorities, and they pretended that he was friendly toward the pro-Italian movement. The British government raised objections against Bishop Gonzi and, going beyond the limits of the 1890 agreement, itself advanced the name of another candidate. And so the appointment of Malta's archbishop brought about a new exchange of diplomatic notes in which courtesy did not conceal intransigence. Gonzi had to wait till October 1943 before becoming Malta's coadjutor-archbishop.

APPOINTING BISHOPS DURING WARTIME

While the British government was attempting to install in Malta an archbishop of its own liking, the German government was demanding a right in regard to episcopal appointments in the occupied territories. Since 1939 Bohemia was under the protectorate of the Reich, but most of the people in the Budejovice diocese were Czech, with a minority being German. The pope appointed A. Eltschkner to be bishop there and informed the German government of this before the appointment was announced in *l'Osservatore Romano*. On 24 July Ambassador von Bergen appeared at the Vatican to meet with Monsignor Tardini: Berlin had instructed him to demand that a German bishop or one of German origin be appointed for Budejovice. Tardini answered that the Holy See usually appointed bishops of the same nationality as their sheep, and since the vast majority of people living in the Budejovice Diocese were Czech, it was appropriate that the bishop also be Czech. The ambassador insisted and recalled that in Alsace-Lorraine the Holy See, after the war of 1914, had appointed French bishops for both Metz and Strasbourg. Tardini replied that these appointments were made only after peace was established and when these cities were once again part of France; the situation was quite different regarding Budejovice. The German ambassador concluded by acknowledging that the Reich had, in fact, no right to interfere in this appointment, but he hinted that J. Remiger, the auxiliary bishop of Prague, would be an excellent candidate. Tardini promised to refer the matter to his superiors. Two days later he made a note of Cardinal Maglione's response: The nuncio will be instructed to tell Berlin that the appointment has been made, and that, furthermore, even in mission countries clergy from the local area are chosen as bishops.

In a message of 21 September Archbishop Orsenigo replied that Berlin felt that the Budejovice appointment, done without prior notice, was a hostile act on the part of the Vatican. The Germans pretended that a broad investigation had shown them that the procedure of giving advance notice was followed for all nations having diplomatic relations with the Holy See. In Budejovice the government was facing a fait accompli. Orsenigo talked with the secretary of state, Weizsäcker, for some time about this, and the nuncio boldly observed that in matters of fait accompli, the government of the Reich was in no position to complain. Finally, Weizsäcker recommended drawing things out and allowing the capitular vicar to govern the diocese. Prepared for by Tardini's notes, the Vatican's response, dated 16 October, refused to accept the claims of the Reich. This appointment to the bishopric of Budejovice could hardly be seen as a hostile act against the German government since special care had been taken to notify Berlin of the appointment several days before its publication in *l'Osservatore Romano*.

Nonetheless, the question was reconsidered by the Congregation for Extraordinary Ecclesiastical Affairs, which concluded that it was necessary to follow through with the appointment that had already been made, again stating that the Holy See had designated a Czech bishop for a Czech population for the good of souls. Should the German authorities hinder the bishop from taking possession of his see, the appointment would not be withdrawn, but provision would be made for the diocese to be governed in a temporary manner, while waiting "for better times that will allow the shepherd to rejoin his flock."

In a second arbitration session, which took place in Vienna on 29 August 1940, Hungary obtained some of the territory taken from Romania and thus was now demanding a reorganization of ecclesiastical administration corresponding to the new political situation. In this regard Monsignor Tardini noted: Too frequent changes in ecclesiastical government harm the good of souls. This is why the Holy See will only make decisions when faced with a situation that is clear and more or less definitive: The oppressed peoples, the Poles, Norwegians, Danes, Belgians, Dutch, Albanians, Greeks, Austrians, Czechs, Romanians are too numerous to be indefinitely held in slavery. "At present they are slaves because Germany and Italy are controlled by an iron dictatorship, but this cannot last for long." Tardini concluded:

> The present historical moment is very serious from this point of view: Hitler, the persecutor of the church and the master of much of Europe, wishes in one way or another to impose the appointment of German bishops within non-German territories, and he wants to exercise an influence on the appointments, more so than previously agreed to.... What can the Holy See do? It can do what it has always done: reaffirm and defend its liberty, firmly maintain its rights against government coercion when such pressure is detrimental to the good of souls. The people will joyfully greet such apostolic firmness on the part of the Holy See and will stand close around it as the sole herald of divine truth and the sole protector of human dignity.

VATICAN RADIO

Just as he did in regard to the bishop of Budejovice, Nuncio Orsenigo in Berlin repeatedly called for prudence in another matter, that of Vatican Radio. Complaints from the German ambassador against both genuine and imaginary broadcasts as well as protests from the Allies regarding the reserve of the pope succeeded one another throughout the war and made especially uncomfortable those who were more or less immediately responsible for the Vatican's information service.

On 17 October 1940 the chargé d'affaires at the German embassy, Fritz Menshausen, went to Cardinal Maglione: His government had instructed him to protest the Vatican broadcast that aired two days earlier regarding the situation in Alsace-Lorraine; it described the German police as being inhumane and barbarian, or something of this kind. The German diplomat demanded to see the precise text of the broadcast. Thereupon he imprudently began to justify the Reich's policy in Alsace-Lorraine, a policy he called restrained and respectful of the rights of the church. Maglione then reminded him that the Nazi police had expelled the bishop of Metz from his see, giving him only two hours to prepare for his departure. The Nazi police had also forbidden the bishop of Strasbourg from returning to that city. The secretary of state added that at Innsbruck the Gestapo had raided the Capuchins, laying hands on all they found—papers, money, and even the meal that had been prepared for the community—and had expelled these religious, giving them also only two hours during which to prepare their departure. And this, concluded Maglione, was the policy the German diplomat presented as restrained and respectful of the rights of the church.

Two days later, Menshausen again came to complain that an English-language Vatican broadcast mentioned that the pope had congratulated the king and queen of Great Britain, who emerged unscathed after Buckingham Palace had been bombed. It was true that, following the information that Osborne had furnished to the Holy See on the bombing of the royal palace, the apostolic delegate in London had been instructed to present the pope's congratulations to the royal couple. Having done so, Archbishop Godfrey sent to the Vatican the thanks of Their Majesties. This exchange of telegrams, related by radio from both London and the Vatican, gave rise to the complaints of the German chargé d'affaires. Yet such objections were completely unjustified since the pope had also congratulated Hitler after he escaped the attack in Munich during November 1939.

Meanwhile, Monsignor Tardini asked the director of Vatican Radio for the text of the 15 October transmission, which was the object of the grievance from the German embassy. On 25 October Menshausen returned to the Secretariat of State and said that ten days ago he had asked for the text of the incriminating broadcast; yet he had received nothing. Tardini's reply was that the director of Vatican Radio had sent not the exact text but rather the news aired in English on 15 October, namely, that in Alsace-Lorraine schools had been shut down, seminaries closed, and priests were no longer permitted to impart religious instruction in schools. All this was true. The only piece of news that could not be confirmed was the closing of the cathedral in Strasbourg. Menshausen became very angry when he found out that he was being refused the text asked for by his government. Then he took out of his briefcase a piece of paper from which he read several sentences, the text of the broadcast as recorded by the Germans: In Alsace-Lorraine national-socialism exercises its "pernicious influence"; the "immoral principles of Nazism" are being spread there. And now becoming more and more angry, the diplomat stated that for a long time the German press and radio had refrained from attacking the Vatican and that Vatican Radio, on the other hand, was taking a hostile stance toward Germany, that the so-called autonomy of Vatican Radio was not admissible, that the Holy See was the most totalitarian of all regimes and that the Secretariat of State should use all possible means to curb the radio, and that, if things should continue in this manner, the Vatican must expect Germany to reply most strongly. Tardini, remaining calm, answered that he completely agreed that Vatican Radio should refrain from broadcasting inexact information, especially since there existed so much accurate news to point out the religious persecution taking place in Germany. Menshausen tried to defend himself but without great conviction, notes Tardini, since he could not deny the facts. To provide himself with an honorable retreat, Menshausen presented another document: Vatican Radio's announcement of the congratulations sent by the pope to England's king and queen after they had escaped unharmed from the bombing of their palace. Tardini explained to the diplomat that according to ordinary diplomatic protocol the Holy See had instructed its representative in London to congratulate Their Majesties for having escaped harm, and nothing more. Menshausen wanted to discuss the matter, saying that the bombing of the palace might have been caused by antiaircraft shells. Tardini had to remark that the Vatican said nothing about the causes of the danger incurred; in Rome antiaircraft defense of the city was regarded as the principal danger from the air.

Nonetheless, the director of Vatican Radio, Father Filippo Soccorsi, was told by the secretary of state to limit broadcasts to news that was well verified and not to season the news with more or less sharp commentaries. According to a saying that seems dear to Maglione: The facts speak for themselves. And on the same day, 27 October, Pius XII personally made the same recommendations to Father Soccorsi.

On 2 November Menshausen raised new objections against Vatican Radio. Here the charges proved to be false since the so-called broadcast never took place. This caused the embassy of the Reich to show more reserve. And yet after three months, on the following 3 April, the German chargé d'affaires ventured to return in order to speak to Monsignor Tardini about the radio. This time it had to do with a broadcast in French that minced no words regarding Nazi neopaganism. The program was immediately repeated by the radio in London, which had it rebroadcast in German. Monsignor Tardini promised to obtain the precise text, while expressing his hope that this time it was not an invention.

There was no general consensus as to the advantages of Vatican Radio. The auxiliary bishop of Kaunas in Lithuania, which was under Soviet occupation, wrote that broadcasts in his language directed against Bolshevik persecution had no effect other than to rile up the Soviet authorities against the church. Among the people at large, such propaganda was totally unnecessary: daily life under Russian occupation constituted the best antidote against Communism.

Monsignor Tardini could well utter sharp replies capable of interrupting what others were saying; and yet it was difficult for him to ignore the cogency of certain protests since it was true that inexact details were sometimes mixed with the information broadcast by Vatican Radio. Allied propaganda profited from the news and commentaries heard over the Holy See's station. On 25 January 1940 the director of the radio himself sent Monsignor Montini the text of a broadcast and added: "I inform you that broadcasts from England have often cited and made reference to this while on its own adding things we have not said." This gave Nazi propaganda an opportunity for picturing the pope as Germany's enemy. Pius XII directed that Vatican Radio be perfectly objective, and he even decided to suspend any broadcasts regarding Germany.

In a letter of 30 April to Cardinal Maglione, Father Ledochoswki, the superior general of the Jesuits, and thereby superior of those Jesuits who had been placed in charge of the station, believed he had to point out the harm caused by this decision: The new program was just being made public and its restrictions might produce an unfortunate impression since, as rumor had it, Germany and Italy were intervening along these lines. These objections were not accepted, and at the bottom of the letter the secretary of state wrote: "As to Germany, no news in any way till there is a new order."

Objections also came from the British, who found these anti-Nazi broadcasts advantageous to their cause. They protested against this silence. And Sir d'Arcy Osborne, the minister of Great Britain, now took the place of his German fellow diplomat in going to the Secretariat of State to complain about Vatican Radio.

In November 1940 Lord Halifax instructed Osborne to send the Secretariat of State a memorandum concerning the attitude of European Catholics who were being confronted with national-socialism. The Nazis, as the note from London pointed out, were waging a campaign to convince people that the Reich was in the process of being reconciled with the Holy See, and that "the new order of the Axis" would comply with the pope's conditions for establishing a just and lasting peace. The argument was that Nazism was more tolerable than Communism, and that in some Catholic countries the idea of a reconciliation between national-socialism and the church was not impossible and even seemed to be gaining ground. The British Foreign Office wanted to be certain that the Holy See was judging the whole extent of the danger; it also wanted to investigate possible ways of opposing such propaganda.

Without mistaking what the English had in mind, Monsignor Tardini nevertheless recognized that some of the observations were correct. The Holy See had to fight against the very real dangers of Nazi propaganda; it also had to respond to certain accusations spread throughout Anglo-Saxon countries, especially in England, according to which influential people in the Vatican favored compromising with the Axis and the new order. And yet a note from the Secretariat of State, dated 22 November, began by rejecting the English pretense of having the Holy See issue a statement, one that would be the equivalent of taking a political position. "The Holy See cannot forget that too often there has been a desire to attribute a purely political meaning to doctrinal and religious actions; by its very nature it is not certain that such a statement will dispel the confusion that is of such concern to His Majesty's legation."

Afterwards, realizing that there was some truth in the remarks of the Foreign Office, the Secretariat of State began preparing a long note that sketched out a very somber picture of the church's situation in regions under Nazi control, Germany itself, and the occupied countries, especially Poland. Mentioned in detail were the Catholic schools and churches that were closed, the religious houses that were invaded and searched, the priests who were arrested, the bishops who were kept far from their flocks, the religious teaching and worship that were impeded in a thousand ways. Personally reviewed and corrected by Pius XII himself, signed by the cardinal secretary of state and dated 18 February, the note was sent to the Holy See's representatives in France, Switzerland, Spain, Argentina, Brazil, and the United States.

This circular letter remained known only to the Vatican offices and the nunciatures, and the information it contained only became public under the form of semiofficial communications. The English government was not informed of all this, and in any case what it wanted were public statements from the pope or at least from Vatican Radio. Also, when the pope's decision to limit and even suspend broadcasts concerning Germany finally leaked out, this provoked the British cabinet to send one of the most astonishing notes in this series of documents:

> It was with astonishment, concern, and profound regret that His Majesty's government has learned that Vatican Radio, toward the end of April, had abruptly suspended all references to Germany, all mention of the steps taken in Germany against the church and of the false affirmations of German propaganda.

Such silence, continues the British note, can only be attributed to German pressure. The Vatican, by thus yielding to German demands, has left a clear field in the occupied countries for Nazi propaganda affirming that the Holy See is entering into friendly relations with the Reich and that Nazi doctrine contains nothing incompatible with Christianity. This is to play Hitler's game and favor his ambitions. England's cause, one supported by the United States, cannot fail to triumph, and the day will come, and sooner than expected, when justice

102

will return: What will Catholics say if the church, which first offered vigorous resistance, has finally agreed to surrender and keep silent?

The note was sent to Pius XII himself on 10 June 1941 by Osborne, who commented on its contents. Pius XII replied that there was no agreement between the Holy See and the Axis powers and that it had not been stated that no one could speak, day after day, about what was happening in Germany. The pope further replied that he was not unaware that some broadcasts were exposing German Catholics and religious to harsh reprisals.

The pope's reply to Osborne did not stop the Secretariat of State from giving a detailed response to the Foreign Office. The secretariat had just received a German memorandum which observed that an obvious opposition was gradually becoming apparent between the impartiality professed by the pope and the attitude of Vatican Radio. The Vatican broadcasts relayed real facts, but they were completely taken out of context: reported was German police repression but nothing was said of terrorism; reported was religious persecution in Germany, comparing this to persecutions undergone by the newborn church; any number of facts were deformed or mutilated and then picked up and unscrupulously used by anti-German propaganda. On the other hand, Vatican Radio said not a word about Polish terrorism, about the English blockade that caused great hunger among people; in a word, the Holy See's impartiality and neutrality, desired in high places, did not appear sufficiently guaranteed.

Fifteen days later, a note dated 28 June 1941 from the Secretariat of State responded in the same tone as that of the note given the pope by the British minister:

> It is not without surprise that His Holiness' Secretariat of State has learned of the content of the memorandum dated 10 June from the royal British legation to the Holy See relative to Vatican Radio.

The fact that for some time Vatican Radio had not been speaking out against religious persecution in Germany and against Nazism was attributed to pressures upon the Holy See, to an attitude of resignation and silence capable of discrediting the fundamental principles of the church. In formulating these criticisms, the British legation forgot how the Holy Father had freely denounced crimes perpetrated against the rights of religion and alerted the faithful about the evils threatening them. However, it happened that the Vatican broadcasts were retransmitted or published in reports "obviously altered in form and denatured in substance." Extracts of these broadcasts were circulated; taken out of context, they contained many and serious inexactitudes "on exceptionally complex and delicate matters." These reports, being "imprecise, tendentious, and sometimes totally false," offered Nazi propaganda a perfect pretext to attack the Holy See, its independence, and its impartiality. The Holy See could not fail to be concerned about the ill effects resulting from this. Nor could it allow what was intended to clarify matters for Catholics be permitted to sow confusion and division among them. Nor was it permissible that a bias falsely attributed to the Holy See be allowed to bring grave consequences upon the religious and the faithful of many countries. When such behavior increased and became more frequent, even to the point of staging forged pseudo-broadcasts from Vatican Radio, then the Secretariat of State had to take action. In concluding, Cardinal Maglione renewed his assurance "that no agreement has been made with any power pertaining to Vatican Radio, and that the Holy See intends to maintain in every circumstance its full independence and its absolute impartiality."

THE ITALIAN PRESS

At a time when the Holy See was protecting its freedom of speech from those wanting to silence it or to have it pronounce certain announcements, the Vatican was the object of repeated attacks on the part of the Fascist press.

Pius XII had shown his desire and hope that Italy might remain apart from the war, this corresponding to the wishes of the majority of the Italian people. In the eyes of those who had cast Italy into the conflict, the Vatican's neutrality appeared to be an unfriendly and a condemnatory position. The Italian government could not officially protest against the Vatican's neutrality through diplomatic notes, but the party's press and especially the *Regime fascista* of Signor Farinacci were soon to attempt this.

The pope's telegrams to the three neutral countries invaded on 10 May 1940 by the Wehrmacht resulted in some exceptionally violent attacks. There is reason to believe that, as a consequence of the protests made by Monsignor Tardini to the Italian ambassador, something was said because Farinacci soon turned his pen in a different direction. To illustrate the anti-Fascist attitude of the Vatican, on 30 August he put the blame on the archbishop of New York. The *Regime fascista* called Archbishop Spellman an "agent of American Jews, someone who sends any amount of dollars to the Vatican in exchange for an anti-Fascist policy approved by the Holy See." And on 1 September the paper again accused the Vatican as it denounced "the wretched alliance between the church and the Jews, an alliance sealed by the dollars the Jews send to the Vatican through Spellman." A note of protest was sent to the Italian embassy which responded that, having submitted the Holy See's grievances to higher authorities, it could offer assurances that the press campaign objected to by the Secretariat of State did not correspond to the mind of the government and that the incriminating articles had been called to the attention of the minister of popular culture, who would deal with the matter as he thought best.

For about two months calm seemed to have been reestablished. But on 7 November Babuscio Rizzo, counselor at Italy's embassy to the Holy See, confided to Tardini that a press campaign was being prepared against the church. Mussolini was alerted by his informants that the atmosphere in the Vatican was becoming more and more Anglophile and Francophile and that in the Vatican there was again hope for an English victory; there were even highly placed prelates and cardinals who did not conceal these sentiments. This mindset of the Fascist party was so well echoed in the press that in June the nuncio again had to protest in an oral note, followed by a letter from the secretary of state to the Italian ambassador:

> His Holiness' Secretariat of State must with the deepest of regret again note that the newspaper *Regime fascista* imperturbably and unconcernedly continues its deplorable campaign against certain important ecclesiastics, against the Holy See, and against the Catholic religion itself.

THE BOMBING OF ROME

It was in this atmosphere of suspicion and hostility that the pope and his coworkers carried out their religious mission and tried to exercise an influence on behalf of peace. Among the Holy See's concerns in its attempt to limit the disasters of the cataclysm ravaging the world, one of the first was to keep the war and its destruction away from Rome.

The question, which was asked since 10 June, when Italy entered the war, became an urgent one after the Luftwaffe began to dump tons of bombs on London and on major English cities. The news spread that Italian airplanes participated in the operations over England. D'Arcy Osborne had to tell the pope that if Italian airplanes were to bomb London, it would no longer be certain that the Royal Air Force would not bomb Rome. Yet the air war against England continued, more intense than ever. The bombing of London, wrote Godfrey on 4 October, continues, especially at night, bringing with it the destruction of human lives and monuments; nonetheless, the population has become accustomed to danger. In spite of the newspaper articles, both pro and con, Godfrey believed that the danger of reprisals was not immediate: The policy of His Majesty's government was to strike down the enemy's military machine.

This news, which was quite comforting as to the fate of Rome, had not as yet reached the Vatican when, on 2 October, the British minister was received by the pope. Pius XII returned to the question of the bombing of Rome and asked Osborne to press his government so that, no matter what, Rome would be spared. Arguments were not lacking: The city is the diocese of the pope; it is rich in artistic monuments and historical memories important to everyone; it is covered with sacred edifices venerated by the whole world. The English government indeed promised to respect the neutrality of the Vatican City, but how would it be possible, and especially at night, to avoid mistakes?

On 5 December Osborne replied to Cardinal Maglione:

> The position of His Majesty's British government in regard to the question of bombing Rome remains as it was defined in the House of Commons on 7 November, namely, that His Majesty's British government has noted the Italian statement that Italian fliers and airplanes have participated in the bombing of London, and that consequently it must retain complete freedom of action in regard to Rome.

Furthermore, declared the Foreign Office, the pressures that the Vatican attempted to exert in order to save Rome from Allied bombing gave "the unfortunate impression that the pope wanted to intervene in order to protect Italy and the Fascist government." Besides, it was regrettable that the pope had not condemned German and Italian bombings of Anglican sanctuaries. Meanwhile, should Rome be bombed, everything possible will be done to spare the Vatican, something that would be facilitated if the boundaries of Vatican City were clearly indicated day and night.

The memorandum from the Foreign Office passed from the cardinal secretary of state to the secretary of the Congregation for Extraordinary Ecclesiastical affairs. On 11 December Monsignor Tardini received Osborne and repeated the Holy See's position, mixing with it his own reactions. That the English government, irritated by actual German bombings and by the Italian bombings claimed by Mussolini, occasionally had a mind to bomb Rome can easily be understood. But to reproach the pope for being interested in the fate of Rome, his diocese, is incomprehensible. It is inadmissible, because it is totally false, to accuse the pope of favoring fascism. As to advising the pope to light up at night the boundaries of Vatican City, this is simply childish. The word *childish* made the minister jump up in protest. But Tardini retracted nothing. The nocturnal illumination of Vatican City, he explained, would have two results: The first, an immediate one, would indicate to the English fliers the location of Rome, which was to be bombed; the second result would be to point out the location of the Vatican so as not to bomb it. Moreover, the Vatican's electricity came from Italy, and so the Holy See would have to request electric power from Italy, which would be used to indicate to the enemy bombers the capital's location. Osborne acknowledged that he had not thought of this. Tardini concluded: If you want to please Mussolini and harm yourselves, bomb Rome!

Things remained such till March 1941, when on 23 March the English government instructed its minister to the Holy See to say that if the Germans or the Italians were to bomb Athens, then Rome would be bombed.

English threats did not save the Balkans. The failure of the Italian army in Greece during October 1940 called for an intervention of the Wehrmacht. Hitler prepared his action against Greece by making sure of Yugoslavia, whose government, feeling itself threatened, signed an agreement on 25 March. But two days later the government of the Regent Paul was swept out by a coup d'état, and on 6 April the German offensive was launched against both Yugoslavia and Greece. Four days later Zagreb Radio announced the formation of an independent Croatian state; on 13 April the German vanguard penetrated Belgrade, and on 17 April the Yugoslavian army surrendered. Despite English aid, Greece could not hold out much longer: At the end of May Crete, the last stronghold of Greek resistance, fell into the hands of General Student's paratroopers.

ANTE PAVELIC

While Greece was under military occupation, Yugoslavia was being dismantled. Hitler kept a Serbia that was theoretically free and yet annexed to the German part of Slovenia; Dalmatia and its islands were ceded to Italy. Croatia, made an independent state, was to form a kingdom under the prince of the House of Savoy; meanwhile, the head of the government was Ante Pavelic, a veteran of the clandestine war for Croatian independence.

One of Pavelic's first acts was to visit Rome, and on 16 May the Italian ambassador to the Holy See requested that he be granted an audience with the Holy Father.

This was a delicate matter, as Monsignor Tardini immediately noted, since an audience with the pope would obviously be exploited as if the Holy See were officially recognizing the new country. And yet both the people of Croatia and Pavelic himself proclaimed themselves to be Catholics. The pope is the father of all the faithful, and refusing to receive Pavelic would perhaps harm the church in these regions, whereas a word of encouragement or of warning might do some good. Monsignor Tardini concluded that an audience should be granted, and yet care should be taken to exclude whatever might politicize this event. So Pius XII decided to meet with Pavelic, but alone, without an entourage, as a Catholic and not as the head of a government.

News of a papal audience requested by the head of the new Croatian state arrived at Yugoslavia's legation, which, having survived the country's collapse, lost no time in preparing a note of protest. After the German invasion of Yugoslavia, "Ante Pavelic...who himself was condemned to death by the French courts for having murdered King Alexander of Yugoslavia," proclaimed Croatia to be an independent country, a situation imposed by forces of occupation and deprived of any juridical foundation.

Nonetheless, Pavelic was received at the Vatican on 18 May at six in the evening. Pius XII spoke of his affection for the Croatian people, whose loyalty he knew so well, but he stressed that he was receiving Pavelic in a simple manner, as a son of the church. To recognize the new country, there would first have to be a peace treaty. On the same day the Secretariat of State distributed to the pontifical representatives a circular letter specifying that the audience given to Pavelic in no way implied recognition of Croatia.

But on 2 June the Yugoslavian minister returned with a note of protest: It was rumored that the Holy See was going to name a representative to Croatia. Monsignor Tardini told him that even though the Holy See was not taking any political position during this time of war, it nonetheless reserved for itself the right to confide a purely religious mission to an ecclesiastic: Neither governments nor their diplomats need to know what pertains to the good of souls.

And Pavelic, having stirred up protests from his enemies, in turn made his own protest. He is furious, Italy's ambassador reported to Monsignor Tardini, because Slovakia has a nuncio, whereas the pope has sent only an observer to Croatia. Tardini replied that the pope's envoy in Croatia was not an observer but an "apostolic visitor." And as the ambassador continued on and requested that the Vatican receive a Croatian representative, Tardini categorically replied in the negative.

ROOSEVELT'S REELECTION

Whereas the war continued to spread in Europe, the United States, beyond the ocean, remained the large neutral power from which the Holy See awaited assistance in carrying out its relief efforts on behalf of the war's victims.

In 1940 President Roosevelt finished his second term; breaking with past traditions, he ran for a third time and was reelected on 6 November 1940. On 14 December the apostolic delegate in Washington cabled the Vatican and suggested that Pius XII write a personal letter of congratulations. The idea was well received, and on 20 December Pius XII sent a private letter to F.D.R. After stressing how this second reelection, occurring at such a critical time, constituted a mark of exceptional confidence on the part of the American people, the pope let it be known that he too was experiencing satisfaction. Pius XII recalled his own meeting with Roosevelt, Myron Taylor's mission, the joint efforts to prevent war, and he concluded by expressing a desire for the return of a lasting peace and of an era of tranquility, collaboration, and progress.

On 9 January the apostolic delegate informed the Vatican of the American government's position. Roosevelt explained his intentions in two speeches, one on 29 December 1940, the other on the following 6 January. They can be summarized in just a few words: to help the British Empire as much as possible and yet not to become involved in the war. Nonetheless, it could have been asked how long such a position might endure, for many believed that the day of armed intervention was certainly inevitable.

Whereas Pius XII was paying close attention to the attitude of the United States, Roosevelt was not indifferent to that of the Holy See. In April the president took the initiative by sending the pope his Easter wishes and by reaffirming that the White House and the Vatican shared a commonality of interests. And here, as Tardini noted, was an attempt to associate the pope with a statement against Germany. The pope's response avoided the trap by reaffirming the superior principles of Christian doctrine. The difference of viewpoints caused no harm, and on 17 May 1941 the apostolic delegate wrote that the White House was completely satisfied as to its relations with the Vatican.

As for the American bishops, Cicognani wrote on 17 June, that the U.S. government was not happy with them. Many prelates did not conceal their lack of enthusiasm regarding a possible armed intervention in Europe, and women's organizations were sending large numbers of petitions to the hierarchy urging the bishops to take a stand against war. Archbishop Spellman in New York was under the impression that those in the upper levels of government were rather unhappy with the attitude of the bishops and the clergy.

When Cicognani's letter arrived at the Vatican, the German offensive against Russia was under way, and this posed new questions to the clergy and faithful in the United States. But the Holy See had already shown Washington that its diplomatic assistance was not negligible.

SPAIN

When the western powers declared war on Germany, Spain had just emerged from its civil war. It was no mystery that Germany and

Italy had given much aid to General Franco so that he could triumph over the "Reds," who were supported by foreign men and arms. In addition, the principles proclaimed by the authoritarian government in Madrid initially appeared rather close to those of Hitler and Mussolini. Till June 1940 the state of material and economic impoverishment in the country excluded Spain from participating in the war. The armistice of June 1940, bringing German troops as far as the Pyrenees, made cooperation easier.

On 2 August 1940 Ribbentrop in Berlin sent a message to Franco's ambassador stating that the Reich wanted Spain to participate as soon as possible in the war. Although conversations took place in Berlin between Serrano Suñer, Ribbentrop, and Hitler, nothing was concluded. The Spanish minister, returning from Berlin, took a detour to Rome, where Mussolini is said to have advised that Spain not enter the war. During his stay in Rome the foreign minister of Catholic Spain failed to request an audience with the pope. Cardinal Maglione did not hide his surprise: Was this to be interpreted as a sign of an ideological rapprochement between Franco's Spain and the Nazi Reich? The Spanish ambassador reassured the cardinal secretary of state: Serrano Suñer had instructed him to assure the Vatican that during his conversations in Germany, he had told his partners that "Spaniards, both as individuals and as a nation, have been and wish to remain totally Catholic and that they will not be influenced to the contrary."

The Holy See did not view with any less concern the influence Germany seemed to be gaining in Spain. The Italian campaign in Greece, which took place in midwinter, restored the center of its operation to the Mediterranean and drew Hitler's attention to Gibraltar. If the British could be driven from Gibraltar, then the Mediterranean would be closed to the British fleet; on the other hand, being able to reconquer a fortress occupied by foreigners since the beginning of the eighteenth century would strike the Spaniards as a prize worthy of the effort.

The German ambassador openly told Franco that the Spanish leader's hesitations seemed to prove that he had doubts about the final conclusion of this war. The Caudillo protested, saying that he was completely confident in an Axis victory and that he was just waiting for an opportune time to join the battle. Yet he would not specify when this moment would occur. On 24 January 1941, in a letter somewhat akin to an ultimatum and addressed to the Reich's ambassador in Madrid,

Ribbentrop called for Spain's immediate entry into the war. The Spanish government once again replied that it wanted to share in the Axis victory, that it had not forgotten the help it had received during the civil war, but—and justifiably so—it did not want to become a burden to its allies. Furthermore, it was continuing its negotiations with England and the United States to replenish its supplies, and then it would enter the war at an appropriate time. Moreover, the severity of winter and the heat of summer in Spain required that the operation be set for the autumn.

Yet in Spain there were highly placed people—and probably Serrano Suñer was one of them—who were betting on an Axis victory. In January 1941 an article in the newspaper *Arriba* enthusiastically reported Hitler's New Year's message to his army. Another paper spoke of Hitler as "the most human person history has known." On 16 January Gaetano Cicognani, the nuncio in Madrid and the brother of the apostolic delegate in the United States, pointed out that a propaganda campaign was being waged whose purpose was to persuade the Spanish people as to the excellence of the national-socialist regime and the respect it was showing to religion. It is also true that somewhat later the same Gaetano Cicognani wrote that enthusiasm for Germany had declined in the country, and Franco's resistance to Axis pressure urging him to enter the war was unanimously approved by the people.

But on 8 April 1941 at half past eleven in the evening the nuncio telegraphed from Madrid that, according to reliable sources, the German government had again begun to pressure Spain to cooperate. It was said that Serrano Suñer, convinced of Germany's final victory and prone to take part in the conflict in order to regain Gibraltar, wished to broaden Spain's sphere of influence in Africa and guarantee his country a privileged place in the new European order. An anti-British press campaign would be launched to prepare public opinion. Twelve days later another telegram from the nuncio confirmed the previous message and added that the government was taking security measures regarding the Pyrenees and Gibraltar. It was concentrating troops in the Canary and Balearic Islands and was enacting the severest penalties for national security violations, as if anticipating some important decisions. This was on 20 April. German successes in the Balkans provoked Hitler to undertake a broad action in the Mediterranean and also to convince Madrid of the advantages of an alliance with the Reich.

England, to ward off the danger, was persuading the United

States to sign a treaty with Spain which would guarantee that country whatever economic assistance it needed. Yet at the same time England was recommending that Washington avoid any interference from Serrano Suñer, who was little disposed to such collaboration. But when the U.S. ambassador, Alexander Weddell, requested an audience with General Franco, he was told that the head of state was very occupied by internal affairs and that the meeting would have to be postponed till the following week. The ambassador replied that he was "naturally surprised and disappointed with this delay, for his government had instructed him to have the meeting as soon as possible."

Notes were successively sent by Weddell on 3 May, 9 May, and 19 May. Serrano Suñer finally responded that it was not possible to grant an audience with General Franco, but if the ambassador had to send a message, he was ready to pass it on to the general. Weddell's answer was that he had been instructed to say that "my government finds it hard to believe that if the head of state had known about my request, he would have approved this unusual delay in order to prepare for the meeting." It seemed that things were on the verge of falling apart. Harold Tittmann, who first was secretary of the U.S. embassy in Italy and who was acting as the chargé d'affaires in the Vatican in the absence of Myron Taylor, was informed of this. On 20 June he sent Cardinal Maglione a note summarizing the dispute and explaining that the ambassador had to talk to the general about the economic assistance the United States was disposed to give Spain. He concluded: "Evidently such behavior will hardly promote sincere and friendly conversations between governments on problems of mutual interest." The following day Maglione telegraphed the nuncio in Madrid to call his attention to the audience that had been refused to the U.S. ambassador and to request information. The nuncio replied that this was a personal dispute between the ambassador and the Spanish foreign minister, having nothing to do with hostile intentions on the part of Spain against the United States: Weddell acted in such a way that Serrano Suñer wanted to attack him.

At the same time, the announcement that Germany was going to war against Russia resulted in violent demonstrations before the British embassy in Spain. Cardinal Maglione telegraphed the nuncio in Madrid with the message that he occupy himself in settling these two incidents as soon as possible to everyone's satisfaction. Gaetano Cicognani indeed intervened and the difficulties were ironed out. On

15 July Osborne, who had informed his government of what the Holy See had accomplished in Madrid, sent to Cardinal Maglione the thanks of the Foreign Office: "Mr. Eden says that the initiative of the nuncio [in Madrid] has been highly effective, and he has instructed me to express to Your Eminence an expression of his great appreciation for your kind intervention."

This, it seems, was the only diplomatic step that circumstances allowed the Holy See to take during the months of incertitude following the armistice of June 1940.

In areas proper to the church, namely, those pertaining to religion, Pius XII was continuing his work on behalf of peace. Praying for peace, requesting the Christian people to pray for peace—these basic themes returned in the pope's addresses: his allocution of 24 November 1940, his radio messages at Christmas 1940, at Easter, and at Pentecost 1941.

The Christmas message sketched out presuppositions for a new political order: renunciation of hatred, fidelity to treaties, renunciation of the principle of unconditional utilitarianism, economic balance among nations, a spirit of law and of collaboration rather than the spirit of egotism. In his Easter message of 13 April Pius XII recalled that his efforts on behalf of peace remained ineffective. Nonetheless, he did not want to resign himself to this, but indeed "to continue to struggle for peace with the arms of prayer, of exhortation, and of consolation on behalf of poor humanity."

Responding to the calls for help coming from the occupied countries and especially from Poland, which had been crushed by the two enemy powers of Germany and Soviet Russia, he reminded the occupying power of their responsibilities:

> Your conscience and your sense of honor should lead you to treat the people of occupied territories with a spirit of justice, of humanity, and with broadness of outlook. Do not impose any burden upon them that you have judged or would judge to be unjust if you were in a situation like theirs....Above all, keep in mind that God's blessing or curse upon your own country may depend on your conduct toward those who, because of the fortunes of war, have fallen under your power.

In June the news of the German offensive, unleashed against the Soviet Union exploded like a clap of thunder. Till the last moment the nuncio in Berne, who was in an advantageous place for gathering information, had been reporting rumors about a German-Russian war, and yet he placed no stock in them. But Pius XII was not taken unawares. He had expected that an offensive to the west would occur at the beginning of May 1940. The same source announced the campaign against Russia. And so the new situation was less unexpected by the pope than it was for a number of European leaders, although it certainly presented him with very complex questions.

CHAPTER 6

From a European War
to a World War*

~·~

O
N THE MORNING OF 22 June 1941 Hitler launched an offensive
against Russia, something he had been planning since the end
of 1940. Everyone could ponder the consequences of what the
dictator himself called the most important decision of his life. For
many politicians of that era, external indignation merely masked internal satisfaction. England could only congratulate itself on emerging
from its isolation in the struggle against the Axis. The U.S. ambassador in Vichy, William Leahy, had reason to say that a feeling of relief
surrounded him: "It is generally said that the two detested powers have
finally come to blows and that there is a vague impression that France,
at least during the hostilities, might find relief from German pressure
and threats." Camille M. Cianfarra, a correspondent for *The New York
Times,* wrote from Rome: "The Vatican was hoping that the German-
Soviet War would give the British Empire and the United States time
to increase their military preparedness." Such an observation rather
quickly identified the Holy See's perspective with that of the Allies.

The Vatican had no reason to feel sorry for the Soviet Union,
which, having divided up what remained of Poland with Hitler, was
now under attack by the Wehrmacht. The church's attitude vis-à-vis
Bolshevism was sufficiently known, and nothing had changed since
Pius XI's encyclical *Divini Redemptoris* stigmatized Communism as
being "intrinsically evil." Nor had anything changed within
Communism itself in regard to the church. This is why Hitler believed
that in launching his airplanes and tanks toward Leningrad and Moscow
he could make the war look like a crusade on behalf of Christian civilization. Ribbentrop, in his audience on 11 March 1940, had already

*Documentation for chapter 6: See *ADSS,* vol. 5. Add *FRUS,* 1941, vols. 1 and 2;
FRUS, 1942, vol. 3.

told the pope that national-socialism, by protecting Germany from Communism, had saved religion in that country. Pius XII simply replied that one could not know what would have happened. Here the pope was already refusing to accept the Nazi pretense of presenting the Third Reich as the champion of Christianity against Communism.

In June 1941 the religious situation in Germany was so bad that nothing could convince the pope that Germany was an ally. From the very beginning of his pontificate Pacelli did everything possible to ease the difficulties with Germany that had characterized the pontificate of Pius XI. According to Diego von Bergen, who was the Reich's ambassador to the Holy See, what resulted was not an understanding but "a stabilization of tension, which at times could give an outsider the false impression of an approaching accommodation."

Reports sent to Rome by the nuncio in Berlin indicated that neither the war in the west nor the offensive against Russia would lead the national-socialist party to back down in its fight against Christianity. Numerous dispatches from Orsenigo during July and the first part of August 1941 listed a series of high-handed measures taken by the Gestapo against the church: religious being expelled, goods and property sequestered and confiscated, Jesuits being excluded from the Wehrmacht and declared unworthy to serve in it. Finally, the pope's speech given on 29 June passed unnoticed in Germany because the official press and radio gave it no mention, and Catholic periodicals had almost completely disappeared.

Despite all, at a date not clearly indicated by the documents, the Reich's ambassador requested that the pope issue a statement in favor of the war against Russia. And on 5 September, during a meeting with Monsignor Tardini, the Italian ambassador, Bernardo Attolico, petitioned the pope to take a position encouraging Germany and Italy in their conflict with Soviet Russia. He stressed that Mussolini had successfully urged Hitler to highlight the anti-Bolshevik character of the war. Given these conditions, was it suitable for the Holy See "to remain silent or, on the contrary, would it not be better to speak out against Bolshevism? Seeing that the war against Russia will be long and harsh and that Italy's participation will continue to expand, it would be good for the Italian people, whose spirit is inimical to Bolshevism, to hear something from the Holy See." The secretary of the Congregation of Extraordinary Ecclesiastical Affairs responded to the Italian ambassador:

The Holy See, whose position regarding Bolshevism does not need to be explained anew, has already reproved, condemned, and anathematized Bolshevism and all its errors. There is nothing to add to or take away from what has been said. Anything asserted today could easily have a political character, whereas the Holy See has clearly spoken *tempore non suspecto*. Clearly whoever in the past has concluded peace agreements with Russia should explain their position. Whoever till yesterday was talking about a Russian alliance as guaranteeing peace in the east and is now waging...a crusade against Russia should evidently explain this change of attitude. But not the Holy See! It has not changed. To speak out at present might be interpreted as submitting to the counsels of Farinacci.

Tardini went on to say:

As for me, in light of the declarations, condemnations, etc. issued by the Holy See, I would be very happy to see Communism put out of action. It is the worst enemy of the church. But it is not the only enemy. Nazism has conducted a veritable persecution against the church and continues to do so. Consequently the swastika is not the cross of a crusade. And yet, to be exact, it was the Germans and not Mussolini who were the first to speak about a crusade.

Attolico wanted to press the matter: it was not a question of preaching a crusade but of reaffirming Catholic principles in the face of Bolshevism. Monsignor Tardini replied that at present it would be difficult to recall "the errors and horrors of Communism" while overlooking "the errors and persecutions of Nazism." The ambassador sought to avoid the parallel by appealing to personal experience: He was acquainted with both Berlin and Moscow. In Russia the religious situation was indeed worse than in Germany, where worship was permitted, whereas in Russia it was forbidden. Tardini replied that this was more or less the present situation, but there were too many reasons for doubting that Germany did not want to proceed still further. "It is precisely for this reason," concluded Tardini, "that for the present, rather than applying the doctrine of a crusade, I apply the proverb, 'one devil chases another,' and so much the better if the other devil is the worst."

The note in which Monsignor Tardini had immediately described his meeting with Attolico was taken to the pope. In reacting to it, the pope merely remarked that the religious situation in Germany had deteriorated since the time Attolico left Berlin.

The days that followed only lengthened the list of the Holy See's interventions ignored in Berlin and the list of German demands rejected by the Holy See. The Reich's pretense of posing as a champion of Christianity appeared more laughable each day. To Diego von Bergen, who was surprised that the pope had not used his Christmas message to express satisfaction that Christianity was again flourishing in territories occupied by the German troops, the response had to be that it was difficult to speak of a Catholic rebirth in regions where even military chaplains were forbidden to minister to the country's inhabitants.

On 24 December Pius XII addressed a new message to a world afflicted by war. Far from praising the Russian campaign and Hitler's new order, the pope spelled out a number of principles condemning the methods of both camps, that of the Nazis and that of the Soviets. In a new order based on justice, said Pius XII, there was no place for violating the liberty and security of other nations, whether large or small, nor for the oppression of minorities, total war, nor a mad arms race; and, finally, there was no place for persecuting religion and the church.

Commenting on this message several weeks later in his diplomatic correspondence, the Reich's ambassador observed that Hitler's Germany was itself implied in the message, as was Stalin's Russia.

Meanwhile, fifteen days later, Bergen was happy to inform Berlin that the Secretariat of State had formally denied there was any truth to rumors about a letter said to have been written by Stalin to the pope: It was a pure invention. Certainly the denial corresponded to reality because no letter originating from the Kremlin has been found in the archives of the Secretariat of State. But records of this Secretariat of State from the same date include dispatches of a less sensational character, which were nonetheless capable of disturbing the masters of the Third Reich.

U.S. CATHOLICS AND AID TO STALIN

Similarly, if a word from the pope might have been able to encourage German and Italian Catholics to join the Axis effort against Russia, there was on the other side of the Atlantic a group of Catholics also attentive to the pontiff's voice and whose attitude could influence the outcome of the war. Responding to appeals from Churchill, Roosevelt was providing England with credit and American materials. But from the very moment Russia found itself at war against Germany, the question for the U.S. president was whether he should also help Stalin against Hitler. An affirmative answer would be open to serious objections since in the eyes of many Americans the political dictatorship and religious persecution raging in Russia presented an insurmountable obstacle to any type of collaboration between the Soviet Union and the United States. At a function held in Chicago on 17 September 1941, former President Herbert Hoover said:

> I believe and ninety-nine percent of Americans believe that totalitarianism, whether Nazi or Communist, is abominable. Both forms are immoral because they reject religion and reject fidelity to one's agreements. They are aberrant because of their unspeakable acts of cruelty and the hideous murder of millions of human beings. I abhor any kind of American compromise or alliance with them. What about the millions of people enslaved in Russia and throughout Europe, and what about our own freedom if we should send our sons to win the war for the benefit of Communism?

Hoover was not alone in his opinion: religious groups and especially Catholic circles were resisting any collaboration whatsoever with Russia. In a detailed report of 1 September 1941 the apostolic delegate in Washington explained the attitude of American Catholics in regard to the conflict. With few exceptions, he wrote, they are against Germany because they know that a Nazi victory would mean an extension of religious persecution. The majority approve aid being given to England, but as to entering the war, that is something else altogether. The pope's speeches favoring the reestablishment of peace lead them to desire that the U.S. government avoid anything that would prolong the war; they also want the government to bring the warring nations to an agreement, giving people their independence and freedom. In general, the bishops have refrained from making any public statements, and those who have done so are against intervention; among these are the cardinal archbishop of Boston and the archbishops of Dubuque, Baltimore, and Cincinnati. Many papers and periodicals make no secret of their isolationist feelings.

If aid to England was a matter of deep concern to many Catholics, the idea of giving assistance to Russia caused even stronger opposition.

Catholics were condemning all cooperation with Russia as they recalled the Soviet regime's religious persecution; they based their opposition on Pius XI's 1937 encyclical against atheist Communism and especially on the following passage: "Communism is intrinsically evil, and no one who wants to save Christian civilization can cooperate with it in any undertaking whatsoever." The American government's cooperation in Russia's struggle with Germany would run contrary to papal teachings, and Catholics would not be able to approve it. This argument, emphasized Archbishop Cicognani, was making an impression on the faithful. And yet some bishops, like Archbishop Mooney of Detroit, believed that this reading of the encyclical *Divini Redemptoris* was not the only one possible, and they feared that American Catholics would be accused of being unpatriotic. Mooney was suggesting that the Holy See itself might furnish an interpretation of the encyclical.

Other prelates, it is true, did not delay in openly pronouncing themselves in favor of Roosevelt's policy. Bishop Hurley, who had just taken possession of the St. Augustine Diocese in Florida and who formerly served the Holy See in the Secretariat of State, declared in a radio address that war appeared inevitable, that it only remained for the United States to choose the moment, and that, on this point, the only route to follow was to rely on the president. This pleased the interventionists but provoked a major scandal among Catholics. It was thought inadmissible that a bishop should appear as giving a call to arms, and he was accused of violating the Constitution by inferring that the president could make the decision in regard to a declaration of war. In any case, the emotion generated by the talk showed how many Catholics were opposed to Roosevelt's policy of intervention.

The president, to have his views accepted by Catholic opinion and to obtain the support of the majority in Congress, understood that he had to appeal to Rome. A year earlier he appointed Myron Taylor as his representative to Pius XII. For health reasons Taylor had to return to the United States, and Roosevelt then replaced him with Harold Tittmann, who was designated the assistant to Myron Taylor. Nonetheless, the president decided to send Taylor once again to the pope for a short mission. On 27 August 1941 Archbishop Cicognani cabled the Vatican that Myron Taylor would leave for Rome on 4 September, and the delegate requested that Taylor be given an audience with the sovereign pontiff on 10 September.

In his personal message, which served as Myron Taylor's credentials, Roosevelt made no secret of Taylor's mission: to persuade the pope to agree to U.S. cooperation with the Soviet Union. According to the president, religion was not completely outlawed in Russia, and there was hope that after the present war the Russian government would consent to religious liberty. "Insofar as I know," he added, "some churches are open in Russia." Roosevelt then insisted that the Nazi peril was much more serious than the Communist one because the former joined armed aggression to the interior subversion of governments.

Carrying this letter, Myron Taylor arrived in Rome on 9 September and was received in an audience on the evening of 10 September. Since we lack direct information on Taylor's meeting with Pius XII, the notes left by Cardinal Maglione relating to his own session with Roosevelt's envoy can give us an idea of the questions treated. In a first meeting Myron Taylor informed Cardinal Maglione of the situation in the United States, both regarding material supplies and morale. All Americans are convinced that Hitler will lose the war; the United States is prepared for a defensive war, and its military potential has already reached "an extraordinary power beyond everyone's imagination." It is true that the newspapers say that this preparation is not sufficient, but the reason for this is to prevent the country from falling asleep. As for the rest, the United States will remain outside the conflict as long as Hitler does not provoke it and as long as the Allies are in no danger of being defeated, but should an incident occur, then the unanimity that exists for peace will become a unanimity in favor of war.

After these preliminaries, Mr. Taylor explained the Atlantic Charter, drawn up the preceding August, that is, the American statement on the objectives of the war being waged by the Allies. Roosevelt and Churchill wanted the pope to lend his voice to theirs "and that he, by means of his own statement, support the ideas expressed by the president and the British prime minister." Cardinal Maglione replied that the pope in his encyclical *Summi Pontificatus* and in his 1939 and 1940 Christmas messages had set forth the conditions for a just peace, and that he had demanded for all people, great and small, the right to independence. If the opportunity arose, the pope could repeat this, and yet he did not wish to mix his voice with that of government leaders, for this would open him up to the accusation of being partial to one camp or the other.

Taylor finally brought up another point, one of greater consequence. In America there were, in addition to the Irish, who were the
hereditary enemies of the English, some Catholics whose interpretation of the encyclical *Divini Redemptoris* led them to state that no distinction could be made between Communism and the Russian people
and that no aid could be given to Russia without supporting
Communism. Some American bishops had told Taylor himself that, to
avoid a deep split among American Catholics, the pope would have to
come out with an interpretation of the encyclical. Cardinal Maglione
answered that he was surprised that something so clear could be the
object of doubt: "The Holy See has condemned and still condemns
Communism. It has never uttered a word, and it cannot do so, against
the Russian people. It has also condemned Nazism. Who can say that
the Holy Father is against the German people? That he is not friendly
to them?" Since Taylor was insisting that the pope himself explain the
encyclical written by his predecessor, the cardinal repeated that he did
not see any necessity for this. But "if the opportunity presents itself for
discreetly distinguishing between Communism and the Russian
people, between Nazism and the German people, the hierarchy can do
so with authority, without fear of contradicting the teachings of the
Holy See."

At noon the following day Cardinal Maglione had still another
session with President Roosevelt's envoy. The precision the cardinal
brought to his statement on the previous day surely expressed the mind
of the pope, with whom he had meanwhile conferred. The prelate
began by saying that at the earliest opportunity the pope would reiter-
ate his teachings both regarding war and regarding the justice and
peace that are to govern relations among peoples. As to the question
asked by many American bishops on the implication of the encyclical
Divini Redemptoris, Cardinal Maglione promised to write the apostolic
delegate in Washington "in order to respond discreetly and with cau-
tion to the prelates who were asking whether there was anything in
Pius XI's encyclical that was against the Russian people. The pope has
condemned Communism, a condemnation that remains. For the
Russian people the pope has had and can only have paternal feelings."
In other words, Catholics need have no scruples in their support of
Roosevelt when he assisted Stalin against Hitler.

Taylor brought up a third point. In the past the pope did everything possible to keep Italy out of the war. Did Maglione see any

possibility whatever of Italy being led to conclude a separate peace treaty? "I see none," replied Cardinal Maglione.

"Perhaps," continued Taylor, "because of the dangers Italy would expose itself to by separating from Germany."

"That is one reason, but not the only one."

"I understand," concluded Taylor.

The main purpose of Taylor's mission concerned the meaning and consequences of the encyclical *Divini Redemptoris*. Roosevelt wanted the pope to approve the American people's support of U.S. aid to Russia, and so he wrote to Pius XII that religious liberty existed in Russia. Yet the Vatican's information in this respect was different from that of the president: The imprisonment of priests and faithful, fiscal surcharges, and even massacres were the reality. As to Catholic churches being open in the Soviet Union, the Vatican knew of only two, one in Moscow and the other in Leningrad. Monsignor Tardini thus had reasons for writing down his reflections, which incorporated numerous objections to the American request.

Roosevelt's position was that religious liberty existed in Russia and that the persistence of Communism was less dangerous than that of Nazism. Tardini admitted the second point, at least to a certain degree and for the time being:

> The president says that Germany is more dangerous than Russia. If limited to the political and military arenas, the thesis is correct. Politically, Nazi Germany is much better organized than Russia, and it is much stronger militarily. But what about the religious arena? Ideologically, Communism and Nazism are equally false and pernicious, both being materialistic, both being antireligious, both destroying the most elementary human rights, both being unyielding foes of the Holy See.

In Germany worship had not disappeared, but this was due to the conditions of a country where Nazism had to reckon "with millions and millions of Catholics, with a large number of courageous clergy, with a united and disciplined hierarchy." Furthermore, Germany did not want to let the rest of the world know about the persecution raging within its borders. But once Nazism was certain of its power, it would rashly move on to implement its antireligious program. And so, neither the survival of Nazism nor that of Communism seemed to offer a more encouraging outlook for religion.

Three days later Monsignor Tardini continued his reflections on the same questions. First, he addressed the meaning of the disputed passage from *Divini Redemptoris*. Had Pius XI in advance condemned military and economic aid to Russia? No, what he condemned was the policy of helping Communism. This was the theory. But, Tardini wondered, in practice, was supporting Russia not also supporting Communism? It is not enough to say that the Russians were attacked since they themselves were making plans to attack: "Stalin is not a peaceful leader who has been forced into war; he is a war-monger who was preceded in his criminal plans by a criminal more daring than he." To be sure, theory has it that helping the Russians win the war does not mean that one is defending Communism and militant atheism. But in practice, "if the Russians win the war, then the victory belongs to Stalin; no one can any longer dethrone him. And for Stalin, it is Communism, victorious Communism, a Communism that is the complete master of the European continent."

Faced with these far from encouraging perspectives, Monsignor Tardini wanted to hope that "from the war now being waged in Russia, Communism would end crushed and Nazism would escape weakened and...ready to be crushed." In conclusion Monsignor Tardini believed that any statement whatever solving the question of assisting Russia would be inopportune.

It is hard to believe that Monsignor Tardini did not share his reflections with the pope. And yet the latter's decision did not correspond to the thinking of the secretary of the Congregation for Extraordinary Ecclesiastical Affairs. In a letter signed by Monsignor Tardini dated 20 September, the Secretariat of State sent to the apostolic delegate in Washington an instruction containing an authentic interpretation of the encyclical *Divini Redemptoris,* as Cardinal Maglione had explained it to Taylor: The pope had condemned Communism, not Russia. This being said, the interpretation of Pius XI's text did not seem to admit of any great difficulty:

> It is, in fact, a fundamental norm of exegesis that every text has to be carefully examined within its natural context. Assuming this to be true, everyone can easily see that in this context Pius XI intended to refer to the well-known ploy of the "holding out one's hand." The pope was warning the faithful not to collaborate with the Communists in their countries, not even in humanitarian

endeavors, because the Communists would use such collaboration for spreading and for securing victory for their Bolshevik program.

This was the obvious meaning of Pius XI's encyclical, and it was this meaning that had to be followed. Obviously Pius XI condemned atheistic Communism and "not the Russian people to whom, in the same document, he sent expressions of paternal good wishes and compassion."

These remarks were easily understood: but Archbishop Cicognani also understood that neither the Holy See nor *l'Osservatore Romano* would publish them. Rather, the delegate would orally and discretely communicate them to Archbishop Mooney and the other bishops. Simply stated, the instruction exhorted the prelates to avoid any reference to the Holy See.

A month later Archbishop Cicognani recalled how he carried out the Roman instructions. Having first consulted several bishops, he called to Washington John McNicholas, the archbishop of Cincinnati, the choice as the most suitable prelate for making a public statement; no one would suspect that McNicholas had caved in to governmental pressure. Archbishop Cicognani brought him up to date on the Vatican's instructions and asked that he issue a statement along the same lines. The archbishop, immediately indicating his agreement, promised to speak on the matter in a pastoral letter addressed to the faithful of his diocese. And he did so. According to Cicognani's report:

> Archbishop McNicholas, first exhorting the faithful to charity and tolerance in matters of political opinion, recalled what Pius XI wrote in his encyclical on Germany and on the distinction the pope made between Nazism and the German people; next he moved on to the same reflections in regard to the Soviet regime and the Russian people; then he examined the passage in question from the encyclical *Divini Redemptoris,* placing it in its true context, and drawing the conclusion that the passage should not be applied to the present time of armed conflict.

The delegate feared that the archbishop's public statement might provoke counter-statements. Just beforehand, the archbishop of Dubuque had declared: "It's time to put an end to a distinction between the Red Army and the Soviet State. The Red Army is the Soviet State insofar as it takes its orders from a godless tyrant."

Six weeks later, Japan's attack on the United States modified the particulars of the problem: The United States and the Soviet Union, by reason of circumstances, had to become allies in the war against the Axis. The event restricted the importance of the practical application of the Roman instructions sent to the U.S. bishops, but it did not lessen the interest of the pope's decision to remove the scruples of American Catholics confronted with Roosevelt's policy.

DIPLOMATIC RELATIONS BETWEEN
THE HOLY SEE AND JAPAN

Two months had not as yet passed since the Japanese attack on the American fleet when on 21 January 1942 Francesco Babuscio, counselor at the Italian embassy, came to inform the cardinal secretary of state that Japan wanted to send a special representative to the Holy See. Cardinal Maglione said that the Holy Father would certainly have no problem with this, but the official request should come through the apostolic delegate in Tokyo. Hope was that this would be a permanent mission and that the Japanese diplomat would be accredited only to the Holy See. Pius XII consented to these proposals: He would gladly receive a Japanese representative, although he added that nationalist China also wanted to have a representative at the Vatican.

On 30 January a cable arrived from Tokyo. Archbishop Paolo Marella, the apostolic delegate, had met with Japan's foreign minister, and the delegate later received a memorandum of the meeting, which he sent on to the Vatican in an Italian translation:

> The Japanese government, considering the world situation and convinced that strengthening the friendly relations already existing with the Vatican is desirable for both parties, desires to accredit an extraordinary envoy to the Holy See. The government asks V. Eminence [!] Most Reverend to immediately communicate this desire to the Vatican for the purpose of knowing the Holy See's mind as to receiving an extraordinary envoy.

The next day the cardinal secretary of state sent a cable to the delegate in Tokyo, which "recorded with satisfaction the feelings and intentions of this government [Japanese] as pertaining to relations with the Holy See." Although the Vatican would have preferred to receive an ambassador, this was not made a condition sine qua non; the Holy See would accept an extraordinary envoy on a special mission. Furthermore, it was presumed that this representative would be accredited only to the Holy See, certainly not to a belligerent state as well.

Three days later, Archbishop Marella cabled the assurances that were requested: The Japanese envoy would be exclusively accredited to the Holy See and, without committing itself in this respect, the Japanese government affirmed its intention to replace, as soon as possible, the extraordinary representative with an ambassador.

The two parties thus had reached an agreement in a minimum of time required, and nothing seemed easier than establishing diplomatic ties between the Holy See and the Empire of the Rising Sun. Undoubtedly this would have been the case several months earlier. But on the preceding 7 December, while diplomatic negotiations were in progress, the American fleet in the Pacific had been surprised and attacked by Japanese bombs at its base in Pearl Harbor. During the following weeks Japanese successes in the Pacific were as striking as the German invasion of Russia: Guam fell within thirty-six hours; Wake Island resisted till 22 December, thus isolating the Philippines, where the Americans held out until May; Hong Kong was immediately captured; Borneo was attacked in mid-December; the Celebes, the Moluccas, Sumatra, Singapore, Java, all fell in January and February. In light of what Japan's diplomacy, not to mention its military successes, had been able to achieve, the prestige of reaching an agreement with the Holy See was evidently not pleasing to the Allies. The cardinal secretary of state certainly had no doubts about this when on 4 February 1942 he confidentially informed the English representative and the American chargé d'affaires that Japan would be having a diplomatic mission accredited by the Holy See.

Tittman himself wrote that upon hearing this news he could not help making a face and saying that this would not go over well in the United States. Cardinal Maglione answered that he well understood this, but that the Holy See was in no position to refuse. On 23 February the British minister, d'Arcy Osborne, sent directly to Pius XII a note that approached the limits of diplomatic propriety:

> His Holiness' acquiescence at this moment in the appointment of a Japanese Representative to the Holy See has caused a most unfavorable impression on His Majesty's Government who find it

128

difficult to reconcile the decision with the frequent Vatican professions deploring the extension of the war.

His Majesty's Government are reluctantly forced to conclude that His Holiness has again deferred to pressure from the Governments of the Axis Powers.

Cardinal Maglione immediately began to prepare a response: The question of diplomatic relations between Japan and the Vatican had been under consideration since 1922; the protection of Catholic interests in the Japanese Empire, now more extended than ever, and the war itself, which was bringing the Japanese into countries where Catholic activity was increasing, had prompted the Holy See to agree to the proposal. The Holy See's decision should not be attributed to political pressure exerted by the Axis, and it was not without regret that the Secretariat of State "has seen opinions of this type placed in a document that was delivered into the venerable hands of the Holy Father."

On 2 March President Roosevelt's chargé d'affaires, Harold Tittman, arrived to present Monsignor Tardini with the first protests from the U.S. government: The State Department viewed the Japanese initiative as designed to spread propaganda among Catholics living in the Far East and in Latin America. Monsignor Tardini repeated the explanations that Cardinal Maglione had already provided. On the following day these were reiterated by the secretary of the apostolic delegation in Washington, Monsignor Egidio Vagnozzi, to Sumner Welles, the undersecretary of state, who was far from being satisfied with them. "I said," as Welles wrote in the minutes of the meeting, "that I believed it necessary to state with all the energy I could muster and with the greatest sincerity that in my opinion this decision of the Holy See was deplorable." The Vatican ventured to receive a Japanese mission at exactly the same time when Japan, at the price of innumerable atrocities, was seeking to eliminate the influence of whites from Asia. Welles hoped that it was not too late to block this plan.

On 5 March the apostolic delegate in Washington, returning from a trip to the west, was informed of Vagnozzi's conversation with Sumner Welles. He hurriedly cabled the reactions of the State Department to Rome, his dispatch leaving shortly after noon. That evening he met with Welles and informed him that he had already sent to Rome the objections recently presented to Monsignor Vagnozzi.

Welles responded that on that very day he broached the question with Roosevelt, who said that, knowing Pius XII as he did, he simply found the news unbelievable. The following day saw another cable from Archbishop Cicognani to Cardinal Maglione: "The president has said that, knowing and valuing the position and feelings of His Holiness, he deems it unbelievable that such a measure could have been agreed to and made public." The whole affair would be considered a Japanese victory, and the Holy See's prestige would greatly suffer in America. Sumner Welles instructed Tittmann to find Cardinal Maglione and then protest vigorously.

The cardinal had already explained to Archbishop Cicognani the Holy See's reasons for accrediting a Japanese mission. Upon receiving a second cable from the delegate, who expressed the personal feelings of Roosevelt, it was the cardinal's turn to send a second cable. Pius XII himself added the following to the preceding remarks: The Holy See's decision was dictated by a concern to protect Catholic interests in a large nation and in order to continue the Vatican's charitable mission and its efforts on behalf of peace. It was not motivated by any political factor. The pope found himself exposed to attacks from the Fascist press because he had not renewed the condemnations previously given and still in force against Communism. Present circumstances required that he not do so since condemnations of this kind could be attributed to political considerations. Pius XII was relying on the president to prevent the Holy See's position from being misinterpreted.

Several days later Archbishop Spellman was received by the president and remarked to him that Catholics made up 33 percent of the armed forces and that this was not the time to stir up trouble in the country. The president was convinced by Spellman, since several days later, during a press conference, he said that the Holy See was unable to act any differently than it did.

But on 22 March England's representative repeated the complaint. The Japanese, he said, threatened to use reprisals against Catholic missionaries if the Holy See rejected their request; and so the Holy See had submitted to blackmail. Cardinal Maglione called in Osborne and explained to him that the Japanese approach had been perfectly correct. On 27 March Welles again sent a message to Tittman instructing him to use his next audience to present the pope with the State Department's "deep rooted objections" to a Japanese mission in the Vatican. As deep as these objections might have been, they were soon meaningless because Tokyo's foreign minister had sent the name of Ken Harada, counselor at the Japanese embassy in France, as the appointee for the anticipated Vatican post. Two days later Cardinal Maglione replied positively to the request of agreement.

On 9 May Pius XII officially received the Japanese ambassador, who presented the pope with his letters of accreditation as a "special envoy with the rank of ambassador." The ceremony stirred up American sensitivities: Tittman noted that Ken Harada was received in the throne room, whereas Myron Taylor had been received in the *"Sala del tronetto."* At the Secretariat of State Tittman was told that the Japanese envoy, being the official representative of the Japanese Empire, was consequently received with the protocol reserved to ambassadors, whereas with Myron Taylor, who was President Roosevelt's personal representative, a slightly different procedure had to be observed. Yet Tittmann was assured that Myron Taylor had been given honors far greater than those accorded the Japanese ambassador.

At the same time, the apostolic delegate in Washington sent the Vatican an official request from Chiang Kai-shek's government that it be accredited with its own representative to the Holy See. Two days later Cardinal Maglione replied that the Holy Father was quite willing to receive a Chinese envoy. But since the Japanese took offense at the idea of finding themselves next to someone from China at the Vatican, the Secretariat of State had to repeat for the sake of the Japanese the explanations given to the U.S. State Department regarding Japan itself. Since the time of Leo XIII, China had quite frequently considered establishing official relations with the Vatican, and the Vatican had always been open to this. China was now repeating its request, and the Holy See could only respond favorably. Clearly, the request came from the China of Chiang Kai-shek. Opposed to his government was the government at Nanking, established by Japan and which Japan wanted to have accredited by the Holy See. Cardinal Maglione recalled that the Holy See had never during a war recognized states whose existence was the result of military activity.

Archbishop Marella proposed that as a substitute measure an apostolic delegate be appointed with instructions to deal with the Japanese authorities in China. On this point agreement was possible, and Archbishop Mario Zanin was told to go into the territory of Nanking to visit the missionaries and to make contact with the government.

FIRST GERMAN FEELERS FOR PEACE

And so the two camps attempted to mobilize for their own benefit the moral and diplomatic influence of the Holy See. But since the
time Hitler began his campaign against Russia on 22 June 1941, the
Führer's hopes were only partially realized. Surely the Wehrmacht had
advanced some twelve hundred kilometers into the Soviet Empire, but
in December, at a time when the German general staff thought Moscow
had been captured, Marshals Timochenko and Joukov sprang a coun-
teroffensive and saved Moscow. The Wehrmacht again formed a front
for the winter and prepared a new offensive for the spring, this time
knowing that the Russians possessed the will and the means for
defending themselves and believing that new victories in Russia did
not mean the end of the war. Many Germans, even in government circles, were anticipating that peace would only come from compromise.

In April 1942 the Reich's ambassador at Ankara, Franz von
Papen, informed Archbishop Angelo Roncalli of his thoughts regarding peace and Germany's future. The ambassador and his host, Baron
von Lersner, suggested that Pius XII sound out various governments.
A week later, Roncalli announced that Baron von Lersner would be
going to Rome and that he was looking forward to meeting various
Vatican officials, perhaps even being received by the pope. Actually it
was on 22 May that Lersner was in Rome where, thinking he was
under surveillance, went to the Vatican to visit the gardens, and from
there he was discretely escorted to the cardinal secretary of state.
Claiming to speak only as a private citizen, he disclosed that all the
German generals believed that victory would not result in peace and
that Turkey was willing to act as a mediator; however, in his opinion,
such a role really fell to the Holy See. Lersner repeated to Cardinal
Maglione pretty much what von Papen had told Roncalli: "The Holy
See could sound out the various powers in order to know what they had
in mind, and next October definite steps could be taken in light of this."
Lersner said the identical thing to Monsignor Montini.

Behind these so-called "personal" words, Monsignor Tardini
caught a glimpse of an initiative on the part of the German government.
In any case, he thought, saying that victory would not bring about
peace meant that the Germans themselves recognized they would not
win the war. They were hoping that by October they might achieve
some successes on the basis of which they could begin negotiations

and, looking forward to these negotiations, they wanted to be certain of the Holy See's cooperation.

Did Washington know about these or similar schemes? At any rate, it wanted to warn the pope and his entourage. In a letter dated 8 August Harold Tittmann refreshed Cardinal Maglione's mind as to the "position of the U.S. government as to peace proposals coming from the Axis powers." It could be summarized in a sentence: "The U.S. government cannot for a moment conceive of peace with the Axis till Hitlerism is completely annihilated." This message, which referred to a statement made to Congress on the previous 6 January, was unambiguous.

But Roosevelt did not want any doubts to remain. On Thursday, 17 September, Myron Taylor arrived at the airport in Littorio. Immediately taken to the Vatican, he stayed with Harold Tittman till Monday, 28 September. Mussolini had given Taylor permission to pass through Italian territory but, throughout his whole stay, the diplomat could not leave Vatican City, where he had three audiences with Pius XII, one on 19 September, a second on 26 September, and a third on 26 September.

In his first audience, which took place two days after his arrival, Myron Taylor read and commented on a long memorandum, presented as a "basis on which to carry out the parallel efforts of His Holiness and of President Roosevelt to bring about a just and moral peace." The first part of the document dwelt on the similarity of views between the United States and the Holy See, recalling pontifical teachings on conditions for a just peace and similar statements from the American bishops. The second section repeated that Washington would never negotiate with the Nazi leaders and warned the Holy See against an eventual Axis tactic. America is certain of victory:

> The world has never seen such an avalanche of war weapons, manned by skilled mechanics and stout-hearted freemen, as we shall loose in 1943 and 1944 against the Axis. In some few sectors, we have already taken the offensive, months ahead of our original plans. That offensive will rise in irresistible crescendo, more and more rapidly, more and more powerfully, until totalitarianism, with its menace to religion and freedom, is finally and utterly crushed.

The memorandum further stated that the Axis powers would attempt to ward off danger by trying "through indirect ways to oblige

133

the Holy See in the near future to confirm proposals for a peace without victory." The Allies wanted to help the Vatican resist such pressure since they were determined to reject any peace arrived at through compromise.

During the second audience, on 22 September, Pius XII responded to many points dealt with on 19 September. In regard to Roosevelt's warning against an Axis plan for a peace compromise, Pius responded that he viewed with pleasure the president's efforts on behalf of "a peace worthy of the importance and great dignity of the human person." As to peace at any price or peace resulting from compromise, the pope said he never had this in mind, as he unequivocally declared in his Christmas messages of 1939, 1940, and 1941: "On certain principles of right and justice there can be no compromise." And he was specific: "We will never approve and We will still less favor a peace that gives free reign to those who undermine the foundations of Christianity and persecute religion and the church." But he also recalled, and the allusion both to Soviet Russia as well as to Hitler's Reich was indeed clear, that this true peace would likewise suppose normal relations between peoples and governments and would require respect for religious convictions and divine worship.

Taylor gave the pope a memoir on Anglo-Saxon collaboration as being a means for introducing religious tolerance into Russia. Tardini's note on this states: "The truth is indeed different; if Stalin conquers, he will be the lion devouring all Europe."

Upon leaving the papal audience, Taylor met with Tardini. The American first spoke to him about "the advisability and the necessity of the pope coming out against the atrocities committed by the Nazis." This desire, said Taylor, has been expressed by many. In fact, just before Taylor's arrival, the ambassadors of Poland, Belgium, and Brazil, as well as England's minister and Roosevelt's chargé d'affaires, joined together asking that the pope issue a solemn condemnation of Nazism and its crimes. Monsignor Tardini, who had endured many attacks from diplomats, repeated to Myron Taylor that the pope had already spoken on numerous occasions, condemning crimes no matter who their authors might be. Some wanted Hitler condemned by name, but this was impossible. Taylor replied: "I never asked for that, I never asked that Hitler be named." And when Tardini replied that in this case the pope had already spoken, Taylor's rejoinder was: "He can repeat it." Tardini agreed. Then Taylor went on to discuss the friendship between the American and Italian people. And when Tardini replied that Italians, and himself included, had nothing against Americans, Taylor, gave the Monsignor to understand what he had in mind, saying that it was precisely for that reason...and he left off with a smile. Tardini understood that Roosevelt's envoy had in mind a separate peace but that he was waiting for an opportunity to speak to others about it.

The third and last of Myron Taylor's audiences, during the morning of 26 September, was devoted to the pope's responses to the envoy's requests and to the many requests addressed to the U.S. president by the pope himself. Pius XII presented Taylor with a private letter for Roosevelt in which the pope thanked him for Myron Taylor's mission and assured him that he would continue to struggle with all the means at his disposal for the establishment of a world order founded on justice and charity.

Pius XII also gave Taylor a note regarding the bombing of cities. The pope did not believe he should ignore a memorandum from the German embassy that called his attention to "the suffering of civilians, helpless women and children, the sick and the aged, for whom an innocent sky has become a deluge of terror, fire, destruction, and ruin." Of the two other notes the pope gave to the ambassador, one concerned the Holy See's information service, and the other was about the fate of Catholic priests and bishops sent to Russian concentration camps.

Finally, acting upon a request from the minister of Lithuania, the pope gave Roosevelt's envoy a note on behalf of this nation, which felt threatened by the Soviet Union. The minister hoped that the United States would guarantee that his country would be protected from all foreign occupation.

On 27 September Taylor made his final appearance at the Secretariat of State, where he gave the prosecretary an unofficial note responding to the pope's request concerning the civilian populations who were victims of the bombing. The American diplomat asked whether the Holy See had intervened against the bombing of London, Warsaw, Rotterdam, Belgrade, and Coventry, all of which had been struck by Luftwaffe bombs. Since it was the Royal Air Force and its American allies who were presently striking the harshest blows, the Holy See might lead people to believe that by its intervention the Vatican was yielding to pressure from the Axis, who were now themselves victims of the weapons whose power they were the first to recognize. Meanwhile, Myron Taylor promised to dissuade London and Washington from bombing indiscriminately, and he would urge these powers to warn civilians that they should withdraw from any military targets.

The fact that Mussolini granted Myron Taylor permission to pass through Italian territory tended to show a certain amount of good will on the part of the Fascist government vis-à-vis the Vatican. In fact, the Vatican's relations with Italy, its neighbor, give the impression of being less strained during this period following the Russian campaign. On 23 July 1942 the new Italian ambassador visited Cardinal Maglione on behalf of Count Ciano in order to deny certain statements made against the church, statements attributed to the head of the Italian government. "The Duce," said Ambassador Raffaele Guariglia, "is anxious to assure the Holy Father and Your Eminence of that." The ambassador expressed his own satisfaction for the haste with which Ciano and Mussolini took steps to refute these statements. The cardinal secretary of state promised to pass these assurances on to the pope: besides, although rumor attributed such remarks to Mussolini, neither the Holy Father nor the cardinal himself wanted to believe them.

Nonetheless, Roberto Farinacci, the director of *Regime fascista,* could not be persuaded to keep silent. On 8 March Archbishop Borgongini Duca, the Vatican's nuncio to the Italian government, had a meeting with Count Ciano; he took in with him a bundle of newspapers in order to protest once again against the Fascist journal. Ciano was not perturbed: "Do as I do," he told the nuncio, "don't read the *Regime fascista.*"

PIUS XII'S EPISCOPAL JUBILEE

Despite all the requests that the Holy See refused to grant, the various governments did not basically fail to appreciate the objectives pursued by the pope, namely, peace with justice. His episcopal jubilee occurred in 1942. The number of telegrams and cables addressed on this occasion to the sovereign pontiff by heads of state and of government, the very expressions used by many of them, showed the esteem the leaders of nations at war with one another had for the accomplishments and very personality of the pope and the value they attached to maintaining proper relations with him.

The most discreet form was that used by Wilhelmstrasse, which instructed Diego von Bergen to "present in the chancellor's name best wishes in a way that seems appropriate." Von Bergen did so on 13 May by visiting the cardinal secretary of state, who, several hours later, went to thank him in the name of the pope. From Italy the pope received not only "the warmest wishes" from the royal couple but also Mussolini's "sincerest greetings and those of the Fascist government." England, for its part, restricted itself to a rather formal cable from George VI. But President Roosevelt sent a private letter in which he repeated that "the efforts you have made to maintain, in a war-torn world, the ideals of Christianity against the actions of the aggressors can be profoundly appreciated, particularly on that day when free men may live together in peace and without fear of attack." Under a less official form and sent through the apostolic delegate in London, General de Gaulle expressed "his filial attachment to the head of the church."

Although the Vatican in turn sent letters and telegrams to thank those who had extended their best wishes, Pius XII also addressed all the faithful in a radio message on 13 May, the very anniversary day of his episcopal ordination. The words of the pope were primarily those of the supreme pastor, words of confidence in the church as "impregnable, indestructible, invincible; it is firm, incapable of being moved; its very charter has been sealed with the blood of Christ." Without doubt, in many areas the church was struggling for its very existence in the face of militant atheism, systematic anti-Christianity, and indifferentism. Its unity had been threatened; the force of its activity had been weakened at a time when its influence could have been so desirable and beneficial for all. Requests for help came to the pope from all sides, reminding the church and its leader that they should "use their authority so that the horrible conflicts presently being experienced come to an end and that the river of tears and blood may flow into a peace that is equitable and lasting for all." Forced to recognize that no prospect for peace was open before him at this time, he again called upon the leaders to end the destruction and the suffering:

> The destruction, both material and spiritual, caused by the war will so increase that we demand that every effort be taken to bring the war to a quick end. We need not mention the random acts of violence and cruelty against which we previously spoke out and

gave warning. We still do so today, with the greatest insistence and solemnity, as we face threats of still more murderous behavior brought about by a war, with the technical perfection of its arms, that causes people unspeakable pain, sorrow, and suffering.

Having enumerated the dead, prisoners, mothers and spouses, broken families and children separated from their parents, Pius XII concluded: "Is it not true that each of these words of evil and ruin recalls a number of cases that summarize and condense all that is the most lamentable, the most cruel, and the most harrowing of what has ever been inflicted on humanity?" It was the image of this humanity, completely torn apart by war, that formed the backdrop against which the pope viewed every particular problem that arose each day. This total vision, hidden from his interlocutors, who were impatiently attempting to win him over to their own positions, gave direction to his words and deeds.

CHAPTER 7

Racial Laws and Persecutions*

~·~

W HEN ITS EFFORTS at warding off the war came to naught and when prospects for reestablishing peace were moved into a very cloudy future, the Holy See concluded that its task was to assist the victims of the conflict by alleviating their physical and moral sufferings. During the First World War Pius XII, who was then known as Eugenio Pacelli and was Benedict XV's nuncio in Bavaria, visited the camps, where he brought the prisoners not only the comfort of his presence and of his words but also gifts of food and clothing. In this new conflict the Holy See wanted to remain faithful to this path, and a note from Cardinal Maglione dated 20 June 1942 mentioned what had been accomplished with the cooperation of Great Britain and the United States:

> Thanks to this spirit of understanding the papal representatives, either personally or through their delegates, were able to visit war prisoners in Australia, Canada, Egypt, England, and Italy, and were able to bring them on behalf of the Holy See words of comfort and of sincere interest; they were able to give them messages from their families and to receive from the prisoners messages for their own families.

One project especially close to the heart of Pius XII was the establishment of an information service whose purpose was to ensure an exchange of news between the prisoners and their families. On 18 September 1939 the pope decided that such an office was necessary, and yet a great disappointment awaited him: The Berlin government,

---

*Documentation for chapter 7: See *ADSS,* vols. 6, 7, and 9; complemented by: *La Chiesa e la guerra. Documentazione dell'uffizio informazioni del Vaticao*, Vatican City, 1941.

which during the first years of the war detained the largest number of prisoners, always refused to provide prisoner lists, which were necessary if the Vatican was to respond to requests for information that came to it from around the world. Nothing was accomplished by repeated and most emphatic demands. Even more, the secretariat of the Fulda episcopal conference, yielding to government orders, told priests not to mention from the pulpit the pope's information service and furthermore not to use its questionnaires.

When the tide of the war turned in favor of the Allies, German and Italian prisoners came to populate the Anglo-American camps. Cooperation from Great Britain and the United States was not spontaneous, and any number of cables were exchanged, but it all came to a satisfactory conclusion. After the Anglo-Americans arrived in North Africa, an American prelate was sent from the Vatican to Algiers; he was to organize an information office for the Holy See, doing so with the help of the English, French, and Americans.

One of the first objections voiced against this work of the Vatican was that such activity belonged to the International Red Cross, which had a specific role and a lawful right based on the 1929 convention officially granting the organization the task of protecting prisoners of war. It had at its disposal a number of ships for transporting food, medicine, and clothing. The organization passed on messages from prisoners of war, and throughout the world it had people qualified to go into prison camps to verify that the Geneva accords were being observed. Finally, it enjoyed the protection of the Swiss government and the financial support of the countries whose nationals it was to protect. All these resources far surpassed the juridical, political, and financial assets of the Holy See. Furthermore, the International Committee of the Red Cross looked favorably upon other charitable organizations, like the Swiss Catholic Mission, whose center was in Fribourg.

Preparation for collaboration between the Vatican and the Geneva organization occurred when representatives of the Holy See took part in the Red Cross congresses held in Tokyo in 1934 and in London in 1938. In mid-October 1939 the nuncio in Berne was instructed to make initial contact with the international committee in Geneva. It would perhaps be fitting, said his instructions, "to enter prudently into contact with this institution in order to inform it as to what the Holy See is doing and to assist by mutual agreement our respective tasks for providing information and assistance." Yet contact between the Holy See

140

and the Red Cross primarily occurred by means of the Swiss Catholic Mission, which was established during the First World War for prisoners of war and was given new impetus during the first days of hostilities in 1939 by M. Besson, the bishop of Fribourg. On his own initiative he offered to the Holy See the assistance of the Swiss Catholic Mission, which was at the time able to contact the chaplains of prisoner of war camps and to send packages there in the pope's name. The Vatican's information service also sent through the Mission a number of messages it had received from German prisoners held by the Allies. And so by the end of 1943 the names of a hundred twenty thousand prisoners had been collected and forty-three thousand packages had been forwarded to these camps.

INITIAL ASSISTANCE TO THE PERSECUTED JEWS

When it joined with the International Red Cross in caring for prisoners of war, the Holy See was thus continuing what it had already begun in the midst of the world conflict of 1914. During the Second World War, in addition to military prisoners and displaced persons, there appeared a new category of people who were appealing to the Holy See for assistance in a manner unknown during 1914–1918: In the language of the time, it pertained to the "non-Aryans," namely, people of Jewish origin, whether by religion or nationality.

The increasingly oppressive measures victimizing the Jews, first in Germany and then in countries that had fallen under the control of the Third Reich, preceded the war. Already during the famous *Kristallnacht* (night of crystal) from 9 to 10 November 1938, hundreds of synagogues and countless Jewish shops were set ablaze. And just as the state of war, far from bringing about any holy union, merely aggravated the hardships facing the church, so too did it give signs that there would be more and more violent persecutions against the Jews.

The Nazi authorities first appeared to seek a solution to the Jewish question by expelling Jews from German territories. And so assisting these Jews meant finding countries willing to accept them. The Holy See began with the fate of baptized Jews, for this group was in very great need since Jewish relief organizations were often unaware of them.

A first step on their behalf was a circular letter dated 30

141

November 1938 and sent to the pope's representatives in North and South America, Africa, the Near East, and Ireland in order to obtain means of subsistence for Jews who were forced to leave their homelands. Then, early in January 1939, another circular letter was sent to the archbishops of free countries; it invited these prelates to create national relief committees whose purpose would be to assist non-Aryan Catholics. The next day Pius XI wrote to the two cardinal archbishops in the United States and Canada, recommending to them the Jewish scholars who were forced to leave Germany. Among the various national committees, the Dutch committee seemed to have enjoyed the most success up to the time when the German occupation put an end to its activity.

Another especially active relief committee was the German St. Raphael Society *(St. Raphaelsverein)*. Established in 1871 "to aid German Catholic emigrants," this church fund had in Germany and beyond an excellent administrative structure, one that benefited a new organization known as the Relief Committee for Non-Aryan Catholics *(Hilfsausschuss für katholische Nichtarier)*, which joined it in March 1935. Through great difficulties and till its suppression by the state police in July 1941, the work of the St. Raphael Society assisted a rather large number of people who were persecuted because of their race, and the Holy See made an important financial contribution to this work.

When threats against Germans because of their race or their Jewish religion continued to increase, one proposal followed another in order to broaden the assistance that was given. One such idea was that Romanian Jews be resettled in Spain: In the summer of 1939 a certain Dr. Kirschberg presented the Secretariat of State with a plan to populate the Portuguese colony of Angola with Jews. Another idea, proposed by Switzerland, strongly recommended that the Jews emigrate to Venezuela. To counteract a plan put forward by the organs of the Nazi party, namely, to place German Jews in Madagascar, others considered settling them in southern Alaska. Dom Odon von Württemberg, O.S.B., came up with the scenario of having the Jews emigrate in several stages, first having them go to Ecuador, then to Australia, and then to Venezuela, with a stop in the Virgin Islands. In view of this odyssey Dom Odon offered the assistance of his relationship with England's royal family.

The Vatican, however, was satisfied with more concrete initiatives. In conjunction with the St. Raphael Society and other European

142

relief agencies, it directed its activity toward what was called the "Brazilian action" *(Brasilienaktion)*, which brought about real though, to be truthful, limited results.

On 31 March 1939 Cardinal Faulhaber, the archbishop of Munich, wrote to Pius XII and requested his intervention on behalf of the Catholic non-Aryans who were forced to leave Germany. It was becoming increasingly difficult for them to find a country willing to receive them. The United States had modified its immigration policy so that applicants now had to wait three or four years. Brazil, on the other hand, was willing to grant three thousand entry visas, but the cardinal's efforts to obtain them were unsuccessful. Faulhaber, however, hoped that the pope might succeed in untangling the situation. On 5 April Cardinal Maglione sent a cable to the nuncio in Rio de Janeiro asking him to speak to the president of the republic about giving three thousand entry visas to German non-Aryans who were Christians.

A year passed while negotiations took place as to the conditions and methods for granting the visas. Finally, on 4 March 1940, following instructions received from his government, Ildebrando Accioly, Brazil's ambassador to the Holy See, suggested to the Secretariat of State a procedure for distributing the three thousand visas granted by President Vargas. Two thousand would be delivered by Brazil's representative in Germany to non-Aryan Catholics remaining in the Reich and who were presented by the St. Raphael Society. A thousand visas could be used by non-Aryan Catholics who had already left Germany and were being detained in other European countries. These visas would be handed over by Brazil's ambassador to the Holy See upon the recommendation of the Secretariat of State.

EMIGRATION BLOCKED

Starting in March 1940 and to the extent that it depended on Brazil's ambassador to the Holy See, the Brazilian action was actually realized. Thus on 30 May the Secretariat of State asked Ambassador Accioly for visas to be used by about fifty non-Aryan Catholics who had taken refuge in Switzerland and had been recommended by the nuncio in Berne. In Germany, on the other hand, the Brazilian initiative was rendered inoperative since Brazil's ambassador in Berlin and its consul general in Hamburg, who had been given the authority to distribute the visas, constantly raised new objections, and in the end not a single visa was issued.

One case, taken from among the many handled by the Secretariat of State during the period between 1939 and 1940, sheds light on Vatican and other ecclesiastical endeavors as well as on the tragic results suffered due to the carelessness of the responsible authorities. On 24 April 1940 Preysing, the bishop of Berlin, requested that the Holy See intervene to obtain quickly a visa for a Catholic non-Aryan from Lwów designed as "A. Th."; arrested in Poland, he had been sent to the Oranienbourg concentration camp. After much effort by the Secretariat of State, on 10 July Preysing received the following message from Brazil's ambassador in Berlin: "I regret to inform Your Grace that this embassy has not as yet been instructed to stamp the visa on the passports of Catholic emigrants of Semite origin. Consequently, the embassy is obliged to await such instructions." In September the bishop entreated the secretary of state to try again. In January 1941 Preysing wrote Cardinal Maglione and informed him that the Brazilian general consulate in Hamburg was again causing difficulties in regard to a visa for M. Th. Even though verbal assurance had been given to the nuncio in Berlin, as though the visa were ready, the consulate still refused to hand it over. After yet another appeal from the bishop of Berlin, the nuncio in Rio was asked, by means of a cable dated 17 March, to become involved in the affair. Everything hereafter was useless. The file on the Polish prisoner was closed on 25 April 1941 with a note from Preysing: "Th. died in the concentration camp."

At the beginning of 1941 the Holy See knew quite well that it was becoming increasingly difficult for political and racial refuges to leave territories now under Berlin's control. The word *deportation* already was appearing in place of *emigration.* On 4 February 1941 a letter from Cardinal Innitzer to the pope reported that the indiscriminate deportation of sixty thousand Jews from Vienna—eleven thousand of these were Catholics of Jewish origin—had begun: "No consideration is given to age or religion." Innitzer's appeal, as the cardinal himself well knew, was darkened with indignation, and he excused himself for his insistence: "Perhaps it will be said that my proposals are too audacious and daring. But whoever knows our inability to offer aid and who is aware of the indescribable suffering of the victims will understand my boldness and will also understand that assistance, if it is to be effective, must be supplied as soon as possible." The letter from Cardinal Innitzer crossed in the mail an explanation sent by Cardinal Maglione in response to a previous appeal sent to the pope by the cardinal on 20 January; it requested money for the baptized Jews, who were not receiving any financial aid. For, he observed, the Quakers, the Swedish mission, and the Jewish community had more funds at their disposal, not to mention that the Brazilian visas had not arrived from Hamburg.

Maglione's response, dated 6 February, was a summary of all that had been done or attempted up to that date. The letter, in its brevity, only partially explains the feeling of helplessness suffered by the Vatican and not only by Cardinal Innitzer. Maglione wrote as if he had believed and perhaps was still believing that the archbishop of Vienna was not fully informed about the Holy See's interventions on behalf of the Jews, whether they were Catholic or not, in territories controlled by the Germans and their allies. These efforts included interventions to mitigate racial laws, to obtain the release of Jewish internees, to improve the conditions of prisoners, and to provide economic aid to families. Encouragement was also given for the formation of national committees to assist refugees and for the issuing of visas allowing immigration to North and South America. A thousand of these visas were in fact granted by Brazil. Maglione concluded by telling Innitzer that the pope himself was sending two thousand dollars for his work, but that there was little hope of obtaining entry visas for the American republics. Innitzer's thoughts on Maglione's letter only attest too clearly the growing tragedy of the situation. In his 28 February response the archbishop said that, as to Vienna, the committee established in 1939 was not very helpful. He only had confidence in the Argentine committee. He reiterated his great disappointment that baptized Jews were being forgotten and the unfortunate contrast with the Quakers, the Swedish mission, and Jewish organizations. Catholics of Jewish origin had been "terribly deceived." In the eyes of their Jewish coreligionists, they were apostates and renegades; their conversion meant that all financial assistance came to an end. But, as Innitzer attested, amidst their trials they give a magnificent example of patience: "Numerous Catholics being sent to Poland undergo their harsh fate with a courage worthy of admiration, and they go to the uncertain fate of their exile with a Christian heroism that edifies the Jews of the Mosaic rite."

At this time transit visas, even by way of the Iberian peninsula, were difficult to obtain. At Rome a member of the *Raphaelsverein,*

Franz Hecht, wrote on the same 28 February that a hundred and fifty people who nevertheless possessed Brazilian visas were detained because they lacked a Spanish exit visa. Furthermore, wrote Hecht, the Italian government has now forbidden the emigration of Jews having a Nansen passport, that is, without nationality, or of those possessing Italian passports. Upon receiving this information on 7 March, Cardinal Maglione immediately instructed Father Tacchi Venturi to tell Mussolini that the Holy See was surprised: It was discriminatory to allow the emigration of Jews with foreign passports and not of those holding the Nansen document or a regular Italian passport. The only bit of good news coming to the Vatican during this period was that Panama agreed to receive Catholic Jews who were coming from Germany and were awaiting future settlement elsewhere, namely, in the United States. On 29 April Archbishop Orsenigo, the nuncio to Germany, passed on to the Vatican a plan from the *Raphaelsverein* to make good use of this permission, a hope that probably went nowhere.

On 16 May 1941 the Delasem *(Delegazione Assistenza Emigranti Ebrei)* sent a message to the pope regarding transit visas that its sister agency in Lisbon was unable to obtain. The Delasem had succeeded in obtaining permission for two thousand Jews (Germans, Austrians, Romanians, and Hungarians) to leave. But toward the end of 1940 the Portuguese government required that Jews pass through Lisbon, where they were to pick up their transit visas. As a result, many who had visas and reserved places were not only impeded but had to start all over again and request a new visa for America. The ideal solution, said the Delasem, would be for the Portuguese government to allow its consulate in Rome to grant transit visas upon the presentation of the proper documents and ship reservations by the *Raphaelsverein.*

A similar proposal was made on 27 June by P. Weber, a member of the *Raphaelsverein.* Two months previous, it had been impossible to obtain transit visas in Lisbon by simply presenting a ticket for the ship. Now, with new delays, the Brazilian visas were about to expire, and the emigrants, almost ready to leave, had to remain in the camps. But already on 26 June a severe blow—certainly not unforeseen—struck the emigration fund for the German refugees. The headquarters of the *Raphaelsverein* in Hamburg was shut down by the police. Orsenigo telegraphed this information on 3 July: "The motive would be the exportation of news defaming Germany." I ask Your Most Reverend Eminence to communicate to the Pallotine Fathers that they suspend correspondence and all activity." And so the last way out of Germany was now closed. Only offices in Rome and in Lisbon continued to function. It is quite likely that various refugees, whether assisted or not by the *Raphaelsverein,* simply "talked too much" once they arrived in a safe place. But the reason given for closing the Hamburg office was merely a pretext to justify a decision already taken in Berlin.

Other bad news befell the refugees in Italy. On 25 July the Delasem wrote from Genoa to Archbishop Borgongini Duca, the nuncio to the Italian government, that the American Service Committee of Friends (Quakers) was forced to suspend the aid it was giving. According to P. Weber, the organization had been furnishing Jewish Catholics in Italy with up to forty thousand liras a month. The Delasem informed the nuncio that it was unable to assist these people even though they were of Jewish origin: "Even with the best of intentions, it is impossible for us to extend our ordinary activity to refugees who do not belong to the Hebrew religion." In the past, according to the note, the Delasem felt it was a pressing duty of human solidarity to furnish Jewish Catholics with "exceptional and temporary assistance."

With the United States soon to enter the war, the growing tension brought with it a progressive restriction on immigration. On 14 November Cardinal Maglione drew the attention of Ildebrando Accioly, the Brazilian ambassador, to the 156 Jews from Holland whom the ambassador had granted permission to obtain visas. Thirty-three of these did in fact receive visas, but these documents were on the verge of expiring and had to be extended. For the 123 others, since they could not go to Berlin, the cardinal asked whether the Brazilian counsel in Lisbon might not be authorized to complete any lacking formalities. Accioly's response was quick and fatal. On 20 November he told Cardinal Maglione that the granting of visas was suspended. At about the same time the Spanish government declared that it would issue no more transit visas. The Portuguese ambassador, who avoided the basic question by simply asking the Holy See to "suspend" or "delay" requests for Portuguese transit visas, said that he still had hopes of obtaining transit visas for persons particularly recommended by the Holy See.

The history of the 156 Jewish Catholics entrapped in Holland and Belgian during 1941 did not end during the following year, 1942. On 15 April 1942 Orsenigo gave the result of his many months' wait: "To my verbal note of this past 25 November, in which I rightly requested

147

that the aforementioned Jews be given the necessary permission to leave occupied territories, the foreign minister has just now responded, notifying me that according to a statement made by internal authorities permission to leave is not granted to Jews of German nationality residing in Belgium and Holland, and this because of general police reasons." Several months later in a report of 28 July Orsenigo wrote that from what he had heard, the Dutch bishops had sent a vigorous protest and they seemed to have succeeded in excluding baptized Jews from measures leading to their deportation. In reality, on Sunday 26 July, two days before Orsenigo wrote so optimistically about the situation in Holland, the Gestapo carried out its well-known raid of reprisals against Jewish Catholics. German Jews were the principal object and, as is known, Edith Stein, who had become a Carmelite, was one of their number. It can be presumed that the 156 candidates for emigration to Brazil were likewise deported.

On 9 October Paolo Giobbe, the internuncio in the Netherlands who had been forced to retire to Rome, sent Cardinal Maglione two documents he had received from Holland regarding deportation. One was the collective pastoral letter of 20 July, which informed the faithful of a common, namely, both Catholic and Protestant, protest addressed to the German authorities: "The object of the request is to stop the mass deportation of non-Aryans including women and children, which has been and is still being carried out." The other document was the letter from the archbishop of Utrecht, Johann de Jong, to Reichskommissar Seyss-Inquart, who much earlier had agreed that non-Aryan Christians would not be subject to the measures taken against non-Aryans in general (this was the subject of the pastoral letter mentioned above). But then this concession was revoked in regard to non-Aryan Catholics. The pretext of this measure, which was hostile to Catholics, was the fact that the above-mentioned (20 July) pastoral was accompanied by the text of the protest sent by the leaders of the Christian confessions to the commissar of the Reich. The internuncio added what is perhaps an implicit reference to Edith Stein: "According to the written information I have received, the recent deportation has even included women religious."

Orsenigo used the phrase "for general police reasons" when explaining why the emigration had come to a halt. This meant that the Gestapo had completely taken control of the fate of the Jews and had interposed its policing authority to block the moderating influence of every other agency, for example, the German Foreign Ministry. Already on 20 April Archbishop Berning of Osnabrück, to whom Cardinal Maglione had sent five thousand dollars for the German Jewish refugees in the Netherlands who were about to depart for Brazil, responded that he was unable to use the money "for general police reasons." One month later, on 20 May, Cardinal Innitzer again made an appeal, which might be considered as his last on behalf of the emigrants. The deportation of which he spoke more than a year earlier had taken on considerable proportions:

> The situation of the non-Aryan Catholics continues to become very bleak; on the one hand, their misery constantly increases; on the other hand, the possibility of assisting them constantly decreases; above all, it is no longer possible to obtain visas so that they might leave. Twenty thousand non-Aryans have gone from Vienna into the General Government, and among them are a thousand Catholics whose situation is hopeless. And so it is almost impossible to help them.

ORSENIGO'S FAILURES AND SUCCESSES

Despite diminishing hopes, the Vatican continued to send requests to the nuncio in Berlin. On 24 June Orsenigo responded to a particular appeal from Monsignor Montini on behalf of a Jewish couple. The fact that these two Jews were not presently in a concentration camp, the nuncio said, made no difference: no exit visa has been given to any Jew. Alluding to some other particular cases that had been called to his attention by Monsignor Montini or by other Vatican officials, he added:

> I regret that, in addition, I must add that these interventions are not only useless but they are even badly received; as a result the authorities show themselves unfavorable to other and even less serious cases, which are not already settled by the general norms, as is the case for non-Aryans.

On 21 July in regard to another situation Orsenigo presented further details regarding the government in Berlin: "The plight of the Jews lies beyond all friendly intervention." More than once he was made to understand at Wilhelmstrasse that the less he spoke about the Jews, the better it would be: "The government official who was hearing the case immediately declared that he could not grant the request from the apostolic nunciature, and he advised the nuncio not even tell anyone that such a request had been made." This took place in May, said Orsenigo, when he presented the especially tragic case of two young Jews under threat of being deported to Poland and who were confined in a synagogue.

A week later, on 28 July, Orsenigo responded to a request from Monsignor Montini on behalf of some Jews who were seeking to receive news about their families in Germany and Poland. Not only was it impossible to do anything to obtain emigration for the Jews or to stop their deportation, but it was absolutely impossible to obtain any news after a person had been deported. It was even dangerous to stop in the street to speak to people wearing the star of David. This was also true for Vienna. As to the tragedy hiding behind this curtain of silence, Orsenigo could only speak in terms of conjecture and fear:

> As is easily supposed, this suppression of news leaves the gate open to the most gruesome suppositions as to the fate of the non-Aryans. Unhappily, there are rumors, difficult to control, of catastrophic journeys and even of large massacres of the Jews. Every intervention, even that in favor of only non-Aryan Catholics, has till now been brushed aside with the customary response that baptismal water does not change Jewish blood, and that the German Reich is defending itself from the non-Aryan race and not from the religious affiliation of the baptized Jews.

Orsenigo, to whom the Secretariat of State continued to appeal, again responded on 9 December to a request for intervention on behalf of a Jew living in Poland who had been refused admittance into Uruguay. In dissembling language Orsenigo pointed out to Maglione: (1) that he could not speak to the Gestapo since this would call attention to the very existence of the individual; (2) that Uruguay was at war with Germany; (3) that no exit visas are given to Jews from Germany much less to those from Poland: "It is here, unfortunately, that we have one of these numerous and very painful cases where one cannot even send words capable of comforting those unfortunates who live in fear of deportation and whose existence is a true agony."

A report sent to the Secretariat of State at the end of 1942 by a counselor at the Berlin nunciature who had returned to Rome after some years in the German capital presents a general picture of the situation of both Catholic and non-Catholic Jews in Germany. During the years 1941–1942 measures against the Jews had become especially violent. The beginning of the Russian campaign had exposed a new contingent of Jews to the same fate; their number was estimated at one and a half million in Poland previously occupied by the Russians, and 260,000 others in the Baltic States, which till 1941 were under Soviet control. Another million and a half lived in Russian territories controlled at the end of 1942 by German armies—altogether four million Jews under German control.

A first reference was now made to the concentration camps. Having mentioned the two ghettos of Lodz and Warsaw, the diplomat explained that all the Jews who had been unable to gather in these ghettos were sent off to concentration camps,

> where they lead a very hard life; they are given but little to eat; and they have to perform extremely heavy work, work that soon brings death. It is said that such concentration camps have till now been established in Poland, which makes one believe that the eastern region has been selected by the German government as the final place of residence for the Jewish population of Europe.

The same counselor noted that the German population did not react as the Nazi party wanted: Goebbels deplored the excessive humanitarianism of the Germans, urging them to consider each bearer of the star of David as a traitor to the German people. He cited a speech of Rosenberg which stated that Germany would not solve the Jewish problem till the last Israelite leaves the Great Reich. The people, however, did not seem to be convinced by the regime's propaganda: "Humorous or mocking gestures in regard to the Jews are never seen. Such an exterior indifference presumes a very strong interior resentment against the inhumane measures which, as the Germans themselves well know, cannot benefit a civilized people, especially a people who claim to be the highest *Kulturtraeger* [bearer of culture] in the world."

Spring 1942 saw the beginning of what the Third Reich's secret documents were already calling "the final solution." The critical moment seems to have been the conference held at Wannsee (Berlin) on 20 January 1942. It was here that Reinhard Heydrich, the head of the Reich's security agency, presented the representatives of the government's ministries and other organizations with the plan for "the final solution of the Jewish question." It was geared, he said, toward eleven million Jews, including 330,000 living in England. Under the pretext of the Russian campaign, the plan took the form of massively transferring the Jewish population of Europe to Poland. In 1942 the possibilities of emigration were completely blocked, and a new phenomenon appeared: the expulsion of Jews—men, women, and children—from their places of residence and their deportation to locations outside Germany.

Henceforth, the Holy See's activity definitely had to assume a new direction: Rather than facilitating emigration, which had become impossible, it was now necessary to oppose deportation, whose tragic end was already being suspected.

It was very difficult for the Vatican to resign itself to the impossibility of doing anything in Germany, even on behalf of the victims of the Nazi ideology. Archbishop Orsenigo found himself in a far from enviable situation. He could satisfy neither his superiors in Rome nor the German bishops, and he had to at least keep up the appearance of having correct relations with the officials at Wilhelmstrasse, who, to tell the truth, were almost as powerless as he was. At the beginning of 1943 the bishop of Berlin insinuated that not only was Orsenigo not up to the task but that the policy of the Reich had fallen so low that it was no longer fitting for the pope to have a representative there: "I wonder," wrote Preysing to Pius XII on 23 January 1943, "whether this is a good time for the august person of Your Holiness to be represented by an ambassador to the government of the Reich."

Nonetheless, requests continued to arrive from the Vatican to the nuncio in Berlin on behalf of persons condemned to death either by civil or military tribunals, even when it concerned especially delicate cases. Should the Holy See, would the Holy See, request clemency for the head of an intelligence network? On 27 October 1942 the Belgian ambassador asked for the Holy See's help on behalf of Count Jean d'Ursel, who had been arrested for espionage and was presently in danger of being put to death. The suggestion was made that the pope propose that d'Ursel be exchanged for a German agent who had fallen into the hands of the Allies. The Holy Father immediately replied that he saw no possibility of an action of this type. Later on, however, following repeated requests from the Belgian ambassador, the nuncio in

152

Berlin was instructed to intervene. Count d'Ursel was rather fortunate to have survived the war.

On 25 June 1943 Orsenigo reported that his appeal in favor of Canon Stanowsky, from Prague, was successful. The nuncio himself had drawn up the text of the request, which was signed by the priest's sister and then sent to Hitler's chancellery. The next day, 24 June, came news that the death sentence had been commuted to eight years in prison. "His sister, totally radiant, came to tell me the good news and to express her most heartfelt thanks for the efficacious interest of the Holy See through its apostolic nuncio." Similar appeals came to the pope on behalf of some Belgians who had been accused of espionage and sentenced to death. On the following 17 November Orsenigo sent a message that three of these had had their sentences commuted.

But when it concerned the Jews, any step was fruitless and even dangerous. The military dreamers now known by Germany only hardened the intransigence of the Nazi leaders. On 12 January 1943, in regard to a special case, Orsenigo reminded the Secretariat of State that it was impossible for a Jew to leave Germany or an occupied country, especially if the person were neither a Catholic nor a foreign citizen. On 19 January, responding to a request in favor of a Jew from Warthegau, he reminded his superiors that the Franciscan Odilo had been sent to Dachau because he had been accused of assisting the Jews. Requests on behalf of the Jews, he said, were immediately dismissed without any examination. In September he recalled the same precedent in regard to a certain Miss Luckner, who was sent to Ravensbrück for having helped the Jews.

One very little known aspect of the Jewish drama during the Second World War concerned German Jews married to Catholics as well as the children of mixed marriages who were raised as Catholics. According to the laws of Nuremberg, Jews who married Christians, as well as their children raised in the Christian religion, were to be considered as Aryans. Consequently a group of approximately three hundred thousand people of Jewish origin had till 1943 been exempt from anti-Semitic measures. However, as early as 1942 the nuncio began to hear rumors that the law would be modified and that thousands of people would consequently be endangered. On 7 September 1942 Orsenigo pointed out to the Vatican that the German hierarchy was greatly perturbed by this and that he had called the government's attention to the injustice and inhumanity of the plan. Months passed, and yet nothing happened till the end of February and the beginning of March 1943, when the arrests began.

The beginning of the crisis was related by Archbishop Orsenigo on 3 March. On 24 February, when the anniversary of the party was being celebrated in Munich, Hitler gave an anti-Semitic speech which, wrote Orsenigo, was distinguished by its tone of unprecedented violence against Judaism the world over. The German leader inflamed all the nations of Europe to follow Germany's example in hunting down Jews. The consequences were not long in coming, so that Orsenigo sent this message: "In fact, 28 February and 1 March were two especially ferocious days for deporting Jews from Berlin to unknown destinations. Included were baptized Jews and Jews married to Aryans, thus destroying families....Once again I used this occasion to tell the foreign minister that all Catholics were disgusted by this; I was heard, but I also know that no one can oppose the physical and unbridled force of the so-called Gestapo."

Finally, by a strange conjunction of circumstances whose details have never been satisfactorily investigated, large numbers of the Jews and semi-Jews thus endangered in Germany escaped deportation. Was this due to the resistance of the population, or did it result from dissensions among rival Nazi organizations? As a whole, the measures considered by Eichmann's departments against Jews married to Catholics and against children of mixed marriages were not carried out in the Reich, either in Berlin or in Vienna.

THE JEWS IN ITALY

Even though Italy was linked to the Reich by the pact of Acier and had entered the war on Germany's side, the situation of the Jews in Italy was considerably different from that in Germany. This, however, did not stop the Holy See from taking an interest in the fate of non-Aryan Italians.

Before the war, in November 1938, an initial law forbade marriages between Aryans and non-Aryans. Discussions on this subject between the Holy See and the government came to naught. In the beginning of November Pius XI sent a private letter to Mussolini and another letter to King Victor Emmanuel III. Nonetheless, the law was made public on 10 November; the cardinal secretary of state then sent a note of protest to the Italian government, and on 6 March 1939 the Holy Office published a warning on the racial doctrine being propagated in Italy.

The number of non-Aryan Catholics in Italy was large. The Holy See's intent was to expand as much as possible the circle of these non-Aryan Catholics, seeking to include there catechumens, Jews who were not yet catechumens, and also half-Jews. The Vatican's primary objectives were the following: that permission be granted for non-Aryan Catholics to exercise their professions; that children of half-Jews not be impeded from attending school; that Jewish converts be allowed to marry Aryans; that marriages between Aryans and non-Aryans not be subjected to racial prejudice but that the new families thus constituted be considered as Aryan families. It is impossible to establish in detail the results obtained by the Holy See when it became involved in particular cases, but they certainly were not negligible. During the first years of the war the Holy See obtained from the government some rather extensive concessions in favor of Italians and of foreigners affected by the anti-Semitic legislation enacted previous to the war. Among these concessions were: complete "discrimination," namely, exemption from every restriction; permission to emigrate; and better physical and moral treatment in internment camps, which the apostolic nuncio could visit. Finally, Jewish Catholics were permitted to remain together with their chaplains.

Among the various internment camps spread throughout the country, the Ferramonti Tarsia camp in southern Italy harbored several thousand Jewish foreigners, mostly Poles, Czechoslovaks, and even some Germans. Much later a group of five hundred Slovak Jews, who had left Bratislava and came down the Danube with the intention of proceeding to Palestine but whose boat foundered in the waters near Rhodes, were captured by the Italians and taken to Ferramonti Tarsia. In 1941 some Catholic Jews, originally from Yugoslavia, were also confined there. A French Capuchin, Père Calliste Lopinot, who was assigned as their chaplain, shared their life and often served as their spokesman, doing so up to the day when Allied troops, who had landed in southern Italy, reached the camp in July 1943.

But throughout 1941 the Holy See's interventions were less and less successful, and the immigration into Italy of Jews fleeing Nazi persecution progressively came to a halt.

Uncertain was the fate of Jews from Yugoslavia who escaped

Croatia to seek refuge in the coastal region occupied by the Italians, for example, Dalmatia and the Slovenian province of Lubiana. On 14 August 1941 the Vatican received a letter from Altari, the president of the Union of Israelite Communities in Italy, who was alarmed about what was happening to Jews in the areas of Dalmatia and Croatia, both under Italian occupation. Without reason they were arrested and, their possessions having been stolen, the men were sent to the salt mines of Bosnia; women, the elderly, and children were sent off to the coast. Alatri asked the Vatican to take up the matter with the Italian and Croatian authorities so that an end might be put to the arrests and confiscations, and he suggested that six thousand of the threatened persons be transported to Italy, where their coreligionists would take charge of them. The nuncio, Francesco Borgongini Duca, was told to make inquiries. On 11 September he replied that the police had assured him that, despite rumors, the Jews taking refuge on the Dalmatian coast were not being forced to return to Croatia. Forbidden to enter Italy, they had to remain in the former Yugoslavian provinces annexed by Italy "because," said the official, "we cannot transform our country into an asylum for the Jews."

Father Tacchi Venturi served as the Vatican's official intermediary not only with Mussolini but also with the various governmental departments, including the heads of police as well as the general board for demographics and race, which was responsible for foreigners and especially the Jews. Bishop G. Rozman from Lubiana, a city occupied by the Italians, appealed to the government, asking it not to send Catholic Croatians of Jewish origin back to Croatia, "where they were being subjected to very harsh punishments." On 10 September 1941 Tacchi Venturi reported that Carmine Senise, the head of the police, had immediately telephoned Lubania's quaestor in order to obtain his support for the request. A month later Father Tacchi Venturi informed the Vatican that the interior minister had agreed that baptized Jews could be admitted into the Ferramonti Tarsia camp. This reception of Jewish refugees into Italy was perhaps the last case of its kind. The following 17 December Tacchi Venturi wrote Cardinal Maglione that any hope of foreign Jews, even if Catholic, entering the country was illusory.

Although the Italian government had closed its borders to Jews coming from the north, to the end, it refused to hand over those who were under its authority.

Thousands of Jews escaped from the Oustachian state of Croatia

156

and took refuge in regions of Yugoslavia occupied by the Italian forces. Likewise, in 1942 when the Germans were occupying the southern section of France, thousands of Jews went over into the southern zone, which was occupied by the Italians. In 1943 there was widespread fear that these Jews would be sent back to the Germans. What followed was a copious correspondence between the Vatican and the Fascist authorities, especially after the appeals sent to the Holy See by Jewish individuals and organizations the world over. At the time it appeared that Mussolini had decided not to send to the Germans those Jews who made their way to territory under Italian control. Pressure from Berlin in this regard was unsuccessful. Never did Mussolini acknowledge this policy, and in his last speech on 24 June he still spoke of "repatriating foreigners." But the concrete decisions taken by his subordinates were always those of refusing and even sabotaging every step taken on behalf of deportation. The Holy See could only reassure those who asked it to intervene with the Italian government.

On 13 February Cardinal Maglione instructed the nuncio to Italy to take action against a deportation, announced as imminent, of seventeen hundred Croatian Jews who had found refuge in Spalato. Word was that refugees not having Italian parents would be sent back to Croatia. Since few of them had family in Italy, the majority would be threatened with deportation, a step, however, denied by the Italian police.

Nonetheless, anxiety remained. On 6 March Archbishop Cicognani cabled Cardinal Maglione with an appeal from Myron Taylor, who himself was alerted by the president of the American Jewish Congress: "About fifteen hundred Yugoslavians of Jewish descent, who are presently in Italy or in areas of Italian occupation, are soon to be handed over to the Germans, and this upon German request, and will be deported to Poland. It means their death sentence." Cardinal Maglione requested Father Tacchi Venturi to see what he could do. The Jesuit met with Giuseppe Bastianini, the Italian undersecretary of state. In his report of 14 April 1943, drafted after the meeting, Tacchi Venturi confirmed that the Italian government refused to align itself with its German ally.

Mussolini's principle is as follows: as to the Jews, separation and not persecution. We do not want to be (and he stressed this) executioners....The more than four thousand Croatian Jewish émigrés

157

in Dalmatia have not been returned to the country from which they came; this saves them from the cruel fate awaiting them in some inhospitable region of Poland.

The same was true for Jews who had come from France: Demands had been made for them, "but Italy is opposed to this." It was only on behalf of Croatian Jews remaining in Slovenian territory annexed by Germany or those in Croatia that the Italian government had no basis for intervening. And still, on 13 June the nuncio confirmed that there was no change in the past policy, and that "consequently no Jew would be handed over to the German authorities."

In August 1943 after the fall of the Fascist regime a number of steps were taken to improve the conditions of the Jews in camps located within the Italian occupation zone of Dalmatia. On 24 August Cardinal Maglione cabled Archbishop Godfrey, the apostolic delegate in London, asking that he inform the Yugoslav government in London that the Italians were presently evacuating the Croatian and Slovenian internment camps following the intervention of the Holy See. Among those being transferred were four thousand Jews, who were to be sent to the island of Arbe. On 24 September an official of the World Jewish Congress wrote Godfrey to tell him that these Jews were no longer in danger because the island had been taken by the partisans. "I am sure that the efforts of Your Grace and of the Holy See have led to this happy result, and I would like to express to the Holy See and to you the warmest thanks of the World Jewish Congress."

FATE OF THE DEPORTEES

The position adopted by the administration and the very leader of the Italian government, notwithstanding the anti-Semitic laws they had promulgated, is better understood by remembering that questions were already being asked as to the meaning of the deportation. What was the fate of the deportees after their expulsion? As early as 1942 the Holy See's chargé d'affaires in Bratislava, Giuseppe Burzio, wrote that deportation was for the most part the equivalent of a death sentence. Several weeks later Angelo Rotta, the nuncio in Budapest, reported that some Jewish circles in Hungary were convinced that the Slovakian deportees were "for the most part doomed to a certain death." What was already known about the conditions under which the deportations were carried out left nothing good to foresee as to what the deportees would find upon their arrival, and this justified affirmations similar to those of the nuncio. And yet this did not destroy any hope against hope that the healthiest would overcome the ordeal. Furthermore, families as well as comrades by race or religion were attempting to learn what was happening. Many times the nuncio in Berlin requested information from Wilhelmstrasse, but always to no avail.

On 26 September 1942 during his brief visit to the Vatican, Myron Taylor delivered an official request for information. A report had been received from the Geneva office of the Jewish Agency for Palestine concerning the desperate situation of the Polish Jews and the Jews who had been deported to Poland. The report, dated 30 August, described the destruction of the Warsaw ghetto and executions in a camp called Belick as well as executions in Lwów and in Warsaw. At the end of the deportation was death: "The Jews deported from Germany, Belgium, Holland, France, and Slovakia," said the report, "are being sent to the butcher's shop, whereas the Aryans from Holland and France, deported to the east, are actually put to work." Taylor's *pro memoria* to Cardinal Maglione said: "I would be most thankful to Your Eminence if you might inform me whether the Vatican has any information that would tend to confirm the report contained in this *pro memoria*. If yes, I would like to know whether the Holy Father has any suggestion concerning a practical means for using the civilized world's forces of public opinion so as to put a halt to the continuation of this barbarism."

On 10 October Cardinal Maglione replied that to his knowledge there was no particular data to confirm the Geneva report. In fact, the most detailed information being received at the Vatican was the same as that received by the United States, the sources being Casimir Papée, who was the Polish ambassador, and the Jewish organizations themselves. In light of this, one did not know how to answer the second question on what practical means should be employed: "Reports pertaining to the severe measures taken against non-Aryans have also arrived at the Holy See from other sources, but thus far it has been impossible to verify their accuracy."

Rather significant are Maglione's annotations after receiving Taylor's document: "I do not believe that we have any information confirming this very serious news. Isn't this correct?" Regarding this the *minutante* wrote: "There is something from Mr. Malvezzi." But the information from Malvezzi, an employee of an Italian business and who had recently returned from Poland, did not correspond to the report from Geneva.

What the cardinal secretary of state understood by "severe measures" can be interpreted in the light of the documents from these two years. The information received in the Vatican was drawn from second- and third-hand reports concerning the brutal treatment inflicted on the Jews in Hungary, Croatia, Slovakia, France, and other countries. But both the final destination of the deportees and the Nazi plan remained at that time an enigma. When, for example, as early as March Giuseppe Burzio, the chargé d'affaires in Slovakia, spoke of the deportees going to "a certain death," it is clear that he based this statement on the inhumane conditions of the departures and on the brutality of the guards. After such a beginning it was easily imagined that the elderly, the sick, and the children would not be able to survive for long, even if typhus did not sweep through the unsanitary and overpopulated camps. It is in a similar vein that we should situate the remark of the Croatian police chief, E. Kvaterni, who told Abbot Marcone that the Germans were responsible for having two million Jews perish and that an identical fate awaited the Croatian Jews. A little later, what he said was not proven to be exaggerated. However, it indeed seems that the Holy See's representative, Abbot Marcone, when reporting this to his superiors, did not believe it should be taken literally. Such remarks, when heard or reported, were taken to mean that a very serious threat existed, a premonition of a tragedy whose real episodes were not yet seen.

The end of 1942 saw many public statements in regard to deportation. On 17 December the Allies published in London a declaration on human rights, which in very general terms denounced the treatment inflicted on the Jews.

On 19 December 1942 the Polish ambassador, Casimir Papée who had taken refuge in the Vatican and who was relating the attack on the Warsaw ghetto, stressed that the deportees were not being sent away to work since the sick, the elderly, and the children were also being expelled. "The deportees are being sent to death inflicted by various methods in places specifically prepared for this purpose." What reality was hidden beneath "various methods" and "places specifically prepared" remains obscure.

Osborne, the British minister to the Holy See, brought to Pius XII the 17 December statement of the Allies and requested that he confirm it in a public speech. The pope concluded his Christmas message by expressing his hope that the fighting come to an end so as to benefit all the victims of war—combatants, widows and orphans, exiles. "This wish," he again said, "humanity owes to the hundreds of thousands of people who, without any fault of their own and sometimes because of their nationality or race alone, have been doomed to death or to progressive extermination."

Upon examining the pope's message, the Reich's security service was not taken in: "He [the pope] virtually accuses the German people of injustice toward the Jews, and he makes himself the spokesman of the Jews, who are war criminals." Nonetheless, the ambassadors of the Allies in Rome were only half satisfied because they wanted a denunciation of Nazi war crimes, with names given, something they thought would better serve their cause. Pius XII, for his part, did not hide from the American diplomat that he thought certain things were being exaggerated by Allied propaganda.

To resolve the questions that continued to surface, the Vatican wanted the Red Cross to help.

The questions facing the Holy See were those also facing this organization. What could be done for the civilian internees, especially for the Jews, for whom there was no international guarantee? The Red Cross had reached the limits of what it could do. Would not its interventions on behalf of the Jews, even as to obtaining information, risk endangering what it was doing for millions of war prisoners? On 4 January 1943 the nuncio in Berne met at the nunciature with Carl Burckhardt, who was the principal assistant to the president of the Committee, with Professor Max Huber, and with Prince Johannes von Schwarzenberg. Despite the 1934 conferences in Tokyo, where an attempt was made to extend to civilians the guarantees that had been established for military personnel, the Red Cross was not able to do very much, and it desired the collaboration of the Holy See.

On 17 February Filippo Bernardini, the nuncio to Switzerland, informed the Vatican Secretariat of State of a meeting held in Geneva on 12 February 1943 by the Red Cross to examine the problem of helping the Jews who fell under Nazi control. A prelate from the diocese of Fribourg, whose note the nuncio sent on to the Vatican, was present together with representatives from various international organizations concerned with the refugees; among these was a pastor from the

Ecumenical Council of Churches. Representing the International Red Cross were Prince von Schwarsenberg and Miss Ferrière, who explained the committee's attitude in regard to the Jewish question. The committee, she said

> is receiving from all quarters numerous requests for information about the Jews residing in lands occupied by Germany. It cannot dissociate itself from these woes. It has done everything in its power, but it is encountering insurmountable difficulties.
>
> There is surprise that the International Committee is not lodging protests with the governments. To begin with, such protests gain nothing; furthermore, they can greatly harm those whom they intend to aid. Finally, the primary concern of the International Committee should be those for whom it was established, namely, prisoners of war. Also, faced with these numerous difficulties, the International Committee has given up on the question of requests for information.

GROWING SUSPICIONS

Nonetheless, on 16 March 1943 Cardinal Maglione again wrote the bishop of Fribourg, who often served as an intermediary between the Vatican and the Red Cross, asking him how to obtain information about the deported Jews "concerning whom there is no positive data."

The information diffused by the Polish government-in-exile continued to focus on the barbaric treatment inflicted on Poles, whether Jewish or not, in the concentration camps. Despite all, the real destination of the deportees remained shrouded in mystery, even in the eyes of the leaders of the Hebrew communities in countries affected by the Nazi persecutions. The silence, the absolute lack of messages from the deported ones once they crossed the Polish frontier, justified all fears. At times the silence was broken by a deceptive letter cleared by those in charge of the camps.

This fearful situation, alternating with snatches of hope, lasted for months, even till 1944. Apparently the papal representatives and the Jewish communities with whom they were in contact had no concrete information. Some very general indications, which were only confirmed later on, came from Archbishops Burzio in Bratislava, Roncalli in Istanbul, Bernardini in Berne, Cassulo in Bucharest, Rotta in Budapest, Valeri in Vichy, and Abbot Marcone in Zagreb. In Berlin Orsenigo knew nothing precise, at least nothing he could guarantee. Of the Allied diplomats residing in the Vatican, the Polish ambassador seemed best placed to furnish details on the Nazi atrocities.

A report from Burzio suggested, though he could not confirm it, that atrocities were indeed the reality. On 7 March 1943 he sent the Vatican a letter he had received from a parish priest in Bratislava who claimed that soap was being manufactured from the bodies of the Jews who had been deported and massacred. "These are not stories. A German officer coldly and cynically confirmed this in the presence of someone I know. Over there the Jews are massacred with asphyxiating gas, by machine gun, or by other means."

It seems that Archbishop Roncalli in Istanbul, a veritable cross-road of information going to Palestine, had no definite information to pass on to the Vatican. However, on 13 March 1943 he transmitted a memorandum from the Jewish Agency on Polish Jews: "The situation in Poland, where about two-thirds of the Jewish population have been cruelly destroyed, needs no commentary." Yet there was no clear information that the Jewish organizations had been informed of the "unknown destination." Perhaps this memorandum inspired the apostolic delegate's response to Franz von Papen, the Reich's ambassador to Turkey. The ambassador spoke in very strong terms of the thousands of Polish officers massacred by the Soviets and discovered in the forest of Katyn. Roncalli, who reported the conversation to Monsignor Montini, wrote on the following 8 July: "With a sad smile I responded that it was first necessary to have forgotten the millions of Jews shipped to and annihilated in Poland."

Already on 23 March the Ecumenical Council of Churches, in touch with the World Jewish Congress, sent the British and American governments a request to relax the restrictions that had been imposed on immigration. Among other things, the document said:

> The secretariat of the Ecumenical Council of Churches and that of the World Jewish Congress possess most trustworthy reports indicating that the campaign, organized by Nazi leaders, of systematically exterminating the Jews has now reached its culminating point. Consequently, they call the attention of the Allied governments to the absolute necessity of immediately organizing a relief effort on behalf of the persecuted Jewish communities.

Pastor Freudenberg, who participated in the Red Cross meeting on 12 February, sent the Council's statement to the nunciature in Berne, and on 4 May 1943 the ad interim chargé d'affaires passed it on to the cardinal secretary of state.

This document may have inspired the Vatican secretariat's memorandum dated 5 May 1943 expressing the reaction of the Roman authorities confronted with the question of deportation:

> The Jews. A dreadful situation. There were approximately four and a half million of them in Poland before the war; today the estimate is that not even a hundred thousand remain there, including those who have come from other countries under German occupation. In Warsaw a ghetto had been established which contained six hundred and fifty thousand of them; today there would be twenty to twenty-five thousand. Some, naturally, have avoided being placed on the list of names. But there is no doubt that most have been liquidated. Nothing is known of the thousands and thousands of persons who month after month have been deported. The only possible explanation here is that they have died, especially considering the enterprising character of the Jew who, if alive, in one way or another makes himself known (*se vive si fa vivo*). There are special death camps near Lublin (Treblinka) and Brest-Litovsk. It is said that by the hundreds they are shut up in chambers where they are gassed to death. Transported in tightly sealed cattle trucks with lime on their floors.

One was now faced with reports that one hesitated to believe. All that was certain was the silence of the deportees. Should the ultimate conclusion be drawn from this?

In any case, Pius XII once again spoke out. In his speech to the cardinals on 2 June, namely, a month after the memorandum had been drafted, the pope gave an indication of his thinking regarding the deportation. Although his address primarily focused on the Poles, he also referred to the Jews:

> Do not be surprised, venerable Brothers and dear Sons, if We respond with a particularly earnest solicitude to the prayers of those who turn toward Us with eyes full of anguished supplication, exposed as they are because of their nationality or their race to still greater calamities and to more heart-felt sorrows; at times they are destined, even without fault on their part, to the threat of

extermination. The leaders of peoples should not forget that, to use the language of Scripture, whoever carries the sword can only dispose of human life and death according to the law of God from whom all power comes.

The pope was content with these carefully measured phrases, and he explained why in the same speech:

Every word from Us in this regard to the competent authorities, every public allusion, should be seriously considered and weighed in the very interest of those who suffer so as not to make their position even more difficult and more intolerable than previously, even though inadvertently and unwillingly.

In both France and Italy even those who were the most interested were unable to discover the exact meaning of the deportation. A typical example of the uncertainty reigning during this period is seen in the reports that a Capuchin Franciscan, Père Marie Benoît, presented to the pope at a private audience on 15 July. The minutes of the meeting contain the requests and the information this religious had received so that he might bring them to the pope's attention. One document is entitled *Information on the Camps of Upper Silesia.* Work camps were believed to be located there. As to camps situated on the Katovice-Birkenau (Auschwitz)-Wadowicz line, the document said: "Morale among the deportees is generally good, and they are hopeful as to their future."

Allied propaganda, which largely dwelt on German atrocities, savage reprisals, and the execution of hostages, said nothing about the death camps. The Poles in London, perhaps the best informed, became increasingly skeptical after Katyn. Yet on 30 August the American secretary of state wrote: "There exists no sufficient proof to justify a statement regarding executions in gas chambers."

Ten days after the roundup of a thousand Roman Jews, the deputy rabbi of Rome, David Panzieri, wrote to Pius XII on 17 October. What was feared for the deportees was the harshness of winter to which the frail bodies of the elderly, the sick, and the children would be exposed. Could not the pope, asked Panzieri, see to it that clothing be sent to them?

The following year, especially in May–June 1944, Angelo Rotta increased his requests to the Hungarian rulers and bishops that the deportation of Hungarian Jews be stopped. Was the nuncio aware of the real fate of the deportees? It is probable that at least in Budapest some Jewish leaders were acquainted with the *Auschwitz Protocol,* in which two young Jews, escapees from this camp during this spring of 1944, denounced the extermination of their Jewish brethren in the gas chambers. But the reports sent by Rotta gave no indication that he had seen the protocol or that he heard anyone speak of it. His reaction during the month of May to the deportations was inspired by the brutality of the arrests and probably by the cries of alarm directed to him by the Jews.

Among all the papal representatives, it was only the chargé d'affaires in Slovakia, Archbishop Giuseppe Burzio, who actually possessed a translation of the "protocol of Auschwitz." On 22 May 1944 he sent to the Vatican a long description of the death camp, twenty-nine pages in German, typed single-space. He gave no commentary except to say that the person who gave him the text requested that it be used in a most confidential manner. Part of the Auschwitz document was published at the end of June, whereas the complete version was not published till November by the War Refugee Board. A victim of obstacles placed in the way of correspondence being sent to the Vatican after the Allies arrived in Rome, the copy sent by Burzio did not arrive at the Secretariat of State till the end of October, at a time when another more summary version was sent by the nuncio to Switzerland. Burzio never explained from whom he obtained his copy, nor did he ever speak of the two escapees from Auschwitz visiting the nunciature.

On 9 June the apostolic delegate in Washington sent an appeal addressed to the Holy Father by four important rabbis. It was absolutely certain, they said, that the extermination of Hungarian Jews had begun: a million human lives were in danger. They requested that the pope issue a public appeal in the strongest of terms in order to save them. The same day, Isaac Herzog, the rabbi of Palestine, sent an identical request. And still, the message sent by Cicognani seemed to presume that the Jews were being exterminated within Hungary itself and by Hungarians, and it contains no reference to deportations and death camps.

On 13 December 1944 Archbishop Cassulo, the nuncio to Romania, sent Rome a petition from some leading Jewish citizens in Bucharest who were disturbed about the fate of 150,000 Jews who had been deported from Transylvania and about whom nothing had been heard. The pope was entreated to intervene with the Reich's ambassador to the Holy See so that the Bucharest Jews would be allowed to send food and clothing to their coreligionists from Transylvania, whom they believed were still alive. In fact, the authors of the petition wrote:

> We request that the Vatican intervene with the German government so that the latter allow the distribution of packages of food, medicine, and clothing, through the intermediary of the apostolic nunciature in Germany and the International Red Cross; this should take place at Christmas so that temporary assistance may be given to these unfortunate ones.

As long as the war lasted, the fate of the deportees was shrouded in obscurity. The homicidal conditions in which the deportations took place was known. There was no doubt that malnutrition, forced labor, and epidemics resulted in thousands and thousands of victims in the overpopulated camps. Serious attention was paid to accounts of massacres committed in Poland, Russia, and elsewhere. But among these notorious facts and the accounts of some escapees concerning death camps, there remained, as it were, a curtain of fog which the parents themselves and those who were linked to the victims by race or religion were unable to lift or had simply given up any effort to do so.

Pius XII never used this continuous shadow regarding an unknown destination as an excuse for abandoning those who were being persecuted. On the contrary, he employed all the means at his disposal to save them. As much as possible he took care to limit what he said in public, expecting nothing worthwhile to come of this. He did not speak, but he took action.

And yet in the territories directly under the Berlin government, every action taken by the Holy See encountered insurmountable obstacles, and every intervention on behalf of the non-Aryans was doomed to failure. But the Vatican could still exert its influence in the allied states or vassals of the Reich, namely Slovakia, Romania, Croatia, and Hungary. As the following chapters will show, the pope by his personal messages and through his representatives in these countries carried out his rescue work till the last days of the war.

CHAPTER 8

Deportations in Slovakia
and in Croatia*

~·~

I N ITALY the Holy See's work on behalf of non-Aryans was facilitated by the secret agenda of the Italian government and administration. But in Germany, however, papal interventions were simply
useless and for the opposite reason: They were predestined to failure in
the face of the inflexible decisions made by the national-socialist state.
But between the two Axis powers, whose positions in this regard were
diametrically opposed, there were also regions that in various degrees
had fallen under the control of the Reich and within which the Holy
See nonetheless felt that in some measure it could exercise an influence and counteract the designs of the Berlin government. This was
true for the allied states, the Axis satellites, namely, Slovakia, Croatia,
Romania, and Hungary.

SLOVAKIA

Toward the end of 1940 Slovakia, which was Catholic and
directly under German influence, began to prepare racial legislation.
For the Holy See this was a unique case since the president of the
republic was a priest, Joseph Tiso, who was first a parish priest and a
dean in Bánovce, and who then succeeded Monsignor A. Hlinka as the
leader of the national Slovak movement. In 1939 he became the first
president of the new Slovak republic. A man of undeniable loyalty to
the church, he was also deeply dedicated to the cause of Slovak independence. His elevation to a position of great political responsibility
caused the Holy See a certain amount of uncertainty. Giuseppe Burzio,
the chargé d'affaires at the nunciature in Bratislava, believed that Tiso

*Documentation for chapter 8: See *ADSS,* vols. 8, 9, and 10.

wanted to escape his delicate situation, and that he only remained at his post in order to save what he could.

Without any public debate in the parliament, an anti-Semitic code was suddenly promulgated in Slovakia on 9 September 1941 under the form of a government decree. Burzio immediately telegraphed this news to the Vatican; details were supplied on 18 September with an explanation of the law's provisions. Immediately Burzio received instructions to protest in writing against the new regulation while the Secretariat of State would be closely studying its text; on 12 November a note of protest was sent to Karol Sidor, the minister representing Slovakia at the Vatican. It was with deep pain, wrote the cardinal secretary of state, that the Holy See had learned that Slovakia, whose population was almost totally Catholic, had enacted racial legislation "containing various provisions directly opposed to Catholic principles."

The Holy See had to wait six months for a response: A note of 23 May 1942 informed the Vatican that the question was no longer apropos since the Slovak government intended to solve the Jewish problem by means of deportation.

DEPORTATION AND PROTESTS

It was Burzio who first reported the deportation to the Vatican when on 9 March 1942 he sent an urgent telegram saying that according to rumor the deportation of the Jews was imminent, with no distinction as to sex, age, or even religion. The destination was to be Galicia or Lublin. The Holy See's representative attributed the paternity of "this atrocious plan" to Vojtekh Tuka, the prime minister, with the agreement of the interior minister, A. Mach. It was said that this scheme had not been conceived under German pressure and that the Slovak government was paying the Germans to accept the deportees. Burzio concluded: "On Saturday I went to Tuka, the president of the council of ministers, and he confirmed the news: He vehemently defended the legitimacy of the measure and dared to say (he who paraded himself as a Catholic) that there was nothing inhumane and anti-Christian with this. Deporting eighty thousand people to Poland where they will be at the mercy of the Germans is the equivalent of condemning most of them to a certain death."

The following day the nuncio in Berne, Archbishop Bernardini, sent a message that Agudas Israel (the international organization of orthodox Jews) wanted the pope to be informed as to the rapidly approaching deportation to take place in Slovakia. They were placing their hopes in the Holy Father since it was said that the Jews in England and in America could do nothing. On 13 March the nuncio in Hungary, Archbishop Rotta, sent an appeal from the Jewish community in Bratislava, a request passed on to the nuncio by a Hungarian prelate.

Following these entreaties, on 14 March Cardinal Maglione sent the Slovak representative at the Holy See, Karol Sidor, a note that in substance repeated what was said in Burzio's telegram and concluded: "With every hope that this information does not correspond to the truth, the Secretariat of State cannot believe that a country intending to be inspired by Catholic principles will take such grave measures which will produce such harmful consequences for so many families."

On 24 March the Vatican received another telegram saying that in Slovakia young Jewish women had been carried off and sent to German brothels in the east. At the pope's orders Cardinal Maglione immediately called in Sidor and, as the cardinal himself noted: "I requested that he intervene as soon as possible with his government in order to stop such a horror." At almost the same time an identical rumor was telegraphed by Burzio, who said that the deportation had been suspended following the Holy See's intervention, something denied the next day. As things actually turned out, these reports were not precise: The young Jewesses who were rounded up were destined not for prostitution but for deportation to Majdanek and then to Auschwitz with the other Jews.

In fact, on 25 March the Holy See's chargé d'affaires in Bratislava again telegraphed to say that, contrary to his previous report, the deportation had not been suspended; indeed ten thousand men and ten thousand women would shortly be deported and that other deportations would follow till all the Jews were expelled. Monsignor Tardini made a note of the instructions he received from Cardinal Maglione: Inform Burzio of the objection that had been made to Sidor and instruct Burzio to protest to President Tiso himself. Tardini added some remarks of his own: "I do not know whether these steps will succeed in stopping...the lunatics. There are two of them. The first is Tuka who does things, and then there is Tiso...the priest who allows them to happen." The telegram, composed by Tardini and immediately sent off, instructed Burzio "personally to speak to the president of the republic, even appealing to his feelings as a priest."

Meanwhile, Burzio continued to report to his superiors. In a message dated 9 April he notified the Vatican that raids against Jewish communities continued daily both in Bratislava and in the provinces. The brutality of the Hlinka Guard knew no bounds. Some Jews succeeded in surreptitiously crossing the Hungarian border; others tried to obtain "discrimination" from President Tiso. Thousands of such requests had already come to the head of state. The Slovak bishops, for their part, were in the process of preparing a pastoral letter.

Sidor, the Slovak representative to the Vatican who had gone to Bratislava to consult with his government, returned after a few days and was received by Cardinal Maglione on 11 April. The diplomat said that he had spoken to President Tiso and the president of the council about the anti-Semitic measures. Tiso assured him that he had personally intervened to mitigate these measures and that he was granting many of the baptized Jews the exemptions that he was legally entitled to give. Minister Tuka was thinking about traveling to Rome where he would explain his policy to the pope. Maglione noted: "Minister Sidor has tried (without much conviction) to present me with some justification for the mass deportation of the Jews. I used the occasion to remind him of the Holy See's thinking, which had often been explained to him, and I then vigorously protested against the treatment recently inflicted on hundreds of young Jewish women, torn away from their families so that they might be sent...to perdition. I told him that such actions were a disgrace, especially for a Catholic country." Maglione insisted that Sidor report this conversation to his government.

On 27 April 1942 Burzio sent the Vatican a copy of the bishops' pastoral letter, which the Catholic newspapers had circulated throughout the country. The letter was finally allowed to be published but at the cost of suppressing its strongest passages, and yet it retained the sentence: "The Jews are also people and consequently should be treated in a humane fashion."

Despite all, the parliament passed a constitutional law—in fact it was retroactive—concerning the Jews, authorizing their deportation, the suppression of their citizenship, and the recent confiscations. Only two categories of Jews were exempt from these severe measures: those who had become members of the Christian community before 1939 and those who had married non-Jews before September 1941, the date on which these marriages came to be forbidden; also exempt were Jews who had obtained an act of "discrimination." Some priest deputies voted for the law, lamented Burzio; some abstained, but none voted against it.

In a note dated 23 May and sent to the Secretariat of State under the form of an official response to the protest of 12 November 1941, the government defended its anti-Semitic policy. This response had been delayed, said the note, because the Jewish question was a very serious one, a question requiring the complete attention of the authorities. The initial plan of Prime Minister Tuka and the foreign minister was to travel to Rome so that they might personally explain everything. But since this trip was impossible within the immediate future, the minister had to explain himself in writing.

The deportation of Jews from Slovakia, according to the note, was part of a general plan and had been put into effect with the concurrence of the German authorities. A half million Jews were going to be transported to eastern Europe. Slovakia would be the first country from which Germany would accept inhabitants of Jewish descent. At the same time, the process had begun for other deportations of Jews in France, Holland, Belgium, in the Protectorate, and in the Reich. Hungary would have to transfer eight hundred thousand Jews; these would be settled in various places near Lublin, where they would ultimately be placed "under the protection of the Reich." The Germans had promised the Slovak government that Christians of Jewish descent would be grouped in a separate area. Finally, "the German government has informed us that the Jews will be humanely treated." The note denied rumors that young Jewish women were being sent to German brothels and stated that Germans had been shot for having had relations with Jewish women. The foreign minister also claimed to justify the prohibition against Jews marrying Christians by citing manuals of canon law. These, he claimed, maintained that civil authority could for the common good at times establish impediments to marriages.

NEW DANGERS AND PROTESTS

Following the deportation of sixty to eighty thousand Jews in the autumn of 1942, a period of relative tranquility fell over Slovakia. But on 7 February the interior minister, A. Mach, gave a speech that predicted new storms. On 26 February Angelo Rotta, the nuncio in Budapest, sent the Vatican a notice from an association of converted Hungarian Jews: Two thousand Slovak Jews were in danger. Cardinal Maglione on 6 March sent a dispatch to the Holy See's chargé d'affaires in Bratislava asking that he verify the accuracy of this report and that he eventually lodge a protest with the government. Burzio replied that, after the speech by Mach and without waiting for instructions, he had already met with Tiso. The president tried to minimize the significance of the minister's speech, and yet he hardly appeared convincing to the Holy See's representative. As for the Slovak bishops, they sent a protest letter dated 17 February to the government requesting that at least baptized Jews, whatever be their date of baptism, not be subject to deportation. Three weeks later the bishops published a pastoral on behalf of the Jews, especially Jews who had become Catholics, and they criticized those elderly Catholics who refused to attend church with the new converts. And especially, as the bishops recalled, people are not to be punished for crimes they themselves did not commit. This was a condemnation of the idea of collective responsibility used by the Slovak officials against the Jewish community.

Meanwhile, the cardinal secretary of state went beyond the protest sent by Burzio to the Bratislava authorities and ordered the preparation of a note along identical lines to be given to the Slovak minister to the Holy See. The scandal was all the greater in Slovakia since the head of state was a priest. The Holy See had to repeat even more clearly what it had already told Sidor in a note given him the preceding year.

While the Vatican was preparing this note, the Holy See's chargé d'affaires was received on 7 April by Vojtekh Tuka, Slovakia's foreign minister. "When I revealed the purpose of my visit," Burzio wrote to Maglione, "he [the minister] changed visibly and rather coolly said: 'Monsignor, I do not understand what business it is of the Vatican as to the Jews in Slovakia. Make the Holy See understand that I reject this action.'" Tuka said that his mission was to clear his country "from this plague, from this band of evildoers, from gangsters." Burzio observed that it was not right to treat as evildoers the thousands of women and innocent children who were included in the previous deportation. "Your Excellency," added Burzio, "is certainly aware of the sad news that is being spread regarding the atrocious fate of the Jews who have been deported to Poland and the Ukraine. Everyone is talking about it.

Even if for the sake of argument one admits that a country cannot take into account natural law and the requirements of Christianity, I do not believe that any country, for the sake of its prestige and future good, can show no interest in international opinion and the judgment of history." Tuka retorted that Jewish propaganda was spreading these accounts of atrocities and that if they were true, he would no longer allow a single Jew to cross the Slovak frontier. "I deplore that the Vatican itself has not completely sheltered itself from such influences," he concluded.

On May 1 Cardinal Maglione returned to the Jewish question with Slovakia's representative, and he insisted that the deportation be stopped. Sidor replied that once he returned to Slovakia he would speak to his government, and he assured the cardinal that Mach's threats would not be put into effect. The substance of Maglione's protest was repeated in a note, dated 5 May, sent to Sidor. The Holy See recalled the preceding protests and its hopes that the Slovak government would end the expulsion of the Jews. And yet it indeed appeared that this government intended to proceed with deporting all the Jews living in Slovakia, including women and children and even those professing the Catholic religion. "The Holy See would shirk its divine mandate if it did not deplore these arrangements and measures which gravely strike at people's natural rights from the simple fact that these people belong to a specific race."

In the end, these moves seemed to have had good results. President Tiso called in the Holy See's chargé d'affaires to express his regret for the position of the interior minister. And Burzio learned from the minister of worship that when Tuka informed the council of ministers of the steps taken by the Holy See, the ministers declared that the Vatican's intervention was an honor for Slovakia; then and there they decided to suspend the deportation of four thousand Jews, a deportation for which everything had already been prepared, and they forbade any baptized Jew from being deported no matter when that person had been baptized. "I hope," concluded Burzio, "that the facts will bear out this information." On 4 June Burzio telegraphed that the deportation of the Jews had, in fact, been suspended. And, as a result, the year 1943 peacefully ended in Slovakia.

Spring 1944 saw forerunners of a new danger for the Jewish community in Slovakia, especially for the Jewish Polish refugees. On 29 January the World Jewish Congress appealed to the apostolic delegate in Washington, asking that he petition the Holy See to request the Slovak government to ensure that the Jews be treated favorably. At the same time the nuncio to Hungary sent the Vatican a memorandum from the Hungarian bishops; it contained some ominous information regarding the Jews residing in the neighborhood of Slovakia. The interior minister had publicly renewed his threat to rid the country of Jews, baptized or not, and a census of all Jews was underway. These measures, together with similar ones, were the prelude to forcing the Jews to live in a ghetto, with all that this meant. And so the pope was being asked to speak out as he did in 1942, when the deportation began.

This warning arrived at the Vatican about 25 February, even though Burzio, responding to two earlier telegrams, had just said that such startling information was exaggerated. No deportation was in sight, and the purpose of the census, which started at the beginning of the month, was to apprehend certain individuals believed to be dangerous. As to the Poles, Tiso had assured him that they would not be mistreated but only kept in a camp from which they could also be helped to reach another country, as had been done for prisoners of war who had escaped from Germany. Burzio's optimism first appeared justified. But Jewish organizations continued to call for the Holy See's intervention against the expulsion of Jews from Slovakia into German territories. The Secretariat of State forwarded these appeals to Burzio on 22 April, instructing him to take whatever steps he judged possible and opportune. On 18 May Burzio repeated that no deportation was in sight, without excluding, however, that the danger might return as a result "of foreign interventions."

FOREIGN INTERVENTIONS

But by the beginning of autumn these foreign interventions had taken place. At the end of August 1944 the approach of the Russian armies resulted in an uprising in Slovakia. Paratroopers sent by the Czechoslovak government in London landed in that country, where they joined up with elements from the local resistance. German reaction was immediate, and the revolt was crushed by Wehrmacht reinforcements. Added to the number of victims was the Slovak republic, now deprived of the little independence it had, and especially the Jews, who were seen as a fifth column. They were led into camps from which most of them had previously escaped, and the deportation resumed, although the destination was no longer Auschwitz, which had been dismantled upon Himmler's orders, but Bergen-Belsen, which was close to Hanover.

On 15 September Burzio alerted his superiors: the Gestapo had begun to take measures against the Jews with mass arrests. Even though nothing had changed in Bratislava, the capital was running the risk of soon being affected. Burzio urged the Vatican to intervene on the highest level: He thought that an action by the Holy See with the government might prove effective. The same day, the nuncio in Switzerland sent on to the Vatican a telegram he had received from Istanbul: Angelo Roncalli, the delegate there, had heard that the Jews in Slovakia were in great danger of death. Without any delay Burzio was told to intervene, first with the foreign minister and possibly with Tiso, "observing that the Holy See is awaiting from the Slovak authorities a position conforming to the Catholic principles and sentiments of the Slovak people." A collective action on the part of the bishops might be helpful. At the same time the Secretariat of State sent Karol Sidor, the Slovak representative to the Vatican, a verbal note that partially repeated phrases already used in the message to Burzio: "The Holy See sends a very ardent plea to the Slovak government, confident that the government wishes to adopt in this respect a position conforming to the Catholic principles and sentiments of the Slovak people." Two weeks later, on 7 October, Sidor informed the Vatican that the Germans had in fact intended to deport the Jews, but that President Tiso had cited the country's constitution in favor of Slovak citizens, and an agreement was reached: The Jews would be assembled in work camps, but they would not be deported.

This agreement, even if it had been taken seriously, lasted only a few days, and appeals again began to flood the Vatican: a message from the War Refugee Board sent to the pope on 23 September by Myron Taylor who was in Rome; a message from Isaac Herzog, the rabbi of Jerusalem, which was sent from Cairo on 30 September by the Vatican's envoy, Arthur Hughes. Burzio had already seen the foreign minister on 22 September, and on 24 September he met with President Tiso. Bishop Kmetko from Nitra also intervened in the name of the Slovak hierarchy. Arrests had already begun in the capital, where about two thousand Jews were taken into custody and mistreated, whether they were Christians or not. The Gestapo invaded many convents while looking for Jews, searching one of them three times in a single night. The protest of the previous week was futile. Burzio went back to the president of the republic in order to obtain his intervention, at least on behalf of the baptized Jews, but to no avail. Tiso, wrote Burzio, "sees the Jews as being the cause of all evils, and he defends the measures taken by the Germans against them as being required by the most important needs of the war." The foreign minister in a note to the Germans had indeed declared that these Jews were protected by the laws and constitution of Slovakia and that the government could not consent to their deportation. But on 26 October Burzio telegraphed that all his efforts were in vain: The deportation was underway, and the search for Jews continued in secret. The government had lost its independence, and the people were asking why President Tiso did not resign.

The pope still wanted to react. A telegram, whose draft bears the handwritten corrections of Pius XII, immediately went out to Burzio. The Holy See's representative was to go to Tiso immediately, inform him of the deep sorrow experienced by His Holiness because of the sufferings inflicted on so many people because of their nationality or race, and "in the name of the sovereign pontiff have him remember that his opinions and decisions are to conform to his dignity and to his sacerdotal integrity." Obeying these instructions, Burzio on 4 November went to President Tiso not to speak to him as a president but as a priest. Tiso promised the papal representative that he would write to the Holy Father, and on 9 November he called in Burzio and gave him the letter. The following day Burzio telegraphed that he had carried out his orders and had sent to the Vatican President Tiso's letter.

TISO'S LETTER

This letter, dated 8 November, handwritten in Latin and signed "Dr. Ioseph Tiso *sacerdos*," arrived in Rome by courier on 19 December. It began with copious expressions of respect for the Holy Father, but then the president began to defend his government. Rumors of atrocities committed by the republic against people because of their nationality and race, he wrote, were being exaggerated by Slovakia's enemies. The Slovak state was established without any blood having been shed, and throughout the five years of the new country's existence it had never condemned anyone to death. The measures taken against

177

the Czechoslovakians and the Jews were designed to eliminate the noxious influence of these elements that the country had endured for so long. The Jews and Czechoslovakians remaining in Slovakia lived in good conditions, but in August they had assisted the paratroopers, and so the weak Slovak government asked help from its German protector. What then took place was situated within the framework of military operations for which the Slovak government was not responsible. Finally, could the Slovaks be unaware that the Germans had recognized and defended their country's independence? As for his sacerdotal dignity and integrity, Tiso asserted that he always kept them in sight and that it was "pharisaism on the part of Slovakia's enemies" to desire to dishonor the clergy who had "defended and served small nations." No commentary has been found in regard to Tiso's letter. Monsignor Tardini simply made the following notation on the original: "*24 dicembre 1944. Visto dal Santo Padre* [seen by the Holy Father]."

CROATIA

The independent state of Croatia, which began in 1941, was even more submissive to the Great Reich than was Slovakia. The situation of the Jews, estimated at forty thousand, was rapidly becoming dangerous. On 14 August 1941 the Delasem asked Cardinal Maglione whether there was any way of contacting the Croatian Jews in order to bring them to Italy. On 6 September Bishop Rozman of Ljubjana expressed his concern and asked that the baptized Jews who had escaped into the province of Ljubjana, which had been annexed to Italy, not be returned to Croatia, where they would be exposed to harsh treatment. And on 21 April 1942 Cardinal Maglione, answering an appeal from American Jews, summed up the situation:

> Abbot Marcone, the Holy See's envoy in Croatia, has often focused the attention of numerous leading citizens in Zagreb on the conditions imposed on non-Aryans. His secretary and the secretary of Zagreb's archbishop have been able to visit various concentration camps where they brought words of comfort and help. For those who have taken refuge in territory occupied by the Italian troops, the Secretariat of State has seen to it that they will not be forced back into their country of origin.

178

At this time the specter of deportation disappeared behind con-cern for the bad treatment inflicted on prisoners held in Croatian camps. But on 17 July Marcone said that whenever information was requested, the Croatian authorities over the past months buried themselves "in an inexplicable silence." Responses were only furnished after repeated protests. In another report bearing the same date Marcone gave some information that by far was the most significant the Vatican had ever received. He met with the chief of police, E. Kvaternik, and complained to him about the cruelty being inflicted on Jews of every age and condition. Kvaternik's answer was that the German government had forced him to transfer all the Jews to Germany, "where, according to what Kvaternik himself reported to me, two million Jews were recently destroyed. It appears that the same fate is awaiting the Croatian Jews, especially if they are elderly or unable to work."

This ominous news had also reached Jewish circles in Zagreb, whose chief rabbi, Salom Freiberger, often met with Marcone to discuss the dangers facing his community. On 4 August Freiberger wrote the pope and asked him to come to the aid of his people.

MARCONE'S SUCCESSES AND FAILURES

The Holy See's efforts had limited success. On 30 September Marcone reported: "Unhappily, we have not been able to change the course of events. Nonetheless, many exceptions proposed by us regarding the deportation of the Jews have been granted, and homes formed by mixed marriages between Catholics and Jews and even nonbaptized Jews have all been spared." And after receiving new instructions from the Secretariat of State, the Holy See's delegate wrote on 8 November that he had done everything possible to alleviate the fate of Croatian Jews, that he had often spoken with Ante Pavelic and with the chief of police, and yet with little success. "Some headway has been made, but not much." A new police chief, an official from the old Austrian school, had openly told him "that one cannot substantially change the measures adopted against these unfortunate people and that sooner or later all will be deported to Germany."

The year 1943, however, opened under favorable omens with a 23 February report from Marcone; the envoy communicated the thanks of

Zagreb's chief rabbi for the assistance given by the Vatican regarding the emigration of Jewish children to Turkey.

But the threat of deportation always hovered over the Jewish community. A police ordinance directing all Jews to appear in person raised new alarms. Marcone went back to the head of state who, before a representative of the Reich, Siegfried Kasche, declared that it was not his intention to persecute baptized Jews and that a statement to this effect had been posted. Following this, it is said that Kasche cried out: "The Holy See is becoming too powerful in Croatia. This time I want to see whether the Holy See or I will get the best of it." Marcone concluded: "I ask the Lord to give [them] the power to resist."

This information arrived at the Vatican on 13 March; on 30 March, following some alarming news, Cardinal Maglione telegraphed Abbot Marcone to take whatever steps were possible to impede the deportation threatening the Croatian Jews, some eighty percent of whom were baptized. The following day Marcone replied that he was continuing to keep an eye on the situation of the Jews, who themselves were following what was happening, coming as they did each day to ask him for information. The government had assured him that there was nothing new in regard to the Jews and that in any case mixed couples and baptized Jews would be spared.

Nonetheless, Marcone was suspicious and justifiably so. Six weeks later all Jews, except for a time those married to Catholics, were arrested and sent to Germany. Even those who had been baptized some time ago were taken. In the middle of the night, while the whole world was asleep, the police showed up among the Jews and had them transported away without any regard for their age, social condition, or even baptism. One of the elderly Jews died of fright. Neither protests from the pope's representative, nor sermons, nor the objections of Archbishop Stepinac of Zagreb prevailed over the influence of national-socialist Germany.

However, on 31 May Marcone notified the Vatican of the assurance given by the foreign minister that mixed marriages were "protected" and that no measure would ever be taken against them:

Large numbers of people who years ago entered into a mixed marriage and till now were living in perpetual fear of being seized at any moment flock into our house and tearfully thank the Holy See which alone during this sad period still gives assistance to the children of Israel.

Receiving this good news, Maglione replied "that he was hoping this government would refrain from taking any measure whatsoever against the Jews, even those not in mixed marriages."

Less than fifteen days later, on 11 June, a letter was sent to the apostolic delegate in Istanbul by Meir Touval-Weltmann, a member of a commission to help European Jews. He expressed to Archbishop Roncalli his thanks "for all the precious assistance given by the Holy See, by Your Excellency, and by Monsignor Righi [secretary at the delegation]." Accompanying this letter was a memorandum that requested the delegate to express the gratitude of the Israelites to the archbishop of Zagreb, because they know "that Dr. Stepinac has done everything possible to aid and ease the unhappy fate of the Jews in Croatia." According to the memorandum, these did not exceed twenty-five hundred in number. Lastly, the memorandum requested Archbishop Stepinac to continue his efforts to save a hundred or so Jews whose chief rabbi was arrested the previous month and to take steps to facilitate their movement from Croatia to Hungary and Italy, from where the commission hoped to transport them either to a neutral country or to Palestine.

CHAPTER 9

Romania and Hungary*

~·~

A RCHBISHOP CASSULO was the nuncio in Romania, where relations with the Holy See were governed by a concordat even
though most of the population belonged to the Orthodox
Church. When war broke out, anti-Semitic legislation already existed,
but it was being modified at the beginning of 1941. On 8 January
Cassulo reported to Rome the difficulties being encountered by children of Jewish converts: They could attend neither religious nor Jewish
schools, and in state schools their enrollment was governed by a quota.
Alerted to this by the bishops, the nuncio spoke to the foreign minister
and to General Ion Antonescu, who was the head of government. Both
assured him that these measures would be modified. In fact, on 21
February Archbishop Cassulo was able to tell Rome that on 19 February
a decree was enacted opening Christian schools to all Christian children, no matter what their origin.

But the next month a press agency announced that the Romanian
government had forbidden Jews, under very severe penalties, to change
their religion. Responding on 31 March to a telegram from Cardinal
Maglione, who was asking for information, Cassulo said that he had
visited the foreign ministry, where the general secretary assured him
that his department had nothing to do with these decrees. Nonetheless,
the nuncio stated that if an attempt were made to tie the church's hands
in this matter of baptizing Jewish converts, then the church would not
fail to protest in order to declare its liberty. On 12 May Maglione
telegraphed Cassulo and asked him whether he had received any written assurances relative to freedom of worship. Three days later Cassulo
replied: "The government has given written assurances."

On 16 May the secretary of the Holy Office sketched out for the
nuncio's use norms to be followed when receiving Jews into the
church. Racial laws, said the instruction, are not to be a reason for

*Documentation for chapter 9: see *ADSS,* vols. 8, 9, and 10. Add: Angelo Martini,
"La Santa Sede e gli ebrei della Romania," in *Civiltà Cattolica,* 1961 / 3, pp. 449–63.

182

refusing baptism to those who sincerely seek it. Nonetheless, in light of present circumstances, a number of precautions are imperative since there are some who "can withdraw from the church just as easily as they have enrolled in it." The past personal life and conduct of each person is to be examined. Where reasonable doubts exist, baptism is to be delayed.

Yet even so, baptizing Jews always caused problems. The number requesting baptism had increased considerably, and it was rumored that the Holy See, "confronted with the danger in which the Jews were placed, ordered that they were to be baptized en masse after receiving a short preparation, with further instruction being delayed till a later time." On 18 April 1942 the Romanian minister to the Holy See told Cardinal Maglione that the number of conversions was high, too high, and thus was suspect. Consequently the government was suggesting that the pope suspend admission into the Catholic Church for the duration of the war, a proposal that was, of course, rejected.

With full right did Archbishop Cassulo intervene when it was a question of the Catholic Jews, but he found himself increasingly taking action on behalf of the whole Jewish community as well. On 7 August 1941 he informed the Vatican of excesses committed against the Jews and of how he had used all his influence in favor of the victims, but that the result of his efforts had been negligible.

On 5 December Cassulo explained to his superiors how the Romanian government had taken harsh measures against the Jews under the pretext that they were Communist sympathizers:

> Having no one in authority who is capable of supporting them, they address the Holy Father's representative, convinced as they are that he is the only person in authority who can help them. And so I find myself in a very delicate and troubling situation. On the one hand, I believe that I have to show interest in so many poor families; on the other hand, I must do so with tact and discretion toward the government so that I am not meddling in the country's affairs.

Nonetheless, the nuncio managed to look after non-Catholic families, "and upon being invited to do so by the government, I presented lists of people who, according to formal statements that were obtained, were exempted from every kind of reprehensible action."

DEPORTEES TO TRANSNISTRIE

And so a close collaboration was established in Romania between the apostolic nuncio and leaders of the Jewish community like A. Safran, who was the chief rabbi, and Dr. Fildermann. Romania never experienced deportations to Poland, but thousands of Jews were slaughtered within the country itself. On 23 September 1942 Cardinal Maglione made a note of information the Vatican had received concerning the imminent deportation of Jews from Transylvania to Transnistrie, a Romanian province made up of territories seized in 1941 from the Soviet Union and located between the Dniester and Bug rivers, and with Odessa as a port on the Black Sea. The cardinal secretary of state told the nuncio to ask the Romanian government for proof that it was at least showing moderation in carrying out this project. Nevertheless, Transnistrie had become something of a penal colony for the deported Jews. On 14 January 1943, following an appeal from the president of the Swiss Jews transmitted by the nuncio in Berne and describing the sad conditions of the Jews in Romania, Cardinal Maglione again directed the nuncio in Bucharest to do everything possible "to mitigate these measures so opposed to the teaching of Christian morality." Archbishop Cassulo in his response of 14 February made it known that some people were attempting to put obstacles in the way of the government, for example, the minister of worship whose actions were directly opposite of what had been decided by Mihail Antonescu, the vice-prime minister. The nuncio again intervened with the minister, who immediately had the measure annulled that had challenged the rights of the church. Cassulo also described the concerns of the Jews for their racial brothers who had been transported into Transnistrie. Antonescu replied "that having given some thought to this, he had no intention of becoming a person who engages in persecution, even if he had to intervene in order to set things right." The head of the Romanian Jewish community had already come twice to thank the nuncio for his help and for the protection given to his coreligionists by the Holy See.

To prove that Romania had nothing to hide, the government allowed the nuncio to visit those interned in Transnistrie. First he went to Odessa and then to Chisinau, the capital of Bessarabie and a city formerly having a large Jewish population whose houses had been burned and destroyed. Next he proceeded to Cernauti and then to Moghilew, visiting throughout the area camps for prisoners of war and Jewish internees. He returned to Bucharest early in May 1943.

On 19 May, subsequent to his visit to Transnistrie, Archbishop Cassulo wrote to the foreign minister to draw his attention to a number of important points, especially certain children. Among the Jews transported to Transnistrie were eight thousand orphans, five thousand of them having lost both father and mother. Would it not be possible to bring these children back to Romania, from where they could eventually emigrate to Palestine? Meanwhile, they could be placed in the care of Jewish families. This was the Fildermann plan, which during the years 1943 and 1944 encountered tenacious opposition and was indeed sabotaged. Cassulo presented the commissioner of Jewish affairs with the suggestions of the Jewish leader, and he was under the impression that the minister was well disposed to the idea. The minister even gave his assurance "that a good number of the orphans will be sent to Palestine." But by 6 September nothing had as yet taken place, for, as Antonescu replied to Cassulo, no concrete plan had been presented for moving the children from Transnistrie.

Although Cassulo did not forget the Jewish community in general, his special mission was to protect baptized Jews, many of whom had been deported to Transnistrie and on whose behalf the concordat offered him a more solid basis for becoming involved. On 26 February 1943 he sent to Cardinal Maglione renewed assurances from the foreign minister that the concordat would be observed in every detail. But on 20 May the nuncio had to complain that these promises were not being kept. Furthermore, on 25 May he wrote to the Catholic bishops of Romania that, despite what any particular official was saying, the bishops could legitimately receive into the Catholic Church those Jews who had been suitably instructed. Giving religious instruction to the children of converts from Judaism as well as allowing these converts' daily practice of the faith were both sanctioned by the government.

Finally, on 7 December Cassulo was able after a cabinet meeting to send the Vatican a "clear and explicit" circular letter from the interior ministry: "The minister of worship has specified in a note of 13 February 1943 that he acknowledges the Catholic Church's right to baptize Jews, it being understood that this change has no effect on the civil status of the newly baptized." The nuncio, in the report that was attached to the document, concluded: "I hope, then, that such an important measure of the government will bring an end to the abuses and that the church will be allowed to exercise freely the rights that have been recognized for such a long time."

Till 1944 Romania had escaped German military control, and the SS squads were not free to execute a policy of deportation to occupied Poland. But Transnistrie was always a center of concern for both the Jewish community and the nuncio, especially now that a deteriorating military situation brought about the fear that, in withdrawing, the Romanians would allow the Jews to fall into the hands of the German forces already present in the area. The Jewish objective here was to secure the transfer of the Jews to the "kingdom" (of Romania) or at least to the western part of Transnistrie, which was judged to be safer, and to organize the emigration of the Jews, or at least of the orphans, to Palestine, for the Romanian government had no fundamental objection to the Jews going to Palestine. In order to obtain this double goal the Jewish community, represented especially by A. Safran, the chief rabbi of Romania, continued to solicit the help of the nuncio and the Holy See.

DEPORTEES FROM TRANSYLVANIA

On 22 January Rabbi Safran brought to the nunciature a memorandum regarding the four thousand orphans whom he was attempting to bring back from Transnistrie to Romania; but the government, however, had fixed their age limit at twelve years, and so the rabbi requested Cassulo to intervene, asking that the age limit be moved to sixteen years. On 26 January the nuncio spoke to the foreign minister and requested that the evacuation take place quickly and that the age of the orphans who would return to the kingdom be raised. And on 2 February he intervened on behalf of the Romanian Jews who had the misfortune of being forced beyond the Bug, into the hands of the Germans.

The case of these four thousand orphans offered a better chance of success; but the deportees in general were not forgotten. On 28 February the Secretariat of State received a telegram from Archbishop Roncalli in Istanbul. Isaac Herzog, the chief rabbi of Jerusalem, came to the delegation in order to thank the Holy Father for his charity over the past months, and he requested the Holy See's urgent intervention on behalf of the Jews in Transnistrie. On 2 March the Vatican sent a message to Bucharest instructing the nuncio to take all steps possible. As in many other cases when various channels were used, the nuncio was well aware of what was happening. It would be superfluous, he wrote on 16 March, to do anything more than had already been done at Rabbi Safran's request. The government was inclined to conciliation, and it would do more in this direction if it did not fear the reactions of those who were the blood enemies of the Jews, namely, the Germans. The nuncio added some very important information: The civil administration of Transnistrie had been recalled, and the people, including the Jewish group, were evacuated to this side of Dniester, that is, to a safe zone. Nonetheless, the nuncio, not being prematurely optimistic, promised to keep an eye on the situation and to send anything he learned to the Vatican. Since the Romanian government had no basic objection against the emigration of the Jews, the War Refugee Board rented a Turkish ship, the *Tari,* which would be used to evacuate in several trips the Romanian Jews, who were to depart from the port of Constanta on the Black Sea. The International Committee of the Red Cross, in whose name the operation was to be carried out, first insisted that the ship obtain a safe conduct from the German government, and it was thought that the Holy See's influence would be useful here. On 21 April the Board asked the Vatican to intervene on behalf of the ship with its fifteen hundred passengers. Finally, with or without safe conducts, several ships were placed into service with either the expressed or the tacit permission of the Romanian government. On 11 July the nuncio informed his superiors that the first group of Romanian refugees, 750 émigrés of whom 250 were from Transnistrie, had arrived in Istanbul several days earlier. Rabbi Safran brought him this news, and Rabbi Herzog sent him a telegram of appreciation.

The Hebrew community in Romania had a special reason for being interested in the fate of the Hungarian Jews. In August 1940 the northern part of Transylvania was detached from Romania and ceded to Hungary. The Jewish population of this region, 150,000 in number, was among the first to have been sent to Auschwitz in May–June 1944. A letter from Rabbi Safran to Archbishop Cassulo on 30 June showed the greatest concern. The rabbi said that his coreligionists from Transylvania were finding themselves "objects of great privations and sufferings." Cassulo conveyed this information in a report dated 11 July: "It appears that for some time now they are finding themselves in a very difficult and perilous situation," and on 28 July he completed this report by speaking of "exceptional coercive measures." He sent on to the Vatican an appeal addressed to the pope signed by six Jews who had parents in Transylvania: "For some time now we have had no news concerning our parents since all our efforts to learn something about their fate have come to naught." Those signing this appeal wanted to know what had happened to their parents, how they could communicate with them, and how they could have aid reach them.

On 8 August Archbishop Cassulo telegraphed to the Secretariat of State the substance of a letter sent to him by Dr. Ernest Grossmann, a delegate of a group of northern Transylvanian Jews having parents there. Two thousand families from northern Transylvania were threatened with deportation by the Hungarians. Dr. Grossmann was asking the Holy See to obtain from the German authorities permission to send these Jewish families to Palestine by way of the Danube, and this would require supervision by the German authorities in Romania. Grossmann's letter is significant because of the way Jewish circles then understood the Vatican's state of mind as well as German intentions:

> I am anxious to stress that the emigration of the Jews from Europe agrees with the views of the German authorities. Since I know what the Catholic Church has done up to the present for the Israelites of all countries, I am convinced that in this matter also we will have its full cooperation, all the more so because this pertains to a deeply humanitarian work for which six thousand souls will thank God.

On 21 April the Secretariat of State answered that it had immediately brought this matter to the attention of the nunciature in Budapest.

Meanwhile, uncertainty continued to hang over the fate of the Romanian Jews evacuated from northern Transylvania. Again on 11 December their parents in Romania addressed the pope on their behalf. In a message bearing the letterhead "*Curatorio generale ebraico per la Transylvania del Nord*," the president, Ernest Martòn, and the secretary, Leo Goldenberg, requested that the Vatican take action. They said that 150,000 Jews had already been deported during May and June, and nothing had been heard about them except the most alarming rumors. The signers of the appeal said that neither Jewish organizations nor the allied governments had any success in contacting them. Could not the Holy See request Berlin to grant permission to distribute packages of medicine and clothing for Christmas? In fact, on 14 November with winter approaching, the Vatican had already issued a general appeal on behalf of all prisoners and internees. Be this as it may, in a letter dated 13 December Archbishop Cassulo summarized what he knew about the situation:

> In northern Transylvania, where for a long time lived a very large number of Jewish families who were well-off materially, the Germans together with the Hungarians took such severe measures that in no time at all almost all these families were forced to abandon their goods and country, deported as they were first to Silesia and then to Germany. We need not speak of the treatment these families were subjected to; it is known by all. The elderly and the infants died on route or in concentration camps; those who survived are now deprived of everything and undergo much suffering.

This report of 13 December, probably arriving in Rome after a long delay, demonstrates the tenacious hope found among the parents of the Jews who had disappeared from Transylvania. On 31 January 1945 the nuncio to Switzerland sent the Vatican an offer that came from Carl Burkhart, president of the International Committee of the Red Cross; it would be happy to collaborate with the Holy See in alleviating the situation of the Jews from Transylvania.

When this report was received—and it arrived late—Monsignor Tardini on 27 February 1945 instructed Archbishop Orsenigo, the nuncio to Germany but who had withdrawn to Eichstätt after the destruction of the Berlin nunciature by Allied bombing, "to see what other steps can subsequently be taken."

It is clear that under such circumstances there was not much the nuncio could still do.

CONCERN FOR THE HUNGARIAN JEWS

In Hungary racial legislation was being prepared as early as spring 1939, and it was finally enacted into law despite the opposition of the bishops who had a vote in the upper chamber. In 1941 there was the expulsion of the Polish Jewish refugees who had taken refuge in Hungary, but mass deportations of Jews did not take place till the Reich had taken complete control of the country in 1944.

At the beginning of 1944 the threat of deportation weighed heavily upon the Polish Jews seeking protection in Hungary. On 29 January Archbishop Cicognani in Washington sent the Vatican an appeal from the World Jewish Congress: Would not the Holy See use its influence with the Hungarian government to support a plan giving these Jews material assistance with costs covered by funds sent from the United States? But on 23 March the Wehrmacht stormed into Hungary, and the Germans seized control of the country. Two days later Cicognani informed the Vatican that the War Refugee Board was asking the Holy See to take urgent measures to assist some two million Jews from Hungary and Romania who were now being threatened with extermination under Nazi occupation. The Board was pressing for the collaboration of the nuncio in Budapest. This appeal, accompanied by a similar instruction, was immediately sent by the Secretariat of State to Archbishop Rotta and Archbishop Cassulo, the nuncios to Hungary and Romania respectively.

On 31 March a message from Rabbi Isaac Herzog in Jerusalem arrived in the Vatican by way of the apostolic delegate in Istanbul. The same day, Archbishop Godfrey sent a petition from the chief rabbi of London. And on 1 April d'Arcy Osborne, the British minister, brought to the Secretariat of State a request from his government that the Holy See use its influence to stop the Jewish refugees in Hungary from being handed over to the Nazis.

The initial information sent during this period by Archbishop Angelo Rotta in Hungary was relatively optimistic. Describing the political situation, he wrote on 30 March that the Jews should be in no immediate danger, even though the fighting would soon aggravate things and despite the fact that many Jews had already been detained. On 7 April he reported that all his previous interventions with the authorities had only obtained for baptized Jews some small modifications in the anti-Semitic laws. The atmosphere in the capital, he wrote, advised against any further action being taken at that time. In a report dated 19 April Rotta explained that immediately after the new government of Dome Sztojay was formed on 23 March, he requested an audience with the prime minister, who was also the foreign minister, in order to protest against the treatment inflicted on members of the Italian embassy who had been arrested or interned. At the same time he recommended to the new government that it show moderation toward the Jews and that it pay special attention to baptized Jews. And when, several days later on 30 March, the anticipated anti-Semitic decrees became generally known, he again protested. Up to this point the question was still not one of deporting the entire Jewish population to an "unknown destination." But on 28 April, after a deceptive calm, pressure increased, especially for Catholics of Jewish origin.

PROTESTS BY ARCHBISHOP ROTTA

Yesterday [wrote the nuncio] I again lodged a serious complaint with the general secretary of the foreign ministry against what the government had done, once more stressing that the manner and extent of the struggle against the Jews was both inhumane and anti-Christian. I said that the Holy Father could only be deeply saddened to see that Hungary also, which till now boasted that it was a Christian nation, had turned down a path that would lead it to contradict the doctrine of the gospel.

Meanwhile, Archbishop Rotta hoped that the combined action of the nunciature and of the cardinal primate would be somewhat productive for the baptized Jews, and as to the others, that their basic human rights would be respected. Cardinal Serédi, the primate of Hungary, actually had a long conversation with the prime minister about the anti-Semitic laws, but he left the meeting without any hope of results. German pressure, according to Rotta, was very strong, and the Germans did not admit any distinction between non-baptized Jews and baptized Jews.

The deportation, which had been some time in preparation, began on 14 May; it was to Auschwitz. The next day Rotta sent a double protest: a letter to the prime minister and a note to the foreign minister. To persecute anyone for the sole reason of that person's race, said the letter, violated natural law. To take measures against the Jews without taking into account the baptism they had received contradicted the Christian state that Hungary claimed to be. The nuncio specified that he had kept the pope up-to-date on what was occurring in Hungary, "I hope," Rotta concluded, "that in his position as supreme pastor of the church, as the one who safeguards the rights of all his children, and as the defender of truth and justice, he [the Holy Father] will not be obliged to speak out in protest."

In his note sent to the foreign minister, the nuncio requested that baptized Jews be exempted from the anti-Semitic laws, and he called for fundamental human rights to be respected in all measures taken by the government. The minister's response was unfeeling and negative.

Dated 27 May, it spoke with irony about the sincerity of the recent converts from Judaism to Catholicism. In any case, he replied, their conversion counted for nothing since the problem was racial and thus was not changed by baptism. Nonetheless, the government would create a special department for Jewish converts; he also agreed to make some exceptions on their behalf, like not being required to bear the yellow star. As to their deportation, the minister pretended, the fact was that the government was simply furnishing the Reich with labor. Christian workers had already been supplied, and as a response to new requests a certain number of Jews were now being sent.

Rotta was not fooled by these explanations, and he knew that his superiors approved of what he was doing. A dispatch of 29 May signed by Monsignor Tardini told Rotta to "continue to do everything possible to alleviate the sufferings of so many unfortunate people"; the nuncio was even invited to send a discrete exhortation to the Hungarian bishops. Encouraged by this approval, Rotta sent the foreign minister a long note, written in French and dated 5 June; its forcefulness was almost unique among diplomatic exchanges.

The apostolic nunciature, wrote Rotta, had been informed that the Hungarian government had decided to deport all the Hungarian Jews, no matter what their religion. Such a deportation was already in progress, and under such conditions many had died en route. In addition, inhumane conditions existed in the concentration camps. It was with bitter irony that Rotta responded to the official version which claimed that it was not a matter of deportation but of forced labor:

It is said that it is not a question of deportation but of forced labor. Words can be debated but the reality is the same. When among those being deported are the elderly who are more than seventy and even eighty years old, elderly women, children, the sick, then we can ask ourselves: for what kind of work can these people be used? The response is that the Jews are allowed to take their families with them; but in this case their departure should be done freely. And what is to be said about cases in which the elderly, the sick, etc. are the only ones being deported, or when there are no parents whom the deportees are to follow? And considering that the Hungarian workers who went to Germany to work were not allowed to bring their families with them, there is indeed astonishment that this great favor was given only to the Jews.

192

Archbishop Rotta forcefully insisted that it was his right and his duty to intervene on behalf of all the Jews who had become Catholics through baptism; he rejected doubts about the sincerity of such conversions. The concessions promised by the government's note of 27 May, continued Rotta, were insufficient; baptized Jews must be exempt from the anti-Semitic laws, and all Jews must be treated humanely, in a way that respects justice and the fundamental rights of every human being. He concluded by expressing the hope

> that the Hungarian people, who have justly acquired the title of defender of the faith and of civilization, do not want to sully their reputation by following methods that the conscience of the Christian world could not sanction, even if it were claimed that these methods were being used as a defense against Bolshevism, and which would merely diminish all the moral value of the people who are still engaged in the campaign they are waging today in defense of Christian civilization.

While informing Rome of his protest, Rotta added that the harassments and deportations were continuing in an inhumane manner, even though they were masked under the name of being sent off for obligatory work: "Force and violence have prevailed over good sense and over the rights of truth and justice."

On 18 June Rotta telegraphed Maglione that three hundred thousand Jews had already been deported. Rumor was that a third of them were sent to work beyond Hungarian borders, but as to the other two-thirds, it was anyone's guess. Reliable people were even speaking about "extermination camps." In any case, the conditions under which the Jews were being transported were "truly horrible." Cardinal Serédi, the prince primate of Hungary, protested in the name of the hierarchy, but no public statement from the bishops as yet appeared in spite of the nuncio's insistence. Rotta said that a direct intervention of the Holy See would be extremely useful, not to say necessary, since vehicles for the next wave of deportations were all in place.

Six days later, 24 June, Rotta telegraphed again: The deportations were continuing, the protests remained useless, and a convoy was to leave within a few days. Moreover, the faithful were surprised at the passivity of their bishops. At this moment the Hungarian hierarchy was divided: Some prelates wanted an energetic protest even though Serédi, the cardinal primate, was not convinced that this was the right time for such a statement. A pastoral letter had already been drafted, but it had not been published due to the government's objections. Furthermore, Serédi believed that threatening to publish the letter was just as effective, if not more so, than the publication itself. On 25 June the secretary of state ordered Rotta that he was to press the Hungarian bishops to take action. Rotta immediately sent the cardinal primate an explicit message: The Hungarian bishops were to intervene, and even openly, in the defense of Christian principles and for the protection of their compatriots—especially for Christians—unjustly affected by the racial decrees. The bishops had to do this so that their complacent attitude would not place them in an unfavorable light and do harm both to the bishops themselves and to Hungarian Catholicism. Now at last the pastoral letter, already close to completion, was signed and dated 29 June. Cardinal Serédi, meanwhile, always believed that the message would be more effective if it remained only a threat, and so he promised the government that the letter would not be issued if the deportation ceased and if the baptized Jews were given the desired concessions.

Meanwhile, on 24 June Harold Tittman brought Cardinal Maglione a message from the War Refugee Board which stated that "according to reports that in every way appear authentic," the Hungarian authorities have begun the persecution of eight hundred thousand Hungarian Jews and intend their mass extermination both in Hungary itself and after their deportation in Poland as well. The Board expressed the hope that the pope would appeal to the authorities and to the Hungarian people, either by radio or through an intermediary of the nuncio or of the clergy, or through a special envoy.

PIUS XII'S TELEGRAM TO ADMIRAL HORTHY

The Refugee Board's request did not catch the pope unawares. As early as 12 June, perhaps following Rotta's telegram, the Secretariat of State had put together the draft of an appeal to Nicolas Horthy. On 25 June Pius XII addressed in plain (not in code) the following telegram, written in French, to Admiral Horthy, the regent of Hungary:

> From many sides We receive requests to use every means so that in this noble and chivalrous country there not be an increase and intensification of the sufferings, already too heavy, that are endured by a large number of unfortunate people due to their

nationality or race. Since Our heart, that of a Father, cannot remain insensitive to these urgent requests, and by reason of Our ministry of charity which extends to all, We personally address Your Royal Highness, appealing to your noble sentiments and being fully confident that you wish to do all in your power in order that so many unfortunate people be spared further afflictions and sorrows.

On July 1 Regent Horthy, who was not Catholic, responded, thanking the pope as follows:

It was with the deepest understanding and thanks that I just received the message sent by wire from Your Holiness, and I ask you to be indeed assured that I am doing everything possible, especially by asserting the Christian requirements of humanitarian principles. May I be permitted to again ask Your Holiness to look with favor upon the Hungarian people in their hour of great trial.

The regent, also greatly affected by an attempted coup d'état on the part of some fanatical anti-Semites, regained power and vigorously took action: The deportations ceased.

Other interventions, apart from those of the pope, were influential here. Five days after Pius XII's appeal Horthy received a message from the king of Sweden, and on July 5 there was a request from Max Huber, president of the International Committee of the Red Cross. On August 9 Archbishop Cicognani in Washington reported that the American Jewish Committee and the Committee to Save the Jews of Europe had asked that the Holy Father and Cardinal Maglione be given an expression of deep thanks for the decisive improvement seen in Hungary. According to news reports the deportation had ceased, and the above-mentioned committee recognized that this was due to the Holy Father.

And yet the Hungarian nightmare did not come to an end. Deportations to Auschwitz were suspended, but surreptitious removals continued as atrocities increased within Hungary itself. Horthy remained regent, but his real power progressively diminished under German pressure, and this led to a resumption of the deportations. When the nuncio was informed of this, he mobilized the heads of the four other diplomatic missions so that together they might issue a

195

protest. On 21 August a combined protest was presented to the regent by Archbishop Rotta; Carl Danielsson, the Swedish minister; Miguel Sanz-Briz, the Spanish chargé d'affaires; Carlos de Liz-Teixeira Branqhuinho, the Portuguese chargé d'affaires; and A. Kilchmann, the Swiss chargé d'affaires. It was "with a feeling of sorrowful surprise" that they had learned that Jewish deportations were to resume. And they were informed by absolutely trustworthy sources as to what in most cases deportation meant, even though the removal was being disguised under the name of working abroad. Furthermore, it was inadmissible that people were being persecuted and sent to death solely because of their racial origin. Horthy replied that notwithstanding German pressure he was determined to resist the resumption of the deportations.

On 30 August Horthy dismissed the Sztojay government and installed General Geisa Lakatos, who remained in power for only six weeks, and yet these were crucial weeks. On 5 September the nuncio reported that the ministers had confidence in Horthy, that they were more moderate as to the Jewish question, and that no deportations would take place.

However, Russian armies were trampling on Hungarian soil. On 15 October Admiral Horthy announced on the radio that Hungary was accepting an armistice with the Soviet Union. German reaction was immediate: Horthy was arrested, the regime was overthrown, and the Nazi party was put into power with F. Szalasi as "guide of the nation, the *Nationsführer*." This change, as far as the Jews were concerned, called everything into question. On 14 October Alex Easterman, from the World Jewish Congress, cabled that according to his sources three hundred thousand Jews were once again in danger. He asked for a public appeal. On 17 October, during an audience, President Roosevelt's representative gave the pope a cable he had received from the World Jewish Congress. This document repeated a message sent directly to the pope by the same organization; believing that the deportations were to resume, it was asking the pope to "issue in the name of humanity an appeal to stop this appalling tragedy." On 19 October Archbishop Cicognani cabled that the Jewish leaders were insisting on a radio appeal sent to the Hungarian people. In their opinion the nunciature could do nothing further, whereas Vatican Radio, with the assistance of a secret propaganda organization, could do more to make the pope's message known. Finally on 28 October Myron Taylor submitted to the pope the text of a message drawn up by the War Refugee Board, which was entreating the pope to give a radio address to the Hungarian people and clergy urging them to assist these unfortunate people by hiding them and by opposing their deportation and extermination.

Yet Pius XII chose another route. Archbishop Rotta had informed the pope that on 29 October a collection would be taken up in all the churches of Hungary for the refugees. A message was immediately prepared, and on 26 October the pope's appeal was sent to the prince primate, who had not asked for it. The pope began by saying that he had received urgent requests that he intervene on behalf of people exposed to persecution and violence because of their religious belief, their race, or their political convictions. The pope was joining his appeal to that of the Hungarian bishops, and he concluded by trusting "that, in conformity with the principles of humanity and of justice, the very grave sufferings caused by this terrible conflict do not become even more horrible." Pius XII called upon the bishops and the faithful to redouble their assistance toward all the victims of the war regardless of their race, in other words, toward the Jews whether baptized or not.

FURTHER PROTESTS

This message was also an invitation that the nuncio continue his work of trying to influence the government. On 10 November Rotta telephoned the foreign minister to protest, once again, the treatment inflicted on the Jews.

> From a humanitarian perspective but also to protect Christian morality, the Holy See protests the inhumane attitude adopted toward the Jews, and even while taking note of the foreign minister's statement, it requests the government to intervene with the greatest determination.

On 17 November, this time accompanied by Carl Danielsson, who was the Swedish ambassador, Archbishop Rotta returned to Prime Minister Szalasi in order to give him a memorandum from the five neutral powers. It summed up the present state of affairs and yet, considering the fanatical hatred of the Nazis toward the Jews, the document harbored few illusions as to practical results. For its part, the nunciature did what it could by intervening with the appropriate government ministers and by delivering more than thirteen thousand letters of protection: For the time being at least, these letters held off the deportation of many baptized Jews.

By this time Auschwitz and its gas chambers had been dismantled, but the fanaticism of those seeking out the Jews had not yet been extinguished. The Jews from Budapest, estimated to have been about forty thousand, were sent on foot to the west, toward Austria, where they had to help prepare the country's defenses against the Soviet armies. On 8 December 1944 the nuncio sent the Vatican a memorandum drawn up by a religious who was sent from the nunciature to the Hungarian borders in order to bring aid to the refugees. The memorandum's author, speaking as an eyewitness, comments: "Only the pen of Dostoïevski would be capable of describing the horrors accompanying the deportation from Budapest to Hegyeshalom, the station at the frontier. Traveling by truck, one passes group after group of deportees as they creep along, starving, frozen, limping, completely exhausted."

The Soviet armies were approaching Budapest, but anti-Jewish measures continued no less. On 8 December the diplomats of the neutral powers who still remained in the city, namely, the Holy See, Sweden, Turkey, Switzerland, and Portugal, were once again with the foreign minister. Meanwhile, the bishop of Veszprém, the future Cardinal Mindszenty, had been arrested by the Arrow-Cross (Hungarian Nazis). The nuncio, although he had been asked to leave Budapest with the government so that he could find another place of residence in the west, responded that he was unable to accompany the government as long as it detained a Catholic bishop, much less the priests who were being held in prison. Furthermore, he complained about the lack of suitable food for the Jews living under the Vatican's protection. This was not the last step for which Archbishop Rotta, as dean of the diplomatic corps, was the spokesman if not the author. Months later, after the Soviets had expelled him from Budapest, he sent the Vatican a copy of a third written protest given on 23 December to the Arrow-Cross government.

The government had decided to place all the Jews inside the ghetto. But at least the children, insisted the diplomats, should be spared. It is not known what effect this plea had upon the government, for on 23 December the Red Army encircled the city, where resistance lasted till 12 February. This final diplomatic effort at least testified to what had been done during the preceding months, and up to the very end, in an attempt to keep in their own country the Jews destined for deportation.

And so up to the very last days the Holy See's representatives were taking action to keep the Jews from the fate planned for them by the Nazi leaders. Even if Pius XII did not issue the public statement that some wanted to draw out of him, it was with deliberation that on 30 April 1943 he wrote to the bishop of Berlin: "To the extent it was able, the Holy See has in fact given charitable aid to non-Aryan Catholics and to members of the Jewish religion....The principal Jewish organizations have expressed to the Holy See their warmest appreciation for its relief efforts." The correspondence exchanged between the Holy See and its representatives fully confirms this assertion.

REACTIONS FROM JEWISH GROUPS

As early as February 1943 the nuncio in Bucharest, Archbishop Cassulo, passed on to the Vatican the thanks of the president of Romania's Jewish community: "The president of the Romanian Israelite community...has twice come to thank me for the Holy See's assistance and protection given to his coreligionists; he has asked me to send to the Holy Father an expression of the gratitude felt by his whole community, which during this difficult time has found in the nunciature an effective support." Fifteen days later the nuncio again sent a message saying that on the previous day Dr. Safran, the chief rabbi in Bucharest, had come to request that he "send to the Holy Father the loving respects and the sincere and gracious wishes of the whole community whose members are well aware that the august pontiff regards them with fatherly solicitude."

It was about the same time that the Holy See's representative in Croatia, Abbot Marcone, wrote along identical lines: "The rabbi of Zagreb asked me to express his deepest thanks to the Holy See for the effective assistance it gave in transporting a group of Jewish children."

The apostolic delegate in Turkey, Archbishop Roncalli, wrote on 22 May of the same year, namely, 1943: "Even today the secretary of the Jewish Agency for Palestine, Mr. C. Barlas, came to thank me and to thank the Holy See for the happy outcome of the steps taken on behalf of the Israelites in Slovakia." And in June he sent on to the Vatican two letters he received, one thanking him for his action on behalf of Jewish refugees, the other being a note of appreciation for the relief work carried out by Alois Stepanic, the archbishop of Zagreb.

The Capuchin Marie-Benoît, called the Father of the Jews, in a letter of 15 July 1943 spoke for the French Jews and expressed "the appreciation they feel toward the Catholic Church for the charity it has shown them."

In a letter of 19 July to the secretary of state, Isaac Herzog, the chief rabbi of Jerusalem, expressed his gratitude to the pope whose efforts on behalf of the refugees "had awoken a feeling of gratitude in the hearts of millions of people." And in a letter addressed to Roncalli on the following 22 November Herzog also expressed "his sincere gratitude as well as his deep appreciation for so kind an attitude toward Israel and for such valuable assistance given by the Catholic Church to the endangered Jewish people." In substantially identical terms the South American Jewish communities—Chile, Uruguay, and Bolivia—wrote to the representatives of the Holy See to express their gratitude to the pope.

Also quite significant is an article that appeared on 27 September 1944 in the paper *Mantuirea*. Written under the signature of Rabbi Safran, the piece's title says it all: "The apostolic nuncio has seen to it that the deportation of Jews to Transnistrie has been halted. May God reward him for what he has done."

Without exaggerating the importance of these words of appreciation, often accompanied as they were by requests for further action, it must be admitted that the Jewish leaders recognized the pope's efforts on behalf of their persecuted communities, and that despite repeated failures and limited results, the Holy See's actions were not completely in vain. Still more remarkable in a way is that, despite the fact that so many repeated interventions ended with only tenuous results in comparison with the efforts expended, the Vatican in the midst of the uncertainty and the darkness within which it had to take action, continued its lifesaving work to the end.

CHAPTER 10

The Fate of the Eternal City*

~·~

A T A TIME WHEN the Holy See was busy responding to the
appeals arriving from Europe and America on behalf of the
Jewish victims of the deportation, it found itself confronted
locally: Rome itself, the capital of Italy, was in danger. The question,
one which arose as early as 10 June 1940 when Italy allied itself with
Germany in the war became increasingly urgent during the first days
of November 1942, when squadrons from England carried out massive
bombings over Genoa, Turin, and Milan.

Having received from the archbishops of the bombed cities
reports on the damage sustained by churches and hospitals and on the
loss of human life, Cardinal Maglione called in d'Arcy Osborne and
Harold Tittman; the cardinal repeated for the sake of their governments
"the Holy See's desire and prayer that civilian populations be spared."
The following day Osborne responded that Genoa was a very important port for provisioning Africa and that the number of civilian casu-
alties was indeed below that suffered by English cities. The following
week Osborne pointed out that the purpose of the air raids was to
destroy military targets, which were found also in Rome. He also
recalled that in 1940 Mussolini requested Hitler that he, Mussolini, be
allowed to participate in the bombing of London. In short, the question
of bombing Rome, first posed when Italy entered the conflict, was
again a topic for discussion.

So it was that in the English press and in the House of Commons
numerous voices were raised demanding that Rome also be bombed.
At the end of October 1942 Cardinal Maglione instructed the apostolic delegate in Washington to inform Myron Taylor that if Rome
were bombed, the pope would have to issue a protest. Faced with a
deteriorating situation, Maglione instructed Archbishop Cicognani to

*Documentation for chapter 10: See *ADSS*, vols. 7, 10, and 11. Add *FRUS*, 1943,
vol. 2, and *FRUS*, 1944, vol. 4; *Akten*, series E vol. 8; O. Chadwick, *Britain and the
Vatican*; Weizsäcker, *Erinnerungen*.

take personal action with the government, to have recourse to the good offices of Ambassador Taylor, to have Archbishop Francis Spellman of New York intervene, and even to look into the expediency of a collective action by the hierarchy on behalf of American clergy and people. Maglione repeated the arguments that had already been proposed: Rome was the diocese of the sovereign pontiff and the capital of Catholicism; the pope would be obliged to protest in case Rome were bombed. The same argument was directed to the British government through William Godfrey, the apostolic delegate in London, and through Cardinal Arthur Hinsley, the archbishop of Westminster. Finally, on 4 December Maglione requested Raffaele Guariglia, Italy's ambassador to the Holy See, to warn the Italian government that if it wished to avoid having Rome bombed, it was necessary to remove from the city all military targets located there.

The apostolic delegate in Washington contacted Taylor, the State Department, and the hierarchy. Roosevelt, Cicognani informed the Vatican, was personally against bombing Rome, but he could not give any assurances in this regard since the enemy could profit from these. More inflexible was the British reaction. On 28 December Osborne confirmed the previous statements of the prime minister. The preceding year Churchill said that the English would not hesitate to bomb Rome to the extent that they could and as heavily as possible if the course of the war warranted this. A protest from the pope against this bombing would be interpreted as the Holy See's taking a position in favor of the Italian state and of the Fascist government. In January Eden returned to the question in the House of Commons, but he only repeated what had been said previously.

Following the bombing of Ostia during the night of 16 May 1943, Cardinal Maglione sent new notes to both parties. Two days later London broadcast the statement of the undersecretary of aviation that the government would not hesitate to bomb Rome if the conduct of the war required it. On 3 June Ciano assured Cardinal Maglione that the headquarters of the Italian forces would be moved outside Rome, but he added, confidentially, that Mussolini had no intention of leaving the city because a Fascist official had strongly claimed for Rome "the honor of being bombed like other Italian cities."

THE HOLY SEE AND THE ITALIAN GOVERNMENT

While the Vatican was sending numerous diplomatic notes, telegrams, and cables to keep the Anglo-American bombers away from Rome, another matter required its attention, both by reason of geographical proximity as well as by the various requests the Vatican received, namely, that of Italy's political situation. Pius XII side-stepped overtures made by Pietro Badoglio and Ettore Bastico, who were attempting to discuss the necessity of changing the government in Italy, and yet he gave more serious consideration to suggestions coming from America. On 18 February 1943 Archbishop Cicognani cabled the Vatican that Myron Taylor had often told him that, in Italy's very interest, the American government would find it useful to have some reliable information on the form any new government would take, on retaining the royalty, and on who might be the prime minister.

And yet, by expressing an opinion the Holy See would appear to be interfering in Italy's internal affairs and in the most fundamental of matters, such as changing the regime. But could the Holy See avoid doing this if it were offered an opportunity to save the Italian people from further destruction and a more disastrous fate? Nonetheless, Cardinal Maglione was in no hurry to reply to Taylor's requests.

In early May fighting came to an end in Tunisia, and it was anticipated that the whole brunt of Anglo-American air power would be concentrated on Italy in order to prepare for a landing on the peninsula; Mussolini's determination to continue the conflict only gave promise of destruction and countless victims. Monsignor Tardini wondered whether the time had not come for the Holy See to become involved. The head of the Italian government had to be forced to face up to his responsibilities toward the Italian people, a people for whom the pope said he was ready to do everything possible. The cardinal secretary of state, in the pope's name, would verbally send a message to Ciano, who would have it sent on directly to Mussolini. Agreeing to this, Pius XII decided to send at the same time a personal message to President Roosevelt.

On 12 May at half past noon Cardinal Maglione read to Count Ciano the pope's message to Mussolini. In it Pius XII recalled his April 1940 letter to the Duce and stated that he "with considerable grief shared in the very great suffering the conflict has caused and is causing to our dear children of Italy." The future threatened ever more terrible sufferings and destruction and, because of his special bonds as being the bishop of Rome and the primate of Italy, the pope wanted once more "to declare to Mussolini that as always he was prepared to do everything possible to come to the aid of this suffering people." First of all, Ciano found the statement to be too vague. However, he then judged it to be very opportune but warned that Mussolini was not yet in a psychological state of mind to understand the necessity, and it was self-understood, "of immediately thinking about how to extract the country from the disastrous situation into which it had been thrown." Ciano sketched a realistic framework of what was really happening: Italian cities lacked any means of defending themselves. In Mussolini's mind the war would go on for still another three or four years, the king would take no action, and the Allies would attack Italy because they believed that its occupation would occasion the downfall of the Reich: "Negotiations were necessary, but Mussolini did not want them, and the Allies will have nothing to do with him." Ciano departed as he kept repeating: "It's tragic!"

What Ciano foresaw turned out to be true. The next day he officially told Cardinal Maglione that Mussolini thanked the pope for thinking about him, for the pope's solicitude on behalf of the Italian people, and for what the pope was suffering, something Mussolini himself also shared; but "under present condition there is no alternative, and Italy will continue to wage war." Ciano added that Mussolini, envious of the prestige enjoyed by the pope, little appreciated the course the Vatican was following and that he had decided to fight on till the last Italian.

Pius XII's letter to Roosevelt, sent eight days later, was, in turn, a call for mercy. Recalling for the president the statement made in his name by Ambassador Taylor, namely, that "America nourished no hatred of the Italian people," the pope expressed his hope that Italy would be treated with consideration and understanding, that it would insofar as possible be spared new suffering and destruction, and finally, that its religious and artistic treasures would be saved from irreparable destruction.

Directly intervening with Mussolini did not cause the Vatican to forget Taylor's request that the Holy See give its opinion regarding political change in Italy. The cardinal secretary of state sketched the broad outlines of a response, and Monsignor Tardini drew up a first draft that had four points. He presented these to Maglione on 18 May:

(1) The Holy See reaffirms its desire to remain above and outside purely political rivalries between countries. (2) The Italian people appear to be attached to and well disposed toward the monarchy. (3) And so, according to the constitution, it belongs to the king and not to outside influences to name the head of the government. (4) As to the person to be designated, the Vatican does not feel itself capable of presenting any suggestions. The text was the object of discussions among Pius XII, Maglione, and Tardini. Although the pope was inclined to put forward several names, he refrained from doing so because of objections raised by Tardini.

The response to Taylor was sent on 21 May to Lisbon by a special courier who carried a letter from Pius XII to President Roosevelt. On 29 May Archbishop Cicognani cabled a new message from Taylor. Considering that the present hour was undoubtedly one of the gravest in Italy's history, the Holy See had to tell "whoever has the means for acting" that since the Allied victory was now certain, it was urgent that Italians separate themselves from Germany and form a new government. The United States would be disposed to negotiate with this government, to support and protect it, and immediately to cease the bombings. But if the opposite were true, then there would only be an increase in the destruction and in the number of victims. Awaiting Italy was nothing other than the fate of the vanquished.

This cable from Washington arrived in the Vatican on 30 May at half past seven in the evening. In passing it on to Monsignor Tardini at noon the next day, Cardinal Maglione, who had received initial instructions from the pope, told Tardini that it was necessary to secretly contact the king, just to inform him of this message. Tardini, thinking about the question and taking pen in hand, wondered what reprisals the Holy See was opening itself to by taking such a step. However, an attempt to stop the "pulverization" of Italian cities, as Eden phrased it, was something totally in conformity with the character of the Holy See. This is what convinced Maglione and Montini on the morning of 1 June. Pius XII decided that Cicognani would be instructed to ask Taylor if he was acting personally or in Roosevelt's name. The cable to Cicognani went out that very afternoon, and the apostolic delegate's response arrived in the Vatican during the evening of 6 June. Taylor had spoken of his own initiative, but he agreed with Roosevelt that he, Taylor, would go to the Vatican if this would be judged useful and there serve as an intermediary between the Holy

See and Washington regarding "every initiative undertaken by Italy to extricate itself from the war."

Two days later Pius XII decided to prepare a message for the king of Italy. Its text was drafted by Monsignor Tardini and then reviewed by the pope. The morning of 11 June Pius XII spoke with Maglione about it and delayed his decision till the following day.

While deliberations were taking place in the Vatican as how to approach Victor Emmanuel, the admiral in charge of the Isle of Pantelleria hoisted the white flag. Several hours later Roosevelt, in a press conference immediately picked up by various radio stations, addressed the Italian people, whom he invited to throw out the Fascist regime and to put an end to German rule on the peninsula. If this were done, the Allies would guarantee that Italy could choose its own government, while hoping that the country would take its place in the family of nations. Taylor explained to Cicognani the meaning of what Roosevelt said: it was an ultimatum. If Italy did not accept it, the Allies, who had decided to overthrow Fascism and Nazism at any cost, would bomb all military and nonmilitary targets, including Rome. Early in the afternoon on 12 June, in a cable marked urgent and intended for the cardinal secretary of state, the apostolic delegate informed the Vatican of the details given to him by Taylor in regard to Roosevelt's message to the Italian people.

The Vatican received the cable the next day at half past seven in the evening. Roosevelt's statements provided a point of departure for the anticipated meeting with the king. Pius XII decided that the nuncio would request an audience with Victor Emmanuel and officially confirm what was being reported by the press agencies. On 17 June Pius XII's nuncio was received at the Quirinal by King Victor Emmanuel. Referring to what Roosevelt said, Borgongini Duca said: "The president's message also corresponds to the intentions of the Allies, which the Holy See knows from an official source." The king understood: "And so you are aware of this from two sides, that of the press agencies and that of diplomacy." Nonetheless, the king remained impervious and distrustful: "To say that 'we will treat you well' can easily mean that 'in place of hanging you we will chop off your head.'" The meeting went on, the nuncio attempting to say all that he was told to tell the king, and the king evading the pressing questions by digressing about the military forces and plans for the landing. As noted by the nuncio, the king, who was rather reserved by nature, spoke so quickly that not a word could be gotten in edgewise. Finally Borgongini Duca found an opportunity to slip in his message: "When the time was right I said that the Most Eminent Cardinal Maglione had been presented with various opportunities to inform the president that the Holy See, which does not intervene in any country's internal affairs, could say that the monarchy is highly regarded in Italy and is loved by the Italian people. The king interrupted me: 'Thank you. Thank you. I have great esteem for Cardinal Maglione: Everyone speaks highly of him. He is good with everyone.' I picked up the thread of the conversation: 'The monarchy is well regarded and loved by the Italian people, and the government depends on Your Majesty.' At this point the king smiled and said to me, and this is word for word: 'I am not like the pope.'"

That same evening the nuncio sent his report to the cardinal secretary of state. The Holy See had done everything possible.

THE BOMBING OF ROME

The following week, on 23 June, a cable arrived from Cicognani that repeated the Allied position regarding the bombing of Rome. The English and American governments did not want to bomb the city, but they would do so if the war necessitated it. The military commanders insisted on having full discretionary power because Rome was a railroad and communications center. After Sicily fell, air strikes would clinch the victory. Writing on 9 July, Eden repeated to Archbishop Godfrey that the British government had the right to bomb the capital of an enemy country. At dawn the next day the Allies landed on the shores of Sicily and within a few days they took the offensive.

In a letter to Pius XII dated 10 July and sent by radio perhaps even before Cicognani had received it, Roosevelt strongly stated that the Allied troops came "to free Italy from Fascism and from Fascism's wretched symbols," and that the president himself, like the pope, longed for the day when God's peace, a just and lasting peace, would again shine on the world.

Five days later Pius XII responded, only to say that he had received the message. But while the Vatican was reflecting on how to reply, decisive events were taking place in Rome.

Eisenhower, who had decided to suspend all activity against the capital till the time of the landing, now took action. On 19 July, from ten after eleven in the morning till three in the afternoon, some five hundred planes attacked the Roman train yard and its adjacent installations. Neighboring residential areas were hit as well as the Basilica of St. Lawrence outside the Walls and the nearby cemetery of Campo Verano. The number of victims was estimated at about fifteen hundred dead with somewhat more having been wounded. At half past four Pius XII, accompanied by Monsignor Montini, arrived in the district of San Lorenzo; they slowly walked through this area till arriving at the basilica, which the bombs had half destroyed. They remained there till eight in the evening. Accompanied by a deeply affected crowd, the pope knelt down to pray among the ruins. The people so crowded in on him that his automobile was damaged, and he had to return in a Vatican staff car.

The next day Cardinal Maglione sent a telegram to the nuncios in Madrid, Lisbon, Dublin, Buenos Aires, Santiago in Chile, Bogota, Rio de Janeiro, Lima, Caracas, and to the apostolic delegates in Ottawa and Washington:

> Yesterday for about three hours Allied airplanes heavily bombed Rome. Even though it had been stated that only military targets were to be hit, homes were demolished, the cemetery was devastated; also destroyed was the Basilica of St. Lawrence outside the Walls, one of the oldest and most venerable of Rome's churches. Because of this the Holy Father is deeply saddened since he was hoping that he could count on more understanding and consideration for his repeated pleas. This event has confirmed the near impossibility of avoiding the destruction of sacred edifices while bombing the very center of Catholicism.

The message added that the pope had gone to these places so that he might get an idea of the damage inflicted and to console his children in their misfortune.

The Vatican then returned its attention to the Italian government. In a note sent to Italy's ambassador on 23 July the pope asked the Italians to verify that they had indeed kept their promise to remove from Rome all military targets so that it could be declared an open city. If the government had done this, then "the Holy See would immediately communicate this to the Allied governments."

THE FALL OF MUSSOLINI

The landing in Sicily dealt a serious blow to Mussolini's prestige: The Allies, rather than being stopped "where the tide ended" as the Duce had promised, were quickly making their way into the island. During the night of 24–25 July the king requested Mussolini's resignation, and he gave the task of forming a new government to Marshal Badoglio.

It seems clear that the Vatican was not aware of what was happening; it was only during the morning of 25 June that a member of the great council informed Monsignor Montini of the events that had occurred during the night. On the other hand, the statements of the king and of Badoglio, affirming their will to continue to fight side by side with the Reich, left unchanged the problems that the Holy See had taken to heart, namely, the war and the threat of bombing, especially the bombing of Rome.

ROME: AN OPEN CITY

As to Rome, the Vatican resolved to take immediate action. On 26 July a note from the Secretariat of State to the Italian ambassador stated that the Holy See "believes it necessary that the new government hasten to declare and to effectively make Rome an open city." The next day Tardini wrote a personal letter to Babuscio Rizzo and insisted that this action "be among the first of the new government."

The Vatican's note arrived just in time. By now Roosevelt's statements during his 23 July press conference were well known. After deploring the fact that the Fascists did not want to declare and actually make Rome an open city, the president repeated his hope that they would decide to do so, especially since Rome, after the occupation of Sicily, had become a very important military center. Several days later, on 27 July and in a speech to the House of Commons, Churchill assumed a very threatening tone. If Italy intended to continue the war under the German yoke, this would not change the final outcome of the conflict, for Italy "will be scorched, destroyed, and annihilated from one end to the other."

On 31 July Badoglio's government informed the Vatican of its decision that Rome would, in principle, be an open city. The Holy See was requested to communicate this to the opposing side so that the Italian government could learn the conditions under which such a decision would be recognized. The following day Cardinal Maglione sent instructions to this effect to the delegate in Washington, and on 2 August to the delegate in London, charging each to make the appropriate government contact and to inform him of the results.

On 4 August Cardinal Maglione gathered in his apartment the cardinals who were present in Rome in order to apprise them of the situation. Fourteen cardinals attended the session as well as the secretary of the Congregation for Extraordinary Ecclesiastical Affairs. First, the cardinal recalled the various steps taken by the Holy See to protect Rome, both with the Allies as well as with the Italian government. The latter, asked to remove the most important military targets, promised to do so, and yet it reneged on its promise. As to the Italian political situation, the Holy See kept itself apart from the discussions, but this did not stop it from bearing the consequences of recent events. These simply made Hitler furious. He refused to hear the explanations given by the military attaché in Berlin, and he rejected the idea that he meet with the king and Badoglio, although he had just permitted a meeting to take place between the two foreign ministers—Guariglia and Ribbentrop—and Generals Ambrosio and Keitel. Since armored divisions were at the time heading toward Rome, the Italian government feared an attack upon the city, even an invasion of the Vatican. This last eventuality was not to be excluded in light of the threats made over the past years by the Germans. Among the rumors circulating, it was said that the Holy Father would be removed to Munich. Italian troops, more numerous than the Germans yet lacking heavy weapons and tanks, were totally unfit to resist the Germans. In Rome itself there were sixty thousand well-armed German soldiers. Under such conditions the Italian government was forced to continue the war. The Holy See tried to be most prudent, but the situation was painful and dangerous.

During this time the governments in London and in Washington responded to Archbishops Godfrey and Cicognani, who had inquired under what conditions would the Allies recognize Rome as an open city. The answer was that the matter was being discussed. And while cables crossed between the Vatican and the two capitals, Rome was bombed a second time, on 13 August. The neighborhood surrounding the train station was hit. Immediately after the alert had been lifted, Pius XII went to the places affected by this disaster. The scene was as emotional as on the previous 19 July. A day later the Italian government officially declared Rome to be an open city. Cardinal Maglione immediately informed the delegate in Washington of this. But Cicognani's reply, cabled the evening of 16 August, was far from encouraging. Italian assertions meant nothing, and they were even inspired by defiance, especially after statements that the war would continue side by side with Germany. "It is for this reason that the Allies seem to have decided to flatten Italy, to wear out the population, which is forced by destruction and slaughter to a complete surrender if this government delays in solving the matter."

On 19 August another cable from Cicognani arrived. The American authorities were surprised to see the present Italian government continuing the policy of the past, and they were wondering why Italy had not immediately separated itself from Germany. The delegate wanted to be able to answer precisely the question of whether the Italian government was freely remaining as an ally of Germany or whether it was being forced to do so. The Secretariat of State hesitated. Although Monsignor Tardini believed that a response was necessary, Cardinal Maglione was less convinced. Pius XII, however, decided to respond. A cable sent on 21 August, drawn up in the Latin and the style of the Curia, gave the requested information:

> As to the doubt proposed by Your Excellency, concerning what they want to know here, we respond *negative* (= no) *ad primam partem* [= whether the apparent Italian cooperation was freely given], and *affirmative* (= yes) *ad secundam* [= is it forced?].

During this time the Quebec conference ended without making any decisions on the question of Rome; and despite the measures taken to demilitarize the city, measures the Secretariat of State brought to the knowledge of the apostolic delegates and the Allied diplomats, communications from Washington were always of a threatening nature.

AN ARMISTICE AND THE GERMAN OCCUPATION

The Badoglio government lost no time in contacting the Allies, but armistice negotiations dragged on and on. On 3 September an envoy from Badoglio, General Castellani, met with Eisenhower in Sicily and signed an armistice, which was to be made public the moment the Americans went ashore at Salerno. On 8 September at half past six in the evening Eisenhower announced over Algiers Radio "that the Italian government has unconditionally surrendered to the armed forces. Hostilities between the forces of the United Nations and those of Italy are ceasing immediately." About an hour later, at quarter to eight, Marshal Badoglio made the same announcement on Italian Radio. It was on this date, although the time of day cannot be determined, that a note from the Italian ambassador informed the Vatican's Secretariat of State as to what was occurring. The next morning the royal family and part of the government, including Badoglio, left Rome and went to Pescara in order to embark for Brindisi.

Ever since the fall of Mussolini, Hitler was expecting this to happen, and he already had Wehrmacht units deployed in Italy. On the morning of 10 September the troops of Marshal von Kesselring were just outside Rome. The cardinal secretary of state called in the German ambassador and requested that he ask Kesselring to show respect to Vatican City. Ambassador Weizsäcker replied that he had no contact with the marshal, but he promised to do everything possible to get in touch with him. At half past eleven in the morning a representative from the Italian general staff arrived to tell Monsignor Montini that the agreement reached with the German command not to have German troops enter Rome was not being observed and that a division of paratroopers was marching on the Via Aurelia toward the Vatican. The Italian troops, he added, were doing well, but they had undergone heavy losses and so it was doubtful whether they could continue on.

Finally, at quarter past four that afternoon Weizsäcker phoned to say that he had been unable to join Kesselring because the roads were blocked by the fighting and that Wehrmacht units were entering Rome; they were at the Coliseum and at St. Mary Major. By evening on 10 September the armed forces of the Reich were in control of the Eternal City.

The Vatican now found itself directly confronting the forces of the Reich, namely, its army, the Wehrmacht, and its state police, the Gestapo. On the other hand, it was enjoying much closer relations than in the past with the German ambassador, Ernst von Weizsäcker, who was the former secretary of state at Wilhemstrasse. From the time he arrived in Rome, Weizsäcker was determined that his policy would be to avoid any rupture between his government and the Holy See. Defining this approach as one of mutual noninterference

212

(Nichteinmischung), he made the Vatican understand that Hitler's reprisals against the pope's pronouncements, however completely ineffectual, could be violent beyond measure. As to Berlin, he made every effort to present the Holy See's position as being, if not favorable to Germany, at least broadminded and basically neutral.

Already on 9 September, the day before the German troops entered Rome, the ambassador came to the Secretariat of State seeking an explanation regarding reports circulated by the paper *Il popolo di Roma* that attributed an important role to the Holy See in concluding the armistice. Monsignor Montini assured him that a denial would appear that very night in *l'Osservatore Romano*. And indeed the Vatican newspaper, dated 10 September and yet appearing as early as nine the previous evening, printed on its first page:

> This morning *Il popolo di Roma* printed a long article on "the Vatican's political activity during the last days of the war." We are authorized to state that this information is totally fanciful.

On 20 September it was Cardinal Maglione who made a request of the Reich's ambassador: Weizsäcker was asked to take urgent action to stop the Germans from demanding six thousand Italian hostages for six German soldiers who were said to have been assassinated in a Roman hospital. The ambassador replied that "his general rule was to keep the Holy See out of such matters" since it could be dangerous to draw Berlin's attention to the Vatican at a time when the Allies were approaching Rome. He was attending to the matter of the hostages, but through the intermediary of friends, since he could obtain more this way than by speaking for the pope.

Cardinal Maglione, thinking of the six thousand young people who were in danger, concluded by expressing his confidence that Weizsäcker would do whatever he thought was most opportune. Moreover, the rumor that six Germans had been assassinated in a hospital proved false, and hostages were never demanded.

Next, London Radio used the occasion of guards being posted in St. Peter's Square, at the borders of Vatican City, to broadcast that the pope was being held hostage by the occupying power.

Furthermore, when Roosevelt stated in a press conference on 1 October that the Allied campaign in Italy was a crusade to free Rome, the Vatican, and the pope from Nazi domination, Ribbentrop told

213

Weizsäcker to request an audience with the pope. This was granted, and so on 9 October the ambassador presented Pius XII with a statement from his government denying the enemy propaganda and affirming that Germany had fully respected the sovereignty of the Vatican City; in return, the German government asked for an identical statement from the Holy See. Although the pope agreed in principle, he reserved to himself the time and the form of its publication. The terms of such a statement were discussed by the German ambassador and the cardinal secretary of state, and finally both agreed on a text that appeared in *l'Osservatore Romano* on 30 October. The notice began by denying the false information coming from Allied propaganda and made note of what the German ambassador had done. The announcement then stated that Vatican City had indeed been respected and that there was a desire to see in the embassy's action a commitment for the future.

THE JEWS IN OCCUPIED ROME

Meanwhile, Rome witnessed certain events that were far more serious than the stationing of guards around St. Peter's Square. The German occupation had naturally thrown into turmoil the Jewish community in Rome, but the Jews hesitated to flee abroad. On the contrary, this was the time when refugees from France were retreating into the city, where they believed they would be safer. Pius XII was immediately worried about the Italian Jews, henceforth in danger of falling into the hands of the Nazi police. A note of 17 September entitled *Measures Feared against the Jews of Italy* contained the pope's directives: "To study the question of deciding whether it would not be fitting to make a general recommendation to Germany's ambassador on behalf of the civilian population of every race, and especially on behalf of those who are more weak, women, the elderly, children, the lower class."

On 20 September the leaders of the Jewish community in Rome were summoned to the general headquarters of the SS by Lieutenant Colonel Herbert Kappler, who called on them to hand over, within twenty-four hours, some fifty kilos of gold. Failing to do so would result in the immediate deportation of all men from within the Jewish population of the city. The Jews were accustomed to this form of extortion. But despite desperate efforts, they could only come up with thirty-five kilos of gold. Rome's chief rabbi, Israel Zolli, appealed directly to

Pius XII who, in turn, ordered that everything necessary be done to supply the missing fifteen kilos. Documents on this incident are very few, but a memorandum from commendator Nogara, a special affairs delegate of the Holy See, reports that on 29 September Rabbi Zolli came and told him that the fifteen kilos were supplied by "Catholic communities." A Vatican contribution was no longer needed.

However, during the early days of October the Jews in Rome were looking toward convents as being places of refuge. On 1 October Monsignor Montini reported to the pope that a Jewish couple, somewhat elderly and in poor health, wanted to withdraw to the Oblate sisters on the Via Garibaldi on the Janiculum. Since these religious were willing to accept the wife but not the husband, the pope gave instructions that the sisters were to help him as well. Two weeks later when the Jews of Rome, finally recognizing that danger was imminent, left their homes and sought refuge with their friends, sympathizers, and especially with religious communities, the barriers of the canonical cloister were lifted, thus allowing men to enter the convents of women religious and also permitting women to enter the cloisters of male religious.

On the night of 15–16 October an SS group, brought to Rome a few days earlier for this purpose, began to hunt down the Jews house by house, with the help of lists prepared in advance. The victims of the raid, about a thousand in all, were brought together at the Military College on the Lungotevere; at the end of three days they were deprived of everything, brutalized, shut up in sealed railroad cars, and sent to Germany, never to be heard from again. The first information about the raid seems to have been brought to Pius XII by a young Italian princess, Enza Pignatelli-Aragona. Early in the morning she hurried to the Vatican, where she was escorted by the *maestro di camera* to a private audience with the pope.

Hardly had the Vatican learned of this when Cardinal Maglione called in the German ambassador and spoke to him as best he could in the name of humanity and Christian charity. The first reaction of this high official of the Reich, who in his heart was opposed to his government's policy, was a personal confession. "I always expect you to ask me, 'So why then are you staying in your position?'" "No," answered Maglione, "I simply tell you: Excellency, you have a soft and good heart. Try to save all these innocent ones. It is painful for the Holy Father, painful beyond measure, that in Rome itself and under the eyes of the father of us all so many people are made to suffer for the simple reason that they are members of a particular race." Then the ambassador asked the practical question: "What would the Holy See do if things were to continue like this?" Maglione's response: "The Holy See does not want to be forced to utter words of disapproval." Weizsäcker observed that up to the present the Holy See had been able to guide its bark through the rocks. Was it now necessary to risk everything at the time when the bark was arriving in port? The directives had come from on high. And he concluded: "May Your Eminence allow me not to make a report of this official conversation?" Cardinal Maglione agreed and emphasized that the Holy See had always taken pains not to give the German people the impression that the Vatican had done or wished to do the smallest thing against Germany during this terrible war. And so Germany must not force the Holy See to protest; but if the Vatican believed that protest was necessary, then the consequences would be left to divine Providence. And the cardinal concluded: "Your Excellency has informed me that he is attempting to do something for the unfortunate Jews. I thank him for this. As to the rest, I leave it to his judgment. If you believe it is more opportune not to mention our conversation, that's fine."

In spite of the confidence the Vatican placed in the intervention of the German ambassador, Pius XII wanted to reinforce it through unofficial means. On the very day of the raid a prelate of Austrian origin who was known for his attachment to the Great Reich, namely, Monsignor Aloys Hudal, rector of the national German church in Rome, had received a visit from Pius XII's nephew, Carlo Pacelli. After this meeting Hudal wrote to General Stahel, the military governor of Rome, and urged him to suspend all actions concerning the Jews. If the arrests were to continue, warned Hudal, the pope would issue a public protest at a time when Germany had every interest in avoiding this. General Stahel immediately sent Hudal's message to the competent authorities and to Himmler himself, who gave the order to suspend the arrests "out of consideration for the special character of Rome."

Meanwhile, Osborne, the English representative at the Vatican, was attributing the suspension of the Nazi roundup to an action taken by his colleague, Weizsäcker. As soon as the cardinal secretary of state "was informed of the arrests of the Jews in Rome, he called in the German ambassador and expressed some type of protest. The ambassador immediately intervened with the result that a good number [of Jews] were released." Osborne specifically told the Foreign Office that his information was strictly confidential since any kind of indiscretion would probably result in new persecutions. In any case, the raid terminated as abruptly as it began. The original plan was to seize all the Roman Jews, believed to number about eight thousand. And yet the roundup that occurred on 16 October was never repeated.

The departure of prisoners to places far from Rome did not stop the efforts employed on their behalf by their parents and by the Vatican. Once again use was made of Father Tacchi Venturi. On 26 October the Jesuit reported that the Jews of Rome were hoping at least to learn where their parents had gone. The next day Rabbi Panzieri, who was functioning as the chief rabbi, asked whether it were possible to send warm clothing to the refugees since winter was approaching. But on 1 November Senator Riccardo Motta told Monsignor Montini that when the Jews were arrested, he went to see General Stahel, who told him that he himself was not responsible for the actions of the police; and several days later the general also informed him that there was no hope: "These Jews will never return home." Nonetheless, Cardinal Maglione, sending an official note to the German embassy, requested information and inquired whether material assistance might be sent to the Jews who had been deported from Rome. On 15 November Weizsäcker let the cardinal know that he, Weizsäcker, could do little if anything, not even obtain information.

During the months that Rome was under German occupation, ecclesiastical establishments provided refuge to a number of individuals sought by the Germans, namely, political refugees, members of the state police who refused to serve the Fascist republic, Jews, and others who felt they were in danger. About a hundred of these found housing in the Vatican, their presence there being officially ignored. Others were in extraterritorial buildings adjacent to various basilicas: St. Mary Major, St. John Lateran, St. Paul outside the Walls. Still others were placed in less favored shelters to which the German embassy had granted letters of protection. Nonetheless, many of these refugees were the objects of Nazi action. During the night of 21–22 December three adjoining buildings—the Oriental Institute, the Russicum, and the Lombard College—were all broken into. Some Jews were arrested, one of them dying of a heart attack. During the night of 3–4 February the Fascist-republican police invaded the monastery of St. Paul outside the Walls, and it was no surprise that high officials, political refugees, and Jews were discovered there, some wearing the cowled robes used by monks. The Holy See strongly protested this violation of pontifical properties covered by diplomatic immunity. Several other incidents infringing upon the extraterritoriality of the Holy See's buildings in Rome also occurred, even though the Basilica of St. John Lateran and its adjacent buildings, located about a hundred meters from Colonel Kappler's headquarters on the Via Tasso, were never broken into: for several months they housed the whole National Committee of Liberation. Finally, the convents and religious institutes generally seemed to enjoy a mysterious immunity despite the paid informants or the Jews found hiding there.

The 16 October raid was directed against Italian Jews. Non-Italian Jews, recent arrivals in Rome, were not at that time bothered. Yet as weeks went on, their situation became perilous. They were helped by the Capuchin monk Père Marie-Benoît, who came to Rome during the last days of the Fascist regime. Using the international Capuchin College on the Via Sardegna as a base of operations, he directed a program of clandestine assistance by supplying refugees with identity papers. On 19 November an official informed the Secretariat of State that the Capuchin had been denounced as someone using the name and stamp of the Commissariat for Emigration and Colonization in order to produce identity cards. Most of the benefici-aries of these forged documents were Jews who together with Père Marie-Benoît would have been handed over to the Germans had the accusation been investigated. Concluding his conversation in the Vatican, the official agreed to hush up the affair "as long as the present situation regarding the Jews lasts." He likewise was suspending all action against the Capuchin, who had falsified the signature and seal of the commissariat.

SAVING ROME

This concern for individuals did not conceal the Vatican's con-cern for the safety of Rome itself. Each day the progress of the Allies in the south of the peninsula brought the line of battle closer to Rome. As early as 2 October 1943 Monsignor Tardini wrote that "the battle for Rome will begin." Consequently he set about preparing a verbal note for the sake of the two parties. With finishing touches by Cardinal Maglione, the note recalled that the Holy See had already intervened for the purpose of avoiding the destruction of Rome, both because of the city's artistic and historical value and because the city is the see of the Holy Father and the center of the Catholic world. Now that the war seemed to come closer and since the Italian government had declared Rome to be an open city, "the Holy See believes that it has the duty of renewing its most ardent entreaties to both parties in the conflict that every effort be made to avoid Rome becoming a battleground. This would cause incalculable damage to human and Christian civilization and bring about, both today and in the future, the reprobation of decent people everywhere." On 7 October the note was sent out by Cardinal Maglione: at noon to Ambassador Weizsäcker; at half past four to d'Arcy Osborne; and at quarter to five to Tittman. That very evening Weizsäcker sent the message, in German translation, on to Berlin.

But during the evening of 5 November an unidentified airplane dropped four bombs on Vatican City. No building was hit, but the bombs fell in the vicinity of the radio station, the palace of the governor, and a building housing some diplomats who were guests of the Holy See. To demands for identifying those responsible for the attack, both the Germans and the Allies replied by blaming one other, although each said that it was not possible to be absolutely certain in this regard. Now the diplomatic battle, begun in order to keep the Anglo-American bombers away from Rome, resumed so that the city would not become a battlefield. Nonetheless, the last months of 1943 and the first of 1944 passed without much change in the local situation.

Another concern of Pius XII throughout the German occupation of Rome was that of providing food and other supplies to the people, whose numbers were growing due to the influx of refugees from the provinces. Replenishing Rome encountered many difficulties; yet these could have been simplified by transporting provisions from northern ports like Genoa. Discussions between the Vatican and the Allies continued without results till 3 June when the latter finally declared that the provisioning of Rome was just an additional burden for the Germans, one that was not to be lightened.

The failure of the plan for maritime transportation was a disappointment for Pius XII, but he insisted that the Germans make a serious effort to replenish the city. On 26 February Count Galeazzi was received by General Westphal, the head of Field Marshal Kesselring's general staff. One of the questions discussed was that of provisioning Rome; Galeazzi insisted that this had to be done. General Westphal complained that voluntary cooperation by the Romans was unhappily in short supply, and he requested that the Holy Father use his influence to obtain it.

Meanwhile, Pius XII's interest in saving Rome intensified when on 23 January 1944 American army units landed at Nettuno, some sixty kilometers south of Rome. Three weeks later, on 15 February, Monte Casino became a target for the Allied bombers. Thanks to caves hallowed out of the rock, the loss of human life was limited, and yet by the evening of 16 February Monte Casino Abbey, the cradle of western monasticism, had become nothing more than a heap of ruins.

At the same time certain areas in the immediate outskirts of Rome were suffering almost continuous bombing. And so even before Pius XII knew of the abbey's destruction, at least as to its details, he had a cable prepared, which was to be sent to the apostolic delegate in Washington. The message, drafted by Monsignor Tardini, reviewed by Cardinal Maglione, and corrected by the pope himself, mentioned the bombing and the machine gunning of many areas close to Rome and made an urgent appeal to the U.S. president that the bombing cease. The message was sent on 17 February. Since the fate of Rome was being discussed in the House of Lords and in the Allied newspapers, the Holy See decided to win over public opinion. Dated 29 February, a circular letter was sent to the nuncios and apostolic delegates in Canada, Argentina, Chile, Brazil, Colombia, Portugal, and Ireland requesting them to persuade the Catholics of these countries as to the "sacred character of the Eternal City, the center of Catholicism and the see of the sovereign pontiff, and of the obligation of the warring parties to preserve the city's integrity."

Roosevelt's response was received the same day. The president confirmed "the ardent desire of the Allies to save the holy buildings and monuments of our common civilization." The military leaders had ordered that they not be destroyed; however, if the enemy entrenches itself in them, then they must be driven out. And so if the pope persuades the Germans to vacate Rome, then he at the same time will have ensured the immunity of the city.

Cardinal Maglione had a note, dated 11 March, sent to the German ambassador. The progress of military operations allowed it to be foreseen that one day soon Rome would become the center of the fighting: to spare Rome, a city which is "unique and incomparable in the political and cultural evolution of the human race and which has been the center and mother of Christian civilization for close to twenty centuries," would be an accomplishment for which Germany could take exceptional credit. The Secretariat of State nourished the hope that the German command would give the necessary orders so that Rome and its surrounding areas would in no event become a theater of military operations.

On 12 March Pius XII received in St. Peter's Square a very large crowd of people. His purpose was to bring some words of consolation to the thousands of people who had fled to what they thought was the protection of Rome, an open city. The English and the Americans had rejected the pope's request that air raids be suspended on this date, and when the day arrived, the sky was so covered with clouds that the bombers could not get off the ground. To the multitude gathered before him the pope repeated that Rome was a holy city, one whose cultural value and religious meaning required the respect of all, and he expressed the hope that no one would ever dare turn Rome into a battlefield and thus become responsible for an action "as little glorious from a military perspective as it is abominable in the eyes of God and of a humanity conscious of the highest and intangible spiritual and moral values."

On 14 March and 19 March bombs again fell on Rome, and this elicited new protests from Pius XII. In a cable sent to Washington Cardinal Maglione stressed that if the Americans intended, and rightly so, to spare the lives of their own soldiers, then they had to understand "the pope's reprobation and deep concern before the useless massacre of human lives."

But while the pope was intensifying his efforts to keep Rome and its inhabitants from suffering harm, a small Italian resistance group, called the GAPO (Group for Patriotic Action) and led by Roman Communists, hoped to incite a popular uprising in Rome. On 23 March at three in the afternoon a bomb exploded on the Via Rasella, a narrow street in the center of the city, as a German column was passing by; the blast killed thirty-two soldiers. From the Wehrmacht's high command and in Hitler's name, an order arrived to execute ten Italians for each German who died and to do so within twenty-four hours. Early in the afternoon of 24 March 335 Italians detained in various prisons—those condemned or under suspicion for political reasons, Jews, and others, none of whom having anything to do with the attack—were taken out of the city to the Ardeantine Caves, where they were executed by an SS squad commanded by Lieutenant-Colonel Herbert Kappler, the head of the SS police in Rome. Only the next day did the German-controlled press report the massacre of the hostages, ten hostages for each German. The documents that remain say nothing about any action taken by the Holy See, a step apparently prevented by the swiftness of the executions. The archives contain only a single piece relating to this incident, and it bears the date 24 March at quarter past ten. It is the note of a *minutante* to whom an official in Rome's city hall had communicated several details about the explosion on the Via Rasella and its victims. The informant concluded: "At present no one knows what measures will be taken in retaliation; one foresees that for each German killed, ten Italians will be shot." He did not seem to consider the possibility of so immediate a reaction.

Throughout the world—in England, the United States, Australia, and Spain—public opinion began to be aroused in favor of the Eternal City. Bishops and faithful alike asked their governments to intervene energetically with the belligerents so that the warring parties consider Rome "as an open city which should not be transformed into a battlefield," as the Spanish bishops told General Franco.

Did such support encourage the secretary of state to undertake a new diplomatic initiative? In any case, on 7 April he sent a message to Great Britain's legation, and two days later to the U.S. representative, informing them of what Weizsäcker told him about the German decision, namely, to remove from Rome every military target, including troop barracks and facilities for resupplying the army and for sending reinforcements to the front. And so an air raid on Rome would target only civilians.

At the same time Spain and Ireland were intervening in Berlin and Washington. The Berlin government repeated in a verbal note of 18 April that the Wehrmacht authorities had brought about a complete demilitarization of the city so that there would be no excuse for a murderous and destructive attack on Rome. Washington's response was more curt; nonetheless, the Americans indeed wanted to consider forming a neutral commission.

While telegrams, cables, and diplomatic notes were crossing one another, the Allied troops were moving to the north. Despite Monsignor Tardini's ironic reflections on their advance toward Rome—it was "more eternal than the Eternal City itself"—he understood that the decisive moment was approaching. On 27 May at quarter past eleven in the morning he had a long conversation with the Reich's ambassador. Speaking on behalf of the cardinal secretary of state and yet giving the conversation its own proper tone, Tardini recalled that at this very moment the fighting was approaching Rome. The Holy See had done everything in its power to prevent the city from becoming a battlefield; Churchill, in a speech to the House of Commons, had expressed his desire that Rome be spared the horrors of war, and the Holy See had told the Allies to take steps that this hope be realized. And now the Holy See was saying to the Germans: You have often declared your intention to respect Rome and your interest in its integrity; so now is the time for you to act accordingly. Besides, during the course of the withdrawal by the German troops, there was a fear of provocations, reprisals, and even destruction. The Holy See instructed its priests to urge calm upon their flocks; on the other hand, it was important that the retreating soldiers avoid every act of violence. The ambassador, Tardini said to Weizsäcker, should assist the Vatican "so that the Holy See itself can more easily, or at least with less difficulty," carry out the task it took upon itself, namely, working for peace and moderation.

On the evening of 31 May the Thirty-sixth American Division entered Velletri, sixty kilometers south of Rome. Without perhaps knowing all the details, Cardinal Maglione prepared on the same day another cable for the apostolic delegate in Washington: "The Holy See wishes to be sure that the military authorities, by using appropriate tactics, will avoid the terrible responsibility and the inexcusable crime of turning Rome into a battlefield; nonetheless, we believe that we must renew to this end our most ardent injunctions and requests." Pius XII crossed out of the draft the words "and the inexcusable crime." On 2 June two American regiments resumed their advance north of Velletri toward Monte Cavo and Rocca di Papa, while a third group was advancing toward the hills east of Lake Nemi. During this time the pope celebrated the feast of his patron, St. Eugene. In his response to the good wishes of the Sacred College, he had to mention the city of Rome, whose fate would be at stake in the hours to come. Speaking both to the ecclesiastics as well as to world opinion, Pius XII reintroduced the harsh condemnations that he had eliminated from the cable prepared by his secretary of state:

It is our hope that a spirit of justice and moderation will triumph over contrary considerations of apparent utility and of so-called military requirements, and that in every case and at all costs the city will be preserved from becoming a theater of war. This is why We do not hesitate to say again, with equal impartiality and with deliberate firmness, that whoever dares to strike Rome will stand guilty of matricide before the civilized world and in the eternal judgment of God.

The hopes of Pius XII did not end in disappointment. Although he failed to obtain any formal bilateral agreement, he did inspire both sides, as Weizsäcker wrote, with a type of reverential respect for Rome. During the evening of 2 June the Second and Sixth American Army Corps forced the Germans to fall back to a final line of resistance, and the latter were left with the choice of either defending Rome or evacuating it as soon as possible. The first option would have allowed Kesselring to gain some time, and yet in so doing he would have left behind a city in ruins. But he had received orders from Hitler to seek, by means of the Vatican, to join the Allies in taking steps to keep Rome outside the area of combat. Kesselring had his troops withdraw north of Rome, taking up a new line of defense, whereas the American command was occupied with capturing the bridges over the Tiber.

And so from the evening of 2 June till 4 June Rome witnessed a continuous passage of soldiers, tanks, trucks, and horses—it was an army in retreat. The Germans had requisitioned all means of transportation: from cars and taxis to oxcarts, all passing by under the eyes of the silent population. "The spectacle is distressing," noted Tardini, "for one sees the military as disgraced, demoralized, worn out...but it is also consoling since one sees the proud now being humiliated, the violent being destroyed."

THE ALLIES ENTER ROME

On the morning of 4 June the American troops were already in Rome's suburbs, where their advance came to an end with the loss of several tanks. But by quarter after seven in the evening elements of the Eighty-eighth American Division arrived at the Piazza Venezia. The morning of 5 June saw the Allied soldiers occupying the Eternal City.

At seven in the morning Pius XII appeared at the window of his apartment to bless the crowd that had already assembled in St. Peter's

Square; he did the same three hours later. At six in the evening the pope again appeared, this time in the central balcony of the basilica. The previous day, Sunday 4 June 1944, was the feast of the Holy Trinity, and it was to the Trinity that the pope referred in his address of thanksgiving:

> In a spirit of praise and adoration and with a heart full of thanks We raise Our mind and heart to the one and triune God, to the Father, to the Son, and to the Holy Spirit. It was on their solemn feast day, and with divine mercy inspiring both belligerent parties with considerations of peace and not of affliction, that the Eternal City was preserved from incommensurable danger.

Rome emerged from the Second World War almost intact. Weizsäcker, the German ambassador, viewed this as the culmination of the Holy See's efforts, and the Romans acclaimed Pius XII as the defender of the city.

CHAPTER 11

Events in France*

~·~

F RANCE, with its two zones, one under military occupation and
the other subject to the Vichy government yet strictly under
Berlin's watchful eye, continued to benefit from the presence of
an apostolic nuncio. Archbishop Valerio Valeri, accredited in 1936 to
the socialist government, followed the Reynaud government when,
faced with the German invasion, it withdrew to Bordeaux, where Valeri
announced on 17 June that the French government had requested
Germany and Italy for an armistice. Shortly afterward, in telegrams
sent on 22 June, 24 June, and 26 June, he informed the Vatican of the
doubts that accompanied the discussion and finally of the signing of
the armistice with Germany and Italy. As early as 24 June he spoke of
the departure of the government, now presided over by Marshal Pétain,
for Vichy. Soon Valeri himself was in this city, where he continued to
carry out his functions as apostolic nuncio.

One of Archbishop Valeri's first concerns was to request the
Vatican for financial resources to alleviate some unspecified miseries—we do not know their precise nature since all we have is
Cardinal Maglione's response. But soon France, both in its occupied
and nonoccupied zones, was experiencing serious difficulties in
replenishing its food supply. Due to the blockades and the interruption
of relations with its colonies, western Europe's food situation had
become a matter of grave concern. The Holy See did not await official
requests to take action, and a note from the French ambassador,
Wladimir d'Ormesson, shows that the Vatican had undertaken a first
step. The cardinal secretary of state informed the French ambassador
that the Holy See "was concerned about the terrible economic situation
afflicting the French people because of the lack of or the insufficiency
of food coming from the colonies or being imported as usual. And so

---

*Documentation for chapter 11: See *ADSS*, vols. 5, 8, 9, 10, and 11. Add: Charles
de Gaulle, *The Complete War Memories*, vol. 2, André Latreille, *De Gaulle, la libéra-
tion et l'Église catholique*, Paris: 1978.

the attention of His Excellency the Ambassador of Italy was drawn to this matter which could easily become a tragedy during the coming winter." Count d'Ormesson informed his government of Cardinal Maglione's message, and in a note dated 20 August he sent to the cardinal the deep gratitude of the head of state, Marshal Pétain, and of the foreign minister. But since the Holy See was preoccupied with reprovisioning the French population, it could easily be seen that recommendations that it be allowed to do so were necessary in both Italy and in Germany. "Nonetheless, the presumption is that England is the key to the problem. In fact, the British blockade is the principal obstacle to a partial resumption of the necessary reprovisioning." The French government would thus be grateful to the Holy See for drawing the attention of His Majesty's government to the urgency of this question, "on which the health and even the existence of millions of families depend."

The Vatican was eager to avail itself of this recommendation. But once the cardinal secretary of state made the first overtures to Sir Osborne, Great Britain's plenipotentiary minister, there was an objection which in future months would often be repeated in regard to other countries, namely, that England feared Germany would hoard for itself the food brought into France. At the end of November the Vatican received an official response. His Majesty's government greatly appreciated the motives behind the cardinal's appeal, but it considered itself bound to the policy resolutely expressed by the prime minister, in other words, the blockade must continue. "And since the purpose of this policy is to hasten the enemy's defeat, His Majesty's government believes that it serves the best interests of all who desire freedom and a future peace."

A VATICAN FLEET?

The question of reprovisioning again appeared in a report from the nuncio to France, but this time it concerned a proposal originating with the head of state. Its purpose was to ease the lack of food and medicine experienced not only in France but throughout Europe in general. On 7 March 1942 Archbishop Valeri was summoned by Marshal Pétain, who showed him two documents; these the nuncio included with his report. One was the draft of a letter from Pétain to the pope; the other was an explanatory note. In his letter Pétain suggested the creation of a Vatican fleet, and for this purpose he offered to send several ships that the pope could use. The objective here was "that this neutral fleet, under a flag that was venerated everywhere, would bring back from America the food and medicine so badly needed in Europe. It would give us great joy," added the marshal, "to place at the disposition of Your Holiness the vessels you would need to carry out this work of international charity."

In a note appended to the draft of the letter Pétain explained that he came up with this idea when he realized that only the Holy See, as a neutral and venerated state, could undertake such shipments without any of the warring parties daring to say no to the project. The marshal then gave the draft to the nuncio and asked whether it was opportune to send an official letter to Pius XII. Immediately the nuncio replied that such a gesture appeared very beautiful and was motivated by the most noble sentiments, and yet it also seemed unrealistic. Nevertheless, the nuncio wanted to refer the matter to his superiors before giving a definitive response.

Valeri's letter, dated 10 March, was in Monsignor Tardini's hands two weeks later. In sketching out the outlines of a response for use by a *minutante,* the head of the first section, who easily gave in to humor, wrote:

In the case [of a positive response] one could:

1. Announce a competition for the position of admiral.
2. Prepare an article for *OR* [*l'Osservatore Romano*]: "From the bark of St. Peter to the Vatican fleet."

Nonetheless, several days later Tardini got hold of himself and began to reflect more calmly. On 2 April he wrote: Ideally, the marshal's gesture would be a recognition of the great and very high esteem that today more than ever surrounds the Holy See and the sovereign pontiff. In receiving such a proposal the Holy See would have an opportunity to reaffirm the high principles of evangelical charity and to show that it is disposed to join undertakings of kindness. And if, as a start toward implementing the marshal's idea, medical supplies for children were received, then the pope's intervention would appear still more moving.

And so the official response, sent to the nuncio in Vichy over Cardinal Maglione's signature, was not as negative as were the initial reactions to the marshal's proposal. And to assist the nuncio in explaining to Pétain the obstacles his proposal would have to surmount, the secretary of state's letter spelled out a detailed account of the Holy See's efforts to assist Greece when this country was starving because of an unrelenting blockade. Here again we have a full page of the Holy See's charitable activity elsewhere, an activity that could now be recalled because of present events in France.

The nuncio first would assure the head of state that the Holy Father, who since the war began had always been involved in alleviating suffering, greatly appreciated the proposal as corresponding to the generous tradition of Catholic France. The nuncio then would tell the marshal of the pope's joy as he considered the proposition, and the esteem it showed for the Holy See's peacemaking mission in a world at war. But it was also necessary to remember the great difficulties that would be encountered in carrying out the idea. Nothing demonstrated this better than what occurred when the Vatican wanted to assist Greece at a time when that country was desperate.

FOOD FOR GREECE

In a note of 20 September 1941 addressed to the British minister at the Holy See, the Secretariat of State requested the English government to permit food to enter Greece, in particular to grant clearance to 350,000 tons of grain that had already been purchased by the Greek government. At the same time the Vatican contacted the occupying powers, who then guaranteed that the food would be distributed exclusively to the Greek population. Although Cardinal Maglione had assured both Sir Osborne and Mr. Tittmann that such guarantees had been given, London's response was negative. According to international law the occupying powers were responsible for providing food, and so the blockade would not be lifted for anyone, not even for Greece. The secretary of state privately repeated to Osborne and Tittmann his deep sorrow at the British position, this having the most painful consequences for the Greek people. And in a verbal note of 21 October the Secretariat of State insisted that, apart from questions of law, the English government "yield to the fact that if help does not arrive, these people will die from hunger, and so we are appealing to the humanitarian and Christian sentiments of the government." Meanwhile, the apostolic delegate in London was instructed to tell the

Foreign Office that Archbishop Roncalli, the apostolic delegate in Athens, had been requested by the civilian and religious representatives of the Greek people to go to Rome for the purpose of requesting the Holy Father's intervention. But on 11 November London replied that it appreciated the Holy See's concern for the Greeks, and yet it repeated "that any breach in the blockade would only provide England's enemies with a means for prolonging the war."

Nonetheless, the Secretariat of State sent a third note to the English government; it explained that the Holy See was only motivated by reasons of Christian charity, without regard to race, nationality, or religious affiliation, and it recalled the steps many countries had undertaken to obtain food for Greece. Cardinal Maglione enclosed a copy of this note with his letter to the nuncio so that the marshal might be better informed, in a confidential way, of the Holy See's charitable works.

At the end of January 1942 English Radio and then the press announced, without alluding to the Vatican's initiatives, that the government was considering the advisability of allowing a certain amount of food to be shipped to Greece. Finally, on 2 February Osborne sent Cardinal Maglione a cable from London communicating the decision taken by London and Washington to authorize, by way of exception, the shipment of eight thousand tons of grain to Greece.

"In light of this," concluded Cardinal Maglione's letter to Archbishop Valeri, "it is easy to imagine the difficulties the Holy See would encounter if it wanted to undertake an initiative of a type suggested by the magnanimity of the marshal." Perhaps there would be less of a problem if the project were limited to shipping food and medicine only to the children. The nuncio could use this information to explain the real situation to Marshall Pétain without dissuading him from sending the letter to the Holy Father if, all things considered, he judged it good, for the nuncio well understood that when it concerned works of charity, the Holy See never withdrew when confronted with difficulties and even unsuccessful ventures. Yet there were successes, for example, obtaining an exchange between England and Italy of seriously disabled prisoners of war.

At the end of the month the nuncio reported on how he was fulfilling his mission. In a meeting with Marshal Pétain, Archbishop Valeri expressed the pope's satisfaction with the marshal's proposal, while at the same time explaining its difficulties. Pétain completely understood and in the end decided not to send the letter in light of recent political events now standing in the way of any steps taken by the Holy See.

THE NUNCIO AND MARSHAL PÉTAIN

Meanwhile, within the strict limits permitted it by Berlin, the Vichy regime hardly had any opportunity to carry on important negotiations with the Holy See, and so the nuncio generally had plenty of time to devote to the church's internal affairs in France. Only occasionally did he send the Vatican a report on his meetings with the head of state and the various ministers. Something said by Marshal Pétain at the conclusion of a dinner for the diplomatic corps in September 1941 reveals much about the situation. The government's difficulties were great, remarked the marshal in a small group composed of the nuncio and the ambassadors of Brazil and Spain. The English were accusing Pétain of rowing toward Germany, and the Germans said he was rowing toward England. In reality, said Pétain, "I'm not rowing at all, I'm floating on my back." Several days later, on 26 September, the nuncio had an audience with the marshal and the conversation turned to military matters. The old soldier was impressed by the news of Wehrmacht successes in Russia, but he feared that the Germans, returning victorious, would propose a separate peace, a prelude to overturning alliances: "I hope," he told the nuncio, "that conditions will be such that I cannot accept." And at the same time he was leaning toward a compromised peace; otherwise, he thought, England will be crushed.

From Paris the nuncio received some news that showed how in these troubled times spirits were divided as to what the country should do. It was not in the least surprising to see the aged Cardinal Baudrillart, a renowned scholar now residing in Paris, yield to the mirages of an anti-Bolshevik campaign as he utilized pen and speech to encourage those who were enlisting on the side of the Germans to fight Bolshevik Russia. Such a position disturbed Cardinal Suhard, the archbishop of Paris, who wanted the pope himself to intervene with his, Suhard's, most esteemed colleague. But Rome remained silent. Finally Cardinal Baudrillart declared that the pope approved of what he was saying. Then the nuncio took it upon himself to write to the archbishop of Paris: "The nuncio believes it opportune that interviews should not be granted, both by reason of present circumstances and by reason of the various interpretations they can be given. *Archepiscopus utatur jure suo.* Namely, if the archbishop believes that his colleague's statements are inopportune, it is his duty to intervene as head of the diocese." In May Cardinal Baudrillart passed away. It was noticed that the occupation authorities did not attend the funeral services for this prince of the church. Some attributed this absence to a personal order from Hitler, who wanted to show his anger toward the Holy See, which in his eyes was guilty of stirring up Catholic opposition against him.

PROTESTS AGAINST RACIAL LAWS AND THE DEPORTATION

Meanwhile, Archbishop Valeri had to speak to the French head of state about more delicate questions than forming a fleet under the papal flag. France, with its northern zone occupied by the German army and its southern zone free though closely watched by Berlin, could not escape the movement unleashed against the Jews by the Nazi authorities.

At Vichy anti-Semitic legislation was passed on 2 June 1941, replacing a former law enacted in October 1940. Two months later Léon Bérard, the French ambassador to the Vatican, was instructed to inquire about any difficulties the Holy See might have concerning the June legislation. During a reception held in Vichy in the middle of September, Marshall Pétain greeted and spoke to the nuncio and told him that he had received a letter from Ambassador Bérard regarding the recent racial legislation. According to Bérard the Vatican "while finding some of the provisions to be harsh and somewhat inhumane, generally had no observations to make."

Perhaps by design, the marshal spoke with the nuncio in the presence of the ambassadors from Spain and Brazil. Valeri did not want to allow any room for misunderstanding: "I reacted quite vigorously," he wrote on 30 September, "especially because of those who were present. I stated that the Holy See had already expressed itself regarding racism, which is at the bottom of every measure taken against the Jews, and which, as a consequence, M. Bérard cannot explain in such a simplistic fashion." The marshal joked that perhaps the nuncio was not in complete agreement with his superiors, and he invited Valeri to come and see Bérard's report. The nuncio accepted the invitation and reported to Maglione on 30 September: "As you noted, the *pro memoria* is much more nuanced than the marshal would have had me believe." Valeri sent Pétain a short note in which he wrote: "I call attention to the grave harm that, from a religious perspective, can result from the legislation now in force, a legislation which in other respects is rather confused." Marshal Pétain answered that he himself deplored many of the provisions taken against the Jews, but that such measures were adopted under pressure from the occupying power.

Ambassador Bérard had indeed, as Cardinal Maglione noted, spoken about this with Monsignor Tardini and Monsignor Montini. Following these conversations Bérard wrote in a report dated 2 September 1941 that the Vatican had not expressed to him any criticism of the law of 2 June and that it had not received from France itself any complaint or request for intervention. The church has condemned racism as it has condemned Communism, but this does not necessarily mean that it condemns every particular provision enacted by a state pertaining to the Jews. He pointed out that the only provision of the law of 2 June that was contrary to the teaching of the church was the first article, which granted no change of legal status to a Jewish person who converted to Christianity. But, on the other hand, French law did not forbid marriages between Jews and non-Jews. In conclusion, he was told at the Vatican that there had been no protest regarding this regulation concerning the Jews. But it was necessary not to impose any regulation on marriages, and the precepts of justice and charity must be considered when applying the law.

No Vatican document arrived in Vichy to confirm Bérard's version of his exchange of views. In any case, a letter from Cardinal Maglione dated 30 October approved the answer the nuncio gave to Marshal Pétain, and the cardinal concluded by expressing the hope that the combined interventions of Cardinal Gerlier of Lyons and of the nuncio would result in mitigating the harshest measures of what was known as "the unfortunate law."

Less than a year later the situation took a far more serious turn. In a report of 29 July 1942 Valeri sent the Vatican a message saying that on the twentieth of that month the occupation authorities, with the cooperation of the French police, had arrested in Paris some twelve thousand Jews, who were temporarily being held in the Vélodrome d'Hiver. For the most part these were Poles and Czechs who were to be sent to the Ukraine. This measure shocked the Parisian people, who were already upset by the fact that Jews had to wear the star of David as well as by the rumor that children over two years old would be separated from their parents.

These events were discussed during a meeting of the French archbishops, who considered making a public protest, but they finally decided that the cardinal archbishop of Paris would send a letter to the head of state. This letter, which the nuncio judged to be rather weak, was in fact sent by Monsignor Chappoulie to the marshal, who promised to bring the matter before the council of ministers. At this meeting Laval stated that the occupation authorities were retracting the decision to separate children from their mothers.

In his next report, dated 7 August, Archbishop Valeri said that the arrests of foreign Jews were now being extended to the nonoccupied zone. Two trainloads of non-Aryans from the camp at Gurs and from other camps had departed the free zone for Germany. "Their final destination, however, is not yet known; the thinking is that they will be sent to Poland in the General Government or indeed to the Ukraine."

These arrangements, explained the nuncio, had provoked much discontent among the people, all the more so because of the fact that the sick and the elderly were being deported—in addition to all the others—proving that they were not being sent into forced labor. On 6 August a commission composed of Catholics and Protestants was received by Marshal Pétain; its purpose was to voice the pain Christians were experiencing. Father Arnou, a Jesuit who was part of the group, reported to the nuncio that the marshal appeared to be greatly troubled *(adoloratissimo)* by all that was happening, and Pétain himself and his closest associates had confirmed that these measures had been imposed by the Germans. Yet, on the other hand, Laval should have assumed responsibility for the whole matter. Finally, the delegation should have obtained a promise that a thousand internees, whose papers were in order, could leave France for America. Finally, Valeri sent Cardinal Maglione an account of what he had done:

> For my part, I have spoken quite frequently to the foreign minister, as Your Eminence well knows, and with the head of state himself about this very sad problem. Nor have I failed to remark on several occasion, especially to diplomats from South America, that it is not true that the Holy See has hidden behind silence in the face of such an inhumane persecution; indeed the Holy Father has often and very clearly alluded to and condemned this. On the other hand, the danger of new severities and of extending these

unduly harsh measures to other parts of Europe, for example, Italy and Hungary, can lead the Holy See to prudent waiting and wise reserve.

In a letter dated 24 August Valeri related a conversation he had two days earlier with the president of the council. The Jews, said Laval, were a danger for France. The nuncio retorted that it was not the detainees in the concentration camps who were a threat to France. The discussion was useless, wrote Valeri, and all that he could obtain were some concessions in particular cases. Laval pretended that Hitler had decided to collect all the Jews into one area because he had learned that anti-German propaganda was increasing among them.

Three days later Monsignor Pacini, a counselor at the nunciature, wrote in place of the nuncio who was ill. Laval had called in a secretary from the nunciature to give him a message that was to be sent to Cardinal Maglione. During the audience the minister read to the secretary a letter sent by the archbishop of Toulouse to all his parish priests. This letter, to be read to the faithful on the following Sunday, 23 August, denounced the measures taken against the Jews. Laval was angry at the archbishop, Jules Saliège, since he anticipated that the English would give much publicity to the letter in radio broadcasts and in the press. Furthermore, the government would look favorably on the archbishop's retirement. Laval also repeated his decision to have the police and the administration cooperate in the deportations, namely, by sending all non-French Jews to Germany. Even those who had found refuge in religious houses would be taken. Their final destination would be Poland where the Germans, said Laval, were thinking about creating "a type of mother house [!]."

THE BISHOPS RESPOND

During the following weeks a series of initiatives took place in France to save what could be saved. On 31 August the vicar general of Fribourg in Switzerland sent the nuncio in that country a plan for assisting the Jews in France. The Laval government, he explained, submissive to what the Germans wanted, was returning the Jews who had come to France from Germany and central Europe. Within the past days some twenty thousand had departed. The vicar general's plan had nothing to do with the adults since this would be absolutely futile; rather, it was to do something for the children under sixteen years of age, whose number was estimated to be from three to five thousand. Thought was given to sending them to the United States or to South America and, while awaiting permission for them to enter, to placing them in Portugal. At the same time it was suggested that the Holy See instruct its nuncios in Portugal, Brazil, Uruguay, Argentina, Venezuela, and Chile to have the bishops prepare public opinion for such an eventuality. As a matter of fact, this proposal was simply unrealistic, although a good number of these children found shelter in French families or institutions.

In a telegram of 5 September Monsignor Pacini kept Cardinal Maglione informed regarding a letter written by the cardinal archbishop of Lyons against the government's anti-Semitic legislation, and three days later Pacini gave specifics in a detailed report. The archbishop of Lyons, Cardinal Gerlier, and the bishop of Montauban, Pierre Théas, each had a letter read in the churches of his diocese against the persecution of the Jews. There was much talk about these letters, with some circles attacking them as a scheme that endangered the government's work of restoring the nation.

Meanwhile, the Jewish children continued to be the focus of the Holy See's attention. On 17 September Maglione telegraphed the nuncio in France to request information on what was happening to them. Monsignor Paulo Bertoli, the Vatican's chargé d'affaires in Port au Prince, sent a message that General Trujillo, president of San Domingo, was offering his country's hospitality to thirty-five hundred Jewish children.

Several days later Monsignor Pacini had further information on the letter written by the bishop of Montauban. It was much stronger than the two preceding letters of Cardinal Gerlier and Bishop Saliège, so much so that it was said that the bishop had been arrested, which is untrue. But the government radio was attacking all who were opposed to its measures, and the Holy See was likewise called to task because of the protests attributed to the nuncio.

Finally, on 24 September Monsignor Pacini telegraphed to Cardinal Maglione a response to the cardinal's request for information on the fate of the Jewish children: "The Jewish children remaining in France have been gathered in special centers and entrusted to various Israelite associations. Other organizations are cooperating in this assistance."

On 9 October Archbishop Valeri once again wrote; in the same envelope he enclosed an issue of the weekly *Je suis partout,* which carried a sketch of Cardinal Gerlier in a posture of protecting the Jews; on its second page was a violent attack on the archbishop of Rouen, Pierre Petit de Julleville. As to the latter, the nuncio had learned that the occupation authorities wanted him to publish in his *Semaine religieuse de Rouen* an article entitled "Measures Taken by Paul IV against the Jews." As a result, the archbishop suspended his religious weekly. Finally, Valeri remarked that the press had recently stressed the measures the papal states had taken against the Jews down through the centuries. He anticipated making a strong protest to the president of the council as soon as his health allowed. But on 22 October Valeri sent another letter informing the Vatican that the deportation seemed to have stopped; now the urgent problem was the sending of workers to Germany. Enclosed in the envelope was a copy of the *Semaine religieuse de Rouen* containing the statement imposed by the Germans and followed by a notice that the publication of the next issue of the paper was being postponed sine die.

Restricting oneself to the information Valeri supplied the Vatican regarding his own activity, it does not seem that the Holy See's representative played much of a role in this suspension. And yet several days earlier the apostolic delegate in the South African state of Orange informed the Vatican on 11 October 1942 that "fifty-nine delegates from the Jewish community had taken notice of, with esteem, the vigorous opposition of the Holy See to the extradition of Jewish refugees in France." In addition to the attacks of the Nazi-controlled press against the nuncio, the testimony of this South African Israelite community leads us to believe that Archbishop Valeri also took steps concerning which he preferred to observe the greatest discretion. Prudent ambassadors have few illusions as to the secrets guaranteed by diplomatic codes and pouches.

THE JEWS IN VITTEL

Somewhat later a Jewish organization in the United States took up the cause of a group, of Jews who were interned in France, and this

237

set Vatican diplomacy into action. On 27 December 1943 Archbishop Cicognani informed his superiors by radio that representatives of the Orthodox Union of Rabbis of the United States and Canada had come to plead the cause of several thousand Polish Jews interned in a camp at Vittel in France and now threatened with deportation, since the government of Paraguay had withdrawn its recognition of the passports delivered by Paraguay's consuls. Four days later the nuncio to Switzerland, Archbishop Bernardini, drew up a report on these Jews:

> Months ago these poor people, who had been interned in German camps, obtained the passports of numerous countries in Central and South America by paying enormous sums of money—and this certainly does not honor the Christian consciences of the consuls involved. But with these passports they were not given their freedom; rather, they were transported to France or elsewhere and treated rather humanely. But just recently, and I do not know why, these passports were withdrawn, and the protecting power, in many cases this being Spain, has suspended its protection. These Jews are now in imminent danger of being massacred.

Upon receiving Cicognani's cable, Maglione instructed the nuncio in Madrid to intervene with the Spanish government, the protective power of Paraguayan interests. It was at least necessary to obtain a delay in order to clarify the matter with Paraguay. The following day the papal representative in Anunció was told to ask for information on this subject.

Almost immediately he reported that the Paraguayan government had decided to recognize the controversial passports. But the problem went beyond Paraguay and its diplomacy. Other South American republics were interested in the matter, and they tended to be more difficult. Haiti's position was stated on 27 January by Monsignor Bertoli, the chargé d'affaires, who explained that the Haitian authorities had voided the naturalization of many people because of the illegal way they had obtained this status. "It is, in fact, known that many counsels and officials of the Haitian legation have distributed or rather sold certificates of naturalization to foreigners, and especially to Jews." As a result a law was passed a year later, stripping away Haitian citizenship from those who had not carried out certain formalities and who had not as yet reached Haitian soil. The multiplication of illegal passports was harming the government. For example, in Rome itself a Jewish refugee had fraudulently obtained a passport, and he was suspected of engaging in espionage in France and Switzerland on behalf of Germany. Haiti's foreign minister said that out of all the Polish Jews holding Haitian passports, only two could be confirmed, the others having lost their naturalization. At any rate, said the minister, the Germans seemed not to recognize Haitian passports, and no hope existed for those holding them.

On 14 January 1944 Archbishop Bernardini in Switzerland again reported that the International Committee of the Red Cross was considering an appeal to its own government in Berne, but it wanted to know whether the Holy See was going to do anything on its own account. Cardinal Maglione made the notation: "We have already cabled Paraguay. So what are we now to do?" Meanwhile, on 24 January the cardinal secretary of state sent identical instructions to most of the Latin American countries interested in the question. Paraguay, Chile, Bolivia, Costa Rica, and Nicaragua responded affirmatively, namely, that they would continue to recognize these papers even if they had been obtained in an irregular fashion. Other countries, including Brazil and Uruguay gave evasive responses. And still others completely refused to recognize the passports, namely, Peru, Cuba, Guatemala, Haiti, and El Salvador.

Berlin's policy at this time was not clear. It is a fact that the question of passports, whether valid or invalid, was in the hands of the German authorities. Did Berlin want to have good relations with Latin America even though some of these countries had declared war on the Reich? Should Spain's intervention as a protecting power be taken into account? During these months the Spanish government, profiting from its position of providing war materials, also intervened on behalf of the Sephardic Jews of the eastern Mediterranean, who were descendants of the Jews expelled from Spain in the sixteenth century. Were the Jews at Vittel being held as hostages with a view to a future exchange with Germans interned in Latin America?

The alarm raised at the end of 1943 seemed to have passed when, in March, the danger reappeared. On 7 March the delegate in Washington cabled that a group of Jews was requesting an intervention with the Swiss government. On March 30 Bernardini, who had been informed of this, telegraphed his superiors that an intervention was necessary not with the Swiss government but with that of Spain. To ward off deportation, the Spanish representatives in Berlin and in

Vichy, on the basis of negotiations in progress, should insist on an exchange between the Vittel Jews and German civilians. The nuncio in Madrid, whom the Secretariat of State had informed of all this, telegraphed on 12 April that the German government was not accepting Spanish intervention on behalf of Jews other than the Sephardic Jews. "Nonetheless," continued Gaetano Cicognani, "concerning the Jews in Vittel, this government will take opportune steps in view of exchanging them with German civilians interned in America."

Finally, some officials of the U.S. government became involved in the question of the Vittel Jews. On 18 April the delegate in Washington reported that "certain officials and representatives of Jewish associations had assured him that the U.S. government was ready to assist these Jews once they were set free, namely, if they were allowed to leave France. The Holy See was asked to intervene either directly or by means of Spain and Switzerland.

But on 26 April Bernardini reported in a telegram that the influence of the protecting powers (Spain and Switzerland) was insufficient and ineffectual. The Jews in question had already been transported from the camp at Vittel to a camp at Drancy. The Holy See was asked by someone, whom the nuncio did not name, to take action in order to impede any further deportation into Germany.

The effort continued, and now for the first time the War Refugee Board entered the scene. On 16 May it turned to Archbishop Cicognani with a new proposal. It said that the recognition of these passports did not mean that those holding them would necessarily emigrate to the countries that had issued these documents. Once the internees had escaped German hands, the United States would take care of them. The Board wanted the Vatican to intervene in Madrid on behalf of those Jews, said to have been 238 in number, who were transferred from Vittel to an unknown destination. First, they had to be returned to Vittel. On 20 May this information was sent to Madrid with the requested appeal. But in writing to the nuncio, Cardinal Maglione was under no illusion: "I do not hide the difficulty of obtaining what is being requested; nonetheless, I ask Your Excellency to consider whether it is possible to do something more here." The landing of the Allies in France on 6 June ended the Vatican's correspondence regarding the Jews from Vittel. Henceforth the Germans had other things to worry about in France.

THE LAST DAYS OF THE VICHY GOVERNMENT

The landing on the Normandy beaches was followed by the Allies rapidly advancing into French territory; on 25 August the armored divisions of General Leclerc entered Paris. Soon afterward the government of General de Gaulle was installed in the newly captured capital. But it was not long before the year 1944 posed new problems concerning the relationship between the Holy See and France.

Meanwhile, Archbishop Valeri continued to keep the Vatican appraised of the French situation. Earlier in 1944, on 5 January, he informed his superiors that Berlin's new representative had arrived in Vichy, namely, Cecil von Renthe-Fink, who immediately removed from office half a dozen ministers. From this point on, the nuncio believed, the policy of collaboration had seen its day, and the Germans wanted to be in a position to remove Marshal Pétain at any moment, for example, in case of an Allied invasion. Perhaps Pétain could retire of his own accord, though it was somewhat late for that, remarked the nuncio, who also noted that having a papal representative in Vichy assured the head of state the loyalty, at least partial, of a certain number of Catholics and members of the hierarchy. But on the other hand, continued the nuncio, there was the "violent and unanimous opposition of the country against the head of the government," Pierre Laval. After this last observation it is easily understood why the nuncio was in no hurry to support proposals that would have encouraged the president of the council to take a hand in church affairs.

Using the occasion of two requests presented to the government—one from the Christian Brothers asking for official recognition of their congregation, and another from the episcopacy, which was seeking an increase of state aid to private schools—Laval responded by placing on the table the question of episcopal nominations. Legal recognition of the Brothers was encountering difficulty in the state council, where Louis Canet, one of the advisors, was requiring that, as a condition for such recognition, the French pronunciation of Latin be followed in schools. Laval, in turn, was willing to defend Canet's position for as long as he, namely, Laval, was excluded from naming bishops. Marshal Pétain, appointing himself spokesman for the council's president, asked Monsignor Chappoulie if candidates for the episcopacy could not be nominated by a commission whose members would be Pétain himself, Laval, the cardinal archbishop of Paris, and the nuncio. To tell the truth,

Laval had never broached this subject with Valeri, who had indeed decided to answer that he did not believe the Holy See "at a time like the present wanted to change its principles in a matter that was so delicate."

Archbishop Valeri also informed the Secretariat of State about the way Marshal Pétain dealt with the occupying power. On 19 April the nuncio reported that the head of state had to insert in a message to the nation a phrase praising Germany, which was saving European civilization by fighting Bolshevism. A second message was ready in case the Allies had already landed. Several days later Valeri related that the marshal had gone to Paris on 25 April to participate in the funeral rites for the victims of the bombing of La Chapelle. This was the first time, noted the nuncio, that the head of state crossed over the demarcation line, and many members of the government, who themselves very frequently stayed in Paris, would have liked to see the marshal remain there. But he had already returned to Vichy by 27 April.

On Thursday 4 May a rumor spread that Marshal Pétain would be invited to take up residence at the chateau de Voisins, located about ten kilometers from Rambouillet. The occupation authorities feared that in the case of an Allied landing a sudden paratrooper raid would seize the marshal, and consequently they were already thinking about moving him. This time talk about a departure was serious, and the nuncio received confirmation of it from the foreign minister, Charles Antoine Rochat. The following day, Saturday, the nuncio was requested, confidentially, to tell the ambassadors of Spain and Turkey not to leave Vichy on the following Sunday. Awaiting an order to the contrary, Valeri did nothing about this. But on Saturday, about six in the evening, he was officially advised that on the next day the head of state would receive him at quarter past ten in the morning, since the marshal's departure was scheduled for one in the afternoon. Valeri, realizing that only he was being invited, went to the Hotel du Parc. The marshal appeared rather disturbed; in the presence of Charles Rochat, the foreign minister, and Jean Tracou, the director of the civilian cabinet, he read three documents: a message to the French representatives abroad specifying that the removal of the head of state did not imply any essential change in the situation; a press release; and, finally, a statement to be read to Cecil von Renthe-Fink, Germany's ambassador at Vichy, who was expected to arrive at quarter past eleven. In this statement the head of state said that he was coerced into going to Voisins. "In view of the desire expressed to him and by reason of circumstances, the marshal will be transported to the Parisian area, but the government's legal seat remains in Vichy, and the marshal will return from Voisins as soon as the reasons behind his removal no longer exist." After the nuncio received a copy of this statement, the conversation went on in a familiar way while awaiting the German minister's arrival. The marshal apologized to the Holy See's representative for not having been able to assist at mass on this Sunday, and he asked whether all the weekday masses he heard in the past at college might make up for this. Adding that he remembered some hymns to the Virgin, he began to sing one of them very softly. And when Rochat made a gesture as if trying to stand, Pétain asked him whether there were nails on his chair. Then he inquired whether Laval would be present for the meeting with Renthe-Fink. When Rochat responded negatively, the marshal turned to the nuncio: "Perhaps he would not be happy to hear something bad said of his friends, the Germans." At the appointed hour, quarter past eleven, Renthe-Fink arrived, and the nuncio departed. Valeri concluded his report of 9 May by relating some details about the trip taken by Pétain, who was acclaimed all along the route, especially at Orleans, where the feast of Joan of Arc was being celebrated. In concluding, the nuncio wondered whether Pétain was still free and whether the heads of the diplomatic missions could visit him.

The marshal's stay at Voisins was of short duration. As early as 26 May the Germans, fearing an Allied landing in the north of France, decided to return him to Vichy. Pétain was in Lyons on 6 June, when the Allies landed in Normandy, and after an absence of little more than a month he returned to his accustomed place of residence.

In the unrest that followed D Day some priests and bishops from Montauban, Agen, and Clermont, as well as Monsignor Bruno de Solages, the rector of the Institut Catholique of Toulouse, were arrested. On 20 June Cardinal Maglione telegraphed the nuncio with instructions that he work energetically to obtain their release. At the same time he advised him that "it seemed opportune to take a temporary leave in Switzerland." Saying he was ready to comply, Valeri also remarked that the Swiss minister was staying in Vichy. Having received this response, on 2 July Pius XII gave a counter order: "All things considered, it is fitting that Your Excellency postpone his leave." And so the nuncio remained at his post. He believed that in the present situation the best thing for France would be an understanding between Pétain and de Gaulle, and he knew one thing that the government did not know, namely, that Marshal Pétain was somewhat disposed to this, but he strongly doubted that General de Gaulle was of the same mind. In any case, he asked whether the Holy See could encourage such a reconciliation. His letter, dated 10 July, only arrived at the Vatican in October, and at that time Marshal Pétain was in Sigmaringen.

But the occupying power had taken precautions. On 17 August the nuncio was informed that the Germans wanted to move the head of state and the diplomatic corps to the east, and he lost no time in informing the Vatican of this "eventual unspeakable act of violence." In such a case the marshal would evidently be a prisoner, and the diplomats could only remain there or head over to Switzerland. Yet on 17 August, in the afternoon, the marshal received an ultimatum to leave Vichy and go to the east. Despite Pétain's protests, Renthe-Fink fixed the departure for 19 August at seven in the morning. Notified of this on the afternoon of 18 August, the nuncio immediately went to the foreign ministry where he and the Swiss ambassador were invited to see the marshal, who was in the midst of telling two Germans (Renthe-Fink and General von Neubronn) that he was not leaving of his own free will and that he was not able to exercise his authority outside Vichy. The Germans left, and the nuncio and the Swiss minister understood that the departure would not be delayed; consequently they decided to return the next day, in the morning, to the Hotel du Parc.

Despite the efforts of his associates, Marshal Pétain had to leave the following morning, 19 August. To show that he was only yielding to force, he had the hotel's entrances closed, although he had his personal guards relinquish their weapons. Several minutes before seven in the morning ten SS troopers forced their way in; Neubronn entered and directed the marshal to prepare to leave. The latter requested one more hour to arrange his affairs, and just before getting into the car, a little after eight, he gave the nuncio the text of his "Declaration to the Head of the Great German State." Before leaving, Archbishop Valeri also received a copy of the speech that Marshal Pétain had prepared for the French people.

Now that the Vichy government had ceased to exist, the nuncio questioned the opportuneness of remaining in Vichy. Through the nuncio in Berne he informed the Vatican that it seemed he should leave in Vichy a counselor and a secretary from the nunciature in order to ensure a liaison with the episcopacy, and he suggested that another diplomat, acting at least as an observer, be assigned to the provisional government that would be installed in Paris. The telegram arrived in the Vatican on 29 August at noon; that same day Tardini responded: "It is fitting that V. Exc. Rev. go to Paris as the Holy See's official representative to the provisional government, just as Minister Guérin is that government's official representative to the Holy See."

This was not the first time that the question of relations with the new government was raised with the Vatican. Shortly after his installation in Algiers on 4 May 1943, General Giraud wrote Cardinal Maglione and expressed his desire to send a representative to the pope, or at least a representative to an apostolic nuncio in a neutral country. Maglione answered by instructing Archbishop Leynaud of Algiers to act as a liaison between Algiers and the Vatican. But General Giraud soon withdrew from the French Committee for National Liberation, over which General de Gaulle alone presided. Toward the end of the year, on 17 November 1943, the commissioner in charge of foreign affairs, René Massigli, wrote to Archbishop Leynaud that the committee was nourishing "the most ardent desire of establishing direct relations with the Holy See as soon as the situation in Rome allows it." This happened when the Allied soldiers, including those of General Juin, entered the city.

THE GOVERNMENT OF GENERAL DE GAULLE

It was during the evening of 4 June that the Allied army occupied Rome. The next morning at half past eight Cardinal Tisserant arrived at the Secretariat of State and gave Monsignor Tardini a letter from General de Gaulle to Pope Pius XII.

The message, bearing the letterhead *"Le général de Gaulle,"* had been handwritten on 29 May in Algiers.

Most Holy Father:

Placed at the head of the French Republic's provisional government, I am happy to bring Your Holiness assurances of our people's filial respect for and their attachment to the Apostolic See.

The trials endured by France for many years now, the suffering of each of its children, have been lessened by the witness of your fatherly affection. We foresee an end to the conflict.

245

But our sorrows could continue on after the conclusion of the combat if the moral, economic, and social upheavals resulting from this war do not find us ready to avoid all disorder, to work in a peace restored between people and between various social classes. And in accord with what you have taught us, we believe that the most underprivileged deserve our greatest care.

At this time the military operations of our armies are and will be carried out with all the respect that we bring to the memories of our Christian faith as well as to the religious, intellectual, and moral patrimony these memories represent. We expect that these operations, God permitting, will soon lead us to victory.

After alluding to the political situation in the capital, the general expressed his confidence in the future and promised:

As soon as the deliverance takes place, the spiritual interests of the French people will again find their primary position, one now endangered by the oppression of the enemy. We are resolved to save them, and we very much hope to do so while benefiting from the special kindness that Your Holiness indeed wishes to extend to France.

May Your Holiness deign to bless our undertakings as well as the faith of the French people whose witness I place at Your feet.

Two days later Monsignor Tardini made a note of the pope's instructions for preparing a response: "a very proper letter; it's something delicate and important."

In his letter dated 15 June Pius XII answered General de Gaulle:

It is with great pleasure that We acknowledge the personal message that you, dear son, have sent to Us under the date of 29 May and which Commander Panafieu has recently delivered to Us on your behalf.

The pope appreciated the acknowledgment given to his charitable works on behalf of the victims of the war, "among whose numbers are rightly placed those of France." He was also very aware of the general's intention not to damage any religious and artistic monuments that the armies might still encounter. He then spoke about his wishes for France:

> Each day we implore the Divine Mercy so that the terrible tragedy, which has already made victims of so many people, will soon end; and we particularly desire that France, which is so dear to us, may emerge from this sorrowful trial spiritually renewed, and that it may continue its journey through history as it follows the glorious footprints of the Christian traditions that once made it strong, great, and respected among nations.

> As you rightly observe, the end of the fighting will not be enough to restore to France the order and tranquility brought by a peace it so ardently desires. It cannot keep within itself the deadly germs of civil discord and social conflict. Doing so would have it lose all the fruit of the sacrifices imposed by this the harshest of wars. In addition, We fervently ask God to free your country from these evil troubles, to enlighten those who will lead it, and to have prevail in the hearts of all sentiments not of rancor and violence but of charity and fraternal reconciliation.

> It is with this prayer and with these heartfelt wishes that We send to you, dear son, our apostolic blessing, doing so in return for your filial homage and as a pledge of the choice graces which We call down from on high upon you and upon your country.

On 16 June Monsignor Tardini gave the letter to M. de Blesson, who was setting out for Algiers.

At the end of the month General de Gaulle was in Rome, going to the Vatican on 30 June. In his *War Memories* he gives an account of this meeting, which began at nine in the morning. The general seems to have been impressed by Pius XII's very personality:

> The Holy Father received me. Under the kindness of the welcome and the simplicity of the moment, I was grasped by how sensible and powerful was his thinking. Pius XII judges everything from a perspective that surpasses human beings, their undertakings and their quarrels. But he knows what these cost them and he immediately suffers with all. One feels that the supernatural burden that he alone carries in the world weighs down his soul, but that he bears it willingly, certain of the end, sure of the way. His reflections and information permit him to ignore nothing in the drama

now upsetting the universe. His lucid thought focuses on the consequences: the outbreak of ideologies identified with Communism and nationalism in a large part of the world. His inspiration reveals to him that only Christian faith, hope, and charity, even if they be submerged for a long time and everywhere, can overcome these ideologies. For him everything depends on the policy of the church, on what it does, on its language, on the way it is conducted. This is why the Pastor makes of that a domain reserved to himself personally and where he displays the gifts of authority, of influence, of the eloquence given him by God. Pious, compassionate, political—in the highest meaning these can assume—such does this pontiff and sovereign appear to me because of the respect that he inspires in me.

The pope and the general discussed the future of Europe, France, Germany, and Italy. Pius XII knew that France could play a large role in the world, but he feared that it would once again succumb to internal divisions. He trembled when thinking about the sufferings that would still overwhelm the German people; the Soviet invasion of Polish territories and of all central Europe filled him with anguish.

After leaving the papal audience the general went to see the secretary of state. He found Cardinal Maglione convinced that the Allies would be victorious and that the Vichy regime would disappear. Henceforth considering de Gaulle as head of the French government, the cardinal expressed hope that the change of governments would take place "without grave tremors, especially for the church in France." In reply, de Gaulle said that this was his government's intention "even though certain French ecclesiastical circles had shown toward him an attitude that would not make things easy for him in the future."

L'Osservatore Romano, on 30 June, mentioned the general audience in terms appropriate to the visit of a head of state:

> This morning at nine o'clock the Holy Father received in a private audience His Excellency General Charles de Gaulle, who then presented to His Holiness the senior officers of his staff. Afterwards, General de Gaulle paid a visit to His Eminence Cardinal Luigi Maglione, His Holiness' secretary of state, and then he went down into the Vatican Basilica [something required by protocol during visits by heads of state] to venerate the tomb of the prince of the apostles.

As a result of this visit Monsignor Tardini had to endure the complaints of the Vichy ambassador, Léon Bérard, who, noted the monsignor, "deplored the manner in which *l'Osservatore Romano* had announced de Gaulle's visit. It completely appeared as if this were the official visit of a head of state." Unable to deny this, Tardini placed the responsibility on the Vatican paper.

Several days later, on 4 July, Comte de Murville, the French delegate on the control commission for Italy, was received by Monsignor Tardini and told him that the Algiers committee intended to send to the Holy See an official representative and it would be Hubert Guérin, the former counselor at the French embassy in Italy, who was accepted. On 15 August Guérin spoke with Tardini about what occurred in Rabat, where a mass was celebrated for Philippe Henriot, the Vichy government's information minister, who had been assassinated in Paris. The parish priest who celebrated the mass had been arrested, and the bishop, strongly intervening on his behalf, threatened to excommunicate anyone who would put priests in prison. Guérin was requesting that an apostolic visitor be sent to Rabat, and he also spoke of Dakar's vicar apostolic and of a third bishop whom he wanted to receive an apostolic visit. With his customary wit Tardini responded to the French representative that "to begin by leading an attack on three bishops was...a bit too...Fascist.

THE NUNCIO RETURNS TO PARIS

On 26 August Pius XII received Guérin and told him that Archbishop Valeri had been instructed to go to Paris and to make contact with the new government, first unofficially and then officially. Guérin seemed satisfied, seeing here a first step toward the official recognition of his government, which was one of his primary objectives.

On 9 September Guérin explained to Monsignor Montini that he was hoping his duties would receive an official status. The substitute objected, telling him of the Holy See's general principle of only recognizing those governments whose existence depended on a juridical title and not on a war in progress. At any rate, the Vatican first had to contact the nunciature and likewise listen to the French bishops. By means of this condition Montini intended to warn the new government about any demands it might make in regard to the bishops, especially since Guérin was not afraid to restate his objections against the apostolic vicar in Rabat.

Meanwhile, on 25 September Archbishop Valeri, accompanied by Monsignor Pacini, the counselor at the nunciature, and by Monsignor Rocco, the secretary, left Vichy for Paris. The Spanish chargé d'affaires and the Irish minister traveled in the same convoy. Their trip required them to travel some 450 kilometers between Vichy and Paris. The following day the nuncio requested an audience with the general secretary at the Quai d'Orsay, where he was received toward five in the afternoon. The general secretary, Brugère, told Archbishop Valeri that he was being received as a private person since, without exception, the government would not recognize any of the diplomats who had been posted to Vichy. Brugère also alluded to some bishops who were to be removed. Valeri replied that he had nothing to find fault with in regard to the government's decision concerning himself, but he was surprised that he was being informed of the decision only after he had been invited to return to Paris. While Valeri was still in Vichy, the general counsel had in fact read to him a message from the ministry asking why the nuncio had not yet returned to Paris and which gave the order that means of transportation be placed at the archbishop's disposal. Likewise, the morning newspapers gave much space to the return of the diplomats to the capital. In conclusion, Valeri asked to see the foreign minister.

A telegram from the nuncio in Switzerland, which informed the secretary of state of the misfortune of the nuncio to France, was in Rome by 9 October, and it did not fail to arouse Tardini's verve. Requiring new credentials when the head of state changed was a matter to be studied. At any rate, for the time being Valeri was only the Holy See's unofficial representative and so he did not need credentials; sufficient was a message to be sent by Guérin, by Archbishop Valeri himself, or by the apostolic delegate in London to the French representative in that city.

On 13 October, through the nuncio in Berne, the Vatican received two more telegrams, several hours apart, from Valeri giving details as to the intentions of the government in Paris. The new regime did not want to recognize any mission head who had been accredited to the Vichy government, even if he had formerly been with the Third Republic, as was true for the nuncio and also the minister from Monaco. On the other hand, the government wished to discuss with the

Holy See the question of the episcopacy which, in its opinion, was the cause of very serious scandal.

The telegrams were immediately taken to the pope, who on the following day gave Tardini his response: Concerning the nuncio, one could complain of injustice but all that could be done was to recall him to Rome. "As to the bishops, on the other hand, no discussion was even possible since each was following his own conscience." Meanwhile, the pope believed that a little patience was necessary so that the government would have some time to change its mind.

On 14 October Archbishop Valeri was received by Georges Bidault, the foreign minister. Their conversation dealt with various topics—the government's desire to maintain good relations with the Holy See, missionary congregations, Catholic schools, bishops who were not equal to their task—and yet the nuncio expressed no strong feelings since he wanted the meeting to be something of a courtesy call. Ten days later, on 25 October, Valeri met with the political director of the ministry, Chauvel, who informed him that General de Gaulle had no problem giving him an audience, but that he was resolute in his decision of not allowing anyone who had been at Vichy to go on as dean of the diplomatic corps. Meanwhile, at Rome on 26 October Guérin, the French representative, said the same thing to Monsignor Montini, namely, that the French government would not recognize Archbishop Valeri as the Holy See's representative in Paris because he had carried out such functions with the Vichy government.

On 1 November the Secretariat of State received a telegram sent four days earlier by Valeri after his meetings with Bidault and with the secretary general at the Quai d'Orsay. Notwithstanding their refusal to receive him as nuncio, Valeri said he favored speedy recognition of the new government.

Since the quickest way of reaching Paris at the time seemed to be by way of London, the apostolic delegate in England was given the task of communicating to Ambassador Massigli the pope's official response. The Holy See noted that the French government in fact had no reason for reproaching the person of the nuncio, that it desired to maintain cordial relations with the Holy See, but that it was requiring the recall of Archbishop Valeri, who had been accredited in France since 1936, the only reason for this recall being Valeri's presence in Vichy. This demand, declared the Vatican's Secretariat of State, was contrary to international norms and customs, and especially as it concerns the Holy See. As a matter of fact, the Holy See has been accustomed to leaving its representatives in the countries where they find themselves, even when the deepest political reversals occur there. And so, for example, the Holy Father remained nuncio in Munich first during the royal government, and then under all subsequent governments, namely, the independent socialist, then the Communist, then the new government with a socialist majority, and finally the right wing republican government. No one ever thought of questioning his diplomatic status.

Finally, this was a troublesome precedent for the future and an action that was hardly amicable toward the Holy See.

This was repeated the next day to the French representative, Hubert Guérin, by Monsignor Tardini. Archbishop Valeri had been accredited with the Popular Front, and his presence at Vichy did not make him responsible for this government's policy, and from a practical viewpoint his knowledge of France as well as the confidence he enjoyed among the French hierarchy would facilitate his efforts toward healing the wounds of the war. As to recognizing de Gaulle's government, Tardini had no trouble in observing "that the French government is precisely engaged...in delaying its recognition of the Holy See; allowing the nuncio to remain at his post, recognizing him as the Holy See's representative would be the best means of facilitating the matter.... To have the nuncio return home is not the best way to request, or to offer an exchange for, recognition by the Holy See."

Tardini, even though he was sure he had won the argument, knew that if the French government did not want Archbishop Valeri, then the nuncio had to be recalled. A telegram signed by Tardini and inviting Valeri to return to Rome was sent on 4 November. The dispatch again told the nuncio that the new government's demand did not involve him personally, and it stressed that Guérin had been told that the provisional government's procedure was inimical toward the Holy See and that it contradicted international norms. Nonetheless, the Holy Father approved of the nuncio returning to Rome on leave, unless an easing of the situation could be foreseen.

As Valeri saw it, two tendencies existed within the government: one demanding his replacement, the other disposed to receive him. Valeri still wanted to wait in order to see which of the two would win the day. Nonetheless, he advised "that the Holy See's juridical recognition of the provisional government not be further delayed and that it should take place even if I have to return on leave." The other powers, except for Switzerland, which was prepared to do so, had already granted this recognition. But the foreign minister, thought Valeri, was unmovable regarding the principle of not recognizing as head of a delegation anyone who formerly was in Vichy. In particular, the minister did not want the dean of the diplomatic corps, who once had presented Marshal Pétain with the customary greetings in addresses required by protocol, to offer similar greetings to General de Gaulle. The nuncio nobly made the best of everything in a 19 November letter to Monsignor Tardini: "At a time so tragic and full of suffering for so many people and nations, how can I complain? Rather, I should thank the Lord for also allowing me to suffer, and I desire to do so with a joyful and tranquil heart as befits our sublime calling."

On 29 November Valeri's report arrived in Rome; it indicated the final positions of the French government. That very day a telegram confirmed to the nuncio in France previous instructions and requested him to take leave and have Monsignor Pacini remain as chargé d'affaires. Three days later the Secretariat of State sent out another message, to Buenos Aires, to inform Archbishop Giuseppe Fietta that the pope was appointing him nuncio to France. He was to leave immediately in order to reach Paris by 1 January so that he could carry out his functions as dean of the diplomatic corps. Two days later in a note sent to Guérin, who this time was called the "minister plenipotentiary," the Holy See declared that it "was officially recognizing the provisional government presided over by General de Gaulle."

ARCHBISHOP RONCALLI AS NUNCIO TO FRANCE

On the same day the Vatican received Archbishop Fietta's refusal. And so on the following day another telegram was sent, this time to Ankara: Pius XII was appointing as nuncio to France the apostolic delegate in Turkey, Archbishop Angelo Roncalli. Should he accept, Roncalli was to reply immediately, and in such a case he was to be ready to leave as soon as Paris agreed. On 13 December at ten in the morning Pius XII received the French minister Guérin and informed him that a nuncio had been approached to serve in France, but that he had not accepted for reasons of poor health, and that the pope then appointed an apostolic delegate to the post, whose reply was being awaited. Roncalli's acceptance arrived that very evening. The next day Tardini called in Guérin and asked him to request his government to approve Archbishop Angelo Roncalli. At this time General de Gaulle was in Moscow and would not return to Paris till 17 December. Four days later Guérin informed the Vatican that his government gave its agreement to Roncalli. Immediately a telegram went out from the Secretariat of State to Ankara; it enjoined the apostolic delegate to "get to Rome as quickly as possible."

The preceding day, in Paris, General de Gaulle met with Archbishop Valeri. The general assured the nuncio that he regretted his departure, "solely due to events that unfolded during these past years," and that the government knew perfectly well all that the nuncio had done for the good of the country. The nuncio replied that his feelings for France remained unchanged, and that, moreover, he had been busy with recognizing the new government. The general then spoke about Russia and about relations between France and Italy, two countries that legally were still at war with one another but were destined to be reconciled. After the meeting General de Gaulle conferred upon Archbishop Valeri the *grand croix* of the Legion of Honor.

On 23 December Valeri was in Rome, and in the afternoon of 28 December Roncalli arrived there. Not much time remained. The two addresses that the new nuncio would have to give shortly after his arrival in Paris, namely, the presentation of his credentials and the New Year's greeting, had been prepared at the Secretariat of State and reviewed by his predecessor. Their texts, after being looked over by the pope, were given to Roncalli on 29 December.

On 1 January 1945 the new nuncio, who had arrived in Paris two days previously, went to present his credentials to General de Gaulle. An hour later, as dean of the diplomatic corps, he extended to the general the customary New Year's Day greetings. And so normal relations between France and the Holy See were reestablished.

CHAPTER 12

The Last Days of the War*

~.~

WHILE RELATIONS between France and the Holy See were passing through turbulent times, the storm of war continued to
roar throughout the world even though the conflict's end
seemed to be approaching. But the war's conclusion and what would
follow was a matter of concern to the Holy See as well as to the ambassadors present in Rome and the Vatican. Throughout the war one of the
most active missions was that of Germany, especially since
Ambassador von Bergen had been replaced by the former secretary of
state at Wilhelmstrasse, Ernst von Weizsäcker, who consented to fill
the post in the hope of being able to work more effectively in the
Vatican than in Berlin to promote the cause of peace. And despite his
more modest diplomatic status as the U.S. president's personal representative, Myron Taylor held one of the foremost positions in the diplomatic corps at the Holy See during the last year of the war.
Furthermore, the Polish ambassador, Casimir Papée, never remaining
silent, always spoke up when it concerned the interests of his own
country.

The fortune of the armies had changed sides since the arrival of
the Anglo-Americans in North Africa, then in Italy, and a temporary
equilibrium of forces would have led to negotiations if the leaders of
the Reich had not been prisoners of an ideology with which their
adversaries refused any compromise. Weizsäcker, however, sought by
means of the Vatican to make contact with the Allies in the hope of
leading his country to peace through compromise. He also counted on
the problem of the Soviet threat as facilitating attempts to meet with
the pope and his counselors. Received by Cardinal Maglione on 6
January 1944, the German ambassador recalled the conference held in
Moscow in October 1943 by the Anglo-Americans and the Soviets, and

*Documentation for chapter 12: See *ADSS*, vol. 11. See also *FRUS* 1944, vol. 3;
FRUS 1945, vol. 1; *FRUS, The Conferences at Malta and Yalta*; Di Nolfo, *Vaticano e
Stati Uniti*.

he deplored the blindness of the former facing the dangers of a Russian victory: "If Germany, a bulwark against Bolshevism, should fall, all Europe will become Communist." The cardinal replied: "What a misfortune that Germany, with its antireligious policy, has stirred up such serious concerns."

The following week, on 14 January, Weizsäcker sent Monsignor Montini a response to a series of particular questions, and he returned to his favorite theme of the danger from the east. This time he spoke of the Communist threat hanging over Germany; this year, 1944, Germany had to decide between the east and the west, with many thinking that it would be advantageous to choose the east "with consequences for all civilization that each person can foresee." The Holy See could have a notable influence in warding off this danger by showing that it was favorably inclined toward the sanest element in Germany.

Returning to these questions six weeks later with Monsignor Tardini, Weizsäcker stressed that the impossibility of making peace with the Anglo-Saxons could possibly throw Germany into the hands of the Russians and consequently into Communism. Tardini recognized that it would be difficult for the Reich to come to terms with the western powers. But, he objected, would the Russians offer better conditions for peace? Weizsäcker pretended that they would and, to prevent any danger of this happening, England had to show that it was European, namely, it first had to stop supplying material to the Soviet Union.

At the end of March the ambassador had an opportunity to develop this viewpoint in a meeting with Monsignor Giuseppe Di Meglio, who spent many years at the Berlin nunciature and was now attached to the first section of the Secretariat of State. After complaining about the ecclesiastics in the Curia, most of whom were openly sympathetic toward England and who desired a German defeat, and of the clergy in northern Italy, who were giving at least moral support to the actions of the partisans against the German troops, Weizsäcker confided his desire to return to active policy making in order to have a direct role in bringing about peace. The Holy See, he said, should persuade the Allies and especially the English that it was in their interests to conclude a peace with Germany so as to have a common barrier against Bolshevism. Di Meglio reminded the ambassador of the Vatican's efforts in 1939 to avert the danger of war. Weizsäcker, then secretary of state in the foreign ministry in Berlin, was aware of such efforts. The meeting ended by discussing the eventuality of a German transition government and the likelihood of Weizsäcker being a member of it.

On 26 April the Reich's ambassador again found himself with Cardinal Maglione, who on the previous evening had received Di Meglio's report. The German representative asked the cardinal whether he thought that the Allies, and especially the English, were now ready to negotiate with the current German government. Maglione's response was that he had no indication of a change in this regard. He knew that Berlin had recently sounded out the Allies and that the latter remained firm in their positions. The diplomat denied that this had occurred, but he gloomily concluded: "The present German government does not want to negotiate with the Russians, and it cannot negotiate with the English since, as it seems to me, the latter do not wish to do so."

UNCONDITIONAL SURRENDER

During these conversations on Europe's future, the Allied armies were approaching Rome, and, as a result, protecting the city was now given priority among the concerns of the Holy See. Once again on 2 June, in an address on the feast of St. Eugene, Pius XII took up the defense of Rome in an especially energetic way. Yet in the same speech the pope touched on the general problem of peace, and he protested against the idea of a peace dictated by the spirit of vengeance, which places the adversary before the dilemma of either complete victory or complete destruction. Such an attitude can only prolong the war, even among those whom realistic considerations dispose to seek a reasonable peace. This alternative, explained the pope who appeared to have foreseen the final obstinacy of the Third Reich's leaders, brings about among the losers the courage of despair: "Those who are animated by such a sentiment move forward as if in a hypnotic dream through the chasms of unspeakable sacrifices and also force others to a destructive and bloody struggle." In all clarity, the pope was here taking a position against the unconditional surrender that the Allies had decided to impose on Germany, and the address did not meet with general approval in the United States. Whereas the Catholic press understood the pope's concern for Rome together with his ardent desire for a universal peace based on justice and charity, other newspapers close to the government had reservations and criticisms.

Not all the Allies were totally convinced that Roosevelt's formula of "unconditional surrender" had merit. Stalin, in Tehran on 28 November 1943, had called into question the principle of unconditional surrender. In his opinion the formula left unclarified the conditions of surrender and this would only unite the German people, whereas drafting precise terms, as harsh as they might be, of surrender and telling the German people what they would have to accept would hasten the end of hostilities. Churchill, although admitting the principle of unconditional surrender, had often said that there was no need to keep repeating the slogan. On 1 June 1944, the day before Pius XII's address, an interdepartmental meeting took place in the British Foreign Office to discuss both the feelers that had been sent out among the German military circles hostile to the Nazi regime as well as some of the responses to them that could be turned into conditions for peace. But no practical resolution was taken to mitigate or make precise the principle of unconditional surrender.

Archbishop Spellman of New York maintained that the formula of unconditional surrender would cause people to believe that the goal of the Allies was Germany's complete destruction, and he decided to talk to Roosevelt about this. The president did not hide his displeasure with the pope's address of 2 June. The archbishop noted that the Allies wanted to eliminate Nazism but not to exterminate the German people and that it would be helpful if this distinction were clearly expressed. The idea pleased Roosevelt, who promised to give it some thought. Archbishop Cicognani, the apostolic delegate, met with Cordell Hull, the secretary of state, who explained that the Allies wanted the complete destruction of Nazism but not of the German people.

TAYLOR RETURNS TO ROME

After 4 June the presence of the Allies in Rome facilitated contacts between the Vatican and the White House. On 14 June Roosevelt wrote to Pius XII to tell him that since the doors of freedom were now being opened for Rome, one of his first thoughts was to send back as soon as possible his personal representative, Myron Taylor. Without any delay Taylor complied with the wishes of Roosevelt and Pius XII; he arrived in Rome on 19 June and two days later was received by the pope.

The representative's audience with Pius XII lasted an hour and a quarter and was followed by an hour's meeting with the cardinal secretary of state. Pius XII expressed his joy that Rome and its monuments had suffered no damage, and he also inquired about the president's health. Taylor alluded to the June 2 address as he stressed "at length that the destruction of the German army and its unconditional surrender remained the policy of our government." In response, Pius XII made a distinction between the German people, the German army, and the Nazi regime. A hardworking people of sixty or seventy million souls could become a respected member of the international community once it demonstrated that it had rejected the policy of aggression and conquest. On the other hand, the pope had concerns about the religious situation in Russia and about the fate of a Poland exposed to Russian ambitions. In light of Taylor's first audience on 21 June, Pius XII had the Secretariat of State prepare a memorandum with one of its pages being devoted to Soviet policy: "The Holy See is greatly concerned with the Soviet government's war objectives. Its intention to occupy the Baltic countries, a part of Poland, and the Balkans does not agree with the Atlantic Charter and could seriously compromise the cause of peace." The Holy See simply could not hope that the present Russian government would tolerate missionary work or even allow the Catholic religion to be free and respected in the territories over which it was extending its control. Both the pope and Taylor agreed to return to these problems the following week.

The White House wanted to convince itself as well as the Vatican that good relations were possible between the Soviet Union and free people. On 23 June Robert Murphy, at that time a member of the Political Committee for Italy, visited Monsignor Tardini. Toward the end of the conversation, which mostly centered on Italy's economic conditions, Murphy told the monsignor that he had a colleague in Rome, A. Bogomolov, who was the Soviet representative and who had often shown interest in relations between his government and the Catholic Church. Once, when Murphy confronted him with the antireligious persecution unleashed by the Soviets, the Russian replied: "These things belong to the past." Bogomolov also expressed a desire to make contact with the Vatican. Monsignor Tardini replied that in no way had Communism changed, and that religious liberty was no more assured in Russia today than it had been in the past. Murphy stressed that Bogomolov wanted at least to visit the museums and the Sistine Chapel; perhaps this could be the first step. Tardini retorted that everyone can visit museums, and that galleries and pictures have nothing to do with diplomatic contacts.

Taylor had two further audiences with the pope, one on 29 June and the other on 12 July. He reaffirmed the principle of unconditional surrender and the necessity of eliminating Hitler and his cohorts and of destroying the Nazi party. On 12 July Taylor again spoke with Pius XII regarding the Russian problem. Upon leaving the audience he unexpectedly paid a visit to Monsignor Tardini and made a statement that Tardini summed up under three headings: (1) The United States desires the sincere collaboration of all people, once Germany has come..."to unconditional surrender...." The American agreed at once. (2) Such sincere collaboration presumes that Russia will have a role in all this—it cannot be otherwise. (3) Russia is presently invading Poland and Germany, countries with large Catholic populations. The church should thus facilitate Russia's collaboration with a pacified Europe; and for its part the United States will do everything possible to ensure that Russia is obliged to respect religious liberty. Tardini responded that he too was hoping for a sincere collaboration among people, even though he could hardly see how unconditional surrender would lead to this; surely peace in Europe was not possible without Russia, but in his opinion it was doubtful whether Russia would respond to American hopes.

Following his meetings with the highest authorities in the Vatican, Taylor wrote to Roosevelt on 17 July:

> My primary efforts are directed as follows: first, to convince the pope and the Vatican authorities that the German army has to surrender unconditionally; second, to convince them that cooperation with Russia is essential to the interests of victory and to permanent world peace; third, to assure them that it is necessary to create as soon as possible an international organization whose purpose would be to solve the problems of war and to guarantee future peace.

On 19 July Taylor sent Pius XII a memorandum on the points discussed during the preceding audiences and in particular on the issues that Communism's expansion into Europe were posing for the Catholic Church. What could be expected from Soviet policy in Poland and in territories inhabited by a population whose majority was Catholic, territories that would soon be annexed to the Soviet Union? What could be anticipated from Stalin in matters of religion? The question was discussed in Washington between President Roosevelt, Cordell Hull, who was secretary of state, and some bishops. One idea was to invite the Russian government to issue a statement proclaiming complete liberty of religious instruction and freedom of worship in all Soviet territories. But Washington concluded that a further stage of discussions "would place the question of religious freedom on the agenda." Taylor did not hesitate to refer to an address by the Communist leader Togliatti, who had just stated that the obstacles hindering a common action on the part of Catholics and Communists were henceforth overcome. Furthermore, Taylor's memorandum again returned to the subject of unconditional surrender: "Granted the Germans cannot win the war; so the more promptly the army surrenders, not only will human lives and goods be spared, but all the sooner will the process begin of leading the German people and the whole world to political stability and economic improvement."

As a response to this memorandum, Pius XII had another prepared by one of Monsignor Tardini's customary collaborators, namely, Monsignor A. Samoré, who the previous year had drafted the letter sent to Ribbentrop on the Polish situation. Samoré compared the known facts with the promises Roosevelt wished to believe. The religious situation in the Soviet Union shows no signs of improving. Antireligious legislation is still in force. Members of the Catholic clergy still living in Russia have not been given their freedom, nor have they been permitted to exercise their ministry. In addition, priests who were deported from Poland have not been set free, and there is no news about E. Profittlich, the apostolic administrator in Estonia. True enough, since December 1940 atheistic propaganda has been suspended, but this is easily explained by the present situation. When *Collier's* magazine printed that about eighteen hundred Catholic churches remained open in Russia, it gave completely false information. Everything leads one to believe that Russia is still disseminating the principles it has never renounced, principles that are basically materialistic and opposed to religion.

Relations with the White House, which nonetheless were characterized by reciprocal candor and confidence, did not hinder the Holy See from continuing to have correct diplomatic links with the Berlin government. When Rome became aware of the unsuccessful 20 July attack on Hitler, the Secretariat of State immediately prepared a telegram instructing the nuncio to "do what diplomatic decorum seems to require in such a case." Afterwards, the radio station in Florence announced that the Führer had received the diplomatic corps' congratulations, including that of the nuncio. Pius XII then instructed Orsenigo not to do any more. But, in fact, the ambassadors simply went to the chancellery, where they signed a book set out for this purpose; the Secretariat of State, informed of this, also told the nuncio not to take any further action.

On September 17 the Secretariat of State received from the nuncio in Madrid a telegram intended for the substitute, Monsignor Montini. Gaetano Cicognani's message was almost identical to that of Weizsäcker: It was urgent that an understanding be reached between the Anglo-Saxons and the Germans if Europe was not to be invaded by the Russians. The latter must have submitted proposals to the Reich: Russia's frontiers previous to 1939 would be recognized, and once an agreement was reached, Russia and Germany would ally themselves with Japan. The German government would reject these proposals since it preferred to come to a direct understanding with the Allies who had to leave Germany's hands open to oppose Russia. On the other hand, if the Allies would continue to demand surrender, then the Reich would be forced to reach an accord with Russia. Furthermore, the German leaders would recognize their errors toward the Holy See and would be disposed to rectify them.

The very next day a telegram, composed by Pius XII himself, told the nuncio that despite little hope of success the Holy See would take action.

On the morning of 21 September the pope received President Roosevelt's representative. Faithful to the promise sent to Madrid, Pius XII related to Taylor the substance of Cicognani's telegram as coming from a source considered to be trustworthy.

At the same time the nuncio to Switzerland requested instructions regarding a message sent by Archbishop Roncalli in Turkey. Roncalli had been asked by a certain individual, who was German and "absolutely trustworthy," to see that Ribbentrop would receive a confidential message. This person, worthy of confidence yet not identified, was visited on 14 September by an American, someone known by the Reich's foreign minister. The American explained that Germany's political and military situation had considerably worsened. The German responded that the morale of the Wehrmacht soldiers far exceeded one's imagination and that the decisive battle had not as yet begun because the Reich's best troops, having new and terrible weapons, were concentrated in Germany behind the most modern and strongest of fortifications. But the American replied that not even the highest morale of the German troops could compensate for the inferiority of their material: "For example," he said, "our superiority in the air is so great that your air force can no longer be counted as a serious adversary." He then invited the Germans to end the war before their country was completely destroyed. The German retorted that the conditions promised the Reich were such that all it could do was to engage in a struggle to the death; nonetheless, he would convey to his government all the advice given him. The American concluded: "Using a special code I'm always ready to cable any German proposal to my friend Roosevelt." The telegram was signed "Marmara."

Tardini's reply to the nuncio in Berne said that the Holy See was not directly interested in this matter, but there was no difficulty in having the message from Ankara transmitted through the Berne nunciature to Berlin, where it would be brought to Ribbentrop's attention.

Amid these anxieties and concerns Vatican diplomacy suffered a terrible loss. On 22 August Cardinal Maglione, the secretary of state, died of a heart attack in Casoria, his native city, where he had gone for a period of rest. During the last year of the war and for the remainder of his pontificate the pope was his own secretary of state.

Meanwhile, weeks and months passed without the war's conclusion being in sight. German troops were certainly retreating on all fronts: in France, where Leclerc's division liberated Paris on 25 August; in Poland, where the Russians stood at the doors of Warsaw. But how much time would it take to overcome Germany which, as Hitler boasted, was a stormproof stronghold?

CONCERN FOR PRISONERS

In autumn 1944, when the German troops were beginning, especially in the east, to destroy what they were unable to carry away, the Allies feared that the Nazis, in their fanaticism, would massacre their hostages and even all foreigners found within Germany. No doubt this fear was inspired by what was initially known about the fate of the Jews. But it also appeared that the Nazi leaders had made a decision to lead their own people to annihilation. Such preoccupation increased with news that the concentration camps, including those at Auschwitz and Brzezinka, were being closed. The other camps, nearer the Russian border, had been taken by the Red Army, and journalists had already visited what remained of the camp at Maidanek, located close to Lublin. Much later it was learned that orders had been given to destroy the gas chambers and the whole Auschwitz-Birkenau camp. In fact, the occupants were not massacred on the spot but were immediately moved, often under murderous conditions, to Bergen-Belsen, close to Hanover.

This alarming information seems to have originated with the Polish government in London, which used firsthand sources. The Vatican received news of this on 25 September from Casimir Papée, the Polish ambassador to the Holy See. The following day the nuncio in Berlin was instructed to take whatever action he deemed to be most effective. This time the Secretariat of State did not require that he first verify the truth of the information; it simply informed the nuncio that the Vatican had been informed "that the German authorities were preparing to massacre prisoners in the Oswiecim concentration camp." Among these prisoners arrested for political offenses were forty-five thousand Poles, a majority, but also Italians and others. Several days later the apostolic delegate in Washington reported that a group of Jewish representatives had requested that the pope appeal to the German government and the German people "as the only way to save the lives of Jews and, in particular, the forty-five thousand Jews and Christians of Polish, French, and Czech nationality interned at Oswiecim and in imminent danger of death." Later on, Cicognani completed his cable by mentioning, in addition to the camp at Birkenau-Näuss, the labor camps in Lithuania.

Ambassador Papée sent his information in a memorandum presented to Monsignor Tardini on 4 October: the occupants of Polish camps, he said, were doomed to extermination. Oswiecim was the principal object of his misgiving, with sixteen thousand men and thirty-nine thousand women being in danger of death. According to Papée the camp commandant, like those of other camps, was prepared to kill all the detainees within a very short period of time, and he was only waiting for a written order before starting the executions. Once again, on 12 October, Papée told Monsignor Montini that a plan of extermination was in place for civilian camps like Oswiecim and

Brzezinka, its purpose being to eradicate all traces of previous atrocities. Men and women in the tens of thousands would be massacred and their bodies burned. The monstrosity of the crime, concluded Papée, should not be a reason for disbelief. The Allies, for their part, took this information seriously, and on 10 October Washington and London published statements threatening the Germans with exemplary punishments if the predicted massacres should occur. Archbishop Bernardini telegraphed from Berne on 18 October: "The situation of the deportees in Germany, already lamentable, could, with events moving quickly, become tragic and end in a massacre." Was this cry of alarm justified or was it inspired by Allied propaganda? The Holy See itself never received any direct information on the murderous intentions attributed to the Nazi leaders, but the Vatican knew from experience that they would not shrink from perpetrating any atrocity.

Even the nuncio in Berlin, Archbishop Orsenigo, while reporting reassuring statements that he had received from Wilhelmstrasse, could not discard the possibility that the Gestapo had received special orders. In his report of 13 October he explained that the German foreign minister had assured him that such rumors were the result of enemy propaganda; moreover, the camps in question had been recently visited by the International Red Cross. Yet Orsenigo commented: "While acknowledging the sincerity of the foreign minister, it cannot be excluded that the unduly famous SS units may have secretly received different orders." Replying on 19 October, Tardini, with irony, requested that Orsenigo find out the precise date when the Red Cross had visited these camps. There are always, he said, complaints relative to the camps in Lithuania, to the camp at Birkenau, and in regard to the Poles seized and taken away after the battle of Warsaw.

In response to a new protest from Orsenigo, Wilhelmstrasse's answer was that the Poles taken prisoner after the battle of Warsaw were probably those removed before the uprising and sent to the camp at Sagan, where they were visited by the YMCA (Young Men's Christian Association). On 14 November the Secretariat of State sent a new verbal note to the Reich's ambassador: The assurances given the nuncio by the foreign minister were a basis for once again insisting on the humane treatment of prisoners. Regarding the alarming rumors of an impending massacre, the note continued in the same style: "As to rumors being recently spread about as to the fate, according to plans prepared beforehand, of the prisoners and the internees of certain races and nationalities, the Holy See has noted with satisfaction the statement made in this respect to the apostolic nuncio by the Reich's foreign minister." Yet this sentence was omitted from the abbreviated version of the note that the German ambassador wrote up and sent to his government.

This concern, which was not completely baseless, was aroused afresh in the last months of the war. On 25 January 1945 Monsignor Tardini, alerted by Papée, sent Archbishop Orsenigo some instructions, which he repeated on 3 March:

> Numerous appeals, all urgent and worthy of consideration, come to the Holy See calling for steps to be taken with the competent authorities so that something can be done to protect prisoners, deportees, internees, foreign workers residing in Germany, regarding both their treatment and their very lives.
>
> Widespread talk about the massacre of a thousand Italian officers in Poland has created great indignation in Italy and a strong reaction abroad.
>
> May Your Excellency see whether it is possible to take effective measures, which would be in the very interest of the German people.

Monsignor Tardini had few illusions about any steps the nuncio could take. On the draft of the telegram he wrote: "This [the telegram] was prepared in the 2nd [section of the Secretariat of State]. I do not know why it has my signature. I should not have put 'in the very interest of the German people' since it is useless to make such references."

However, was Archbishop Orsenigo, who by now had withdrawn to Eichstätt, still able to exert any influence? On 18 March the apostolic delegate in Washington reported that the Jews were terrified by rumors that all the Jews then in German hands, about six hundred thousand of them, were to be liquidated. Meanwhile a report arrived on the alleged massacre of a thousand Italian officers in the camp at Siedlice. Tardini in his responses of 27 March and 28 March explained the various steps the Holy See had taken to protect people; then, alluding to the rumors that Germans were being sent to work in Russia, he stressed that this was not the best way of ending the massacre of Jews and of Poles: "The eventual indiscriminate deportations of both prisoners and

German civilians for forced labor would seriously compromise such a humanitarian work by offering the German government a pretext for violent reprisals, and consequently the number of innocent victims would be increased."

CONDITIONS FOR ENDING THE WAR

Meanwhile, Myron Taylor, henceforth residing in Rome, continued his contacts with Pius XII in order to keep him informed of Allied policy in the conflict. On 28 November he explained to the pope the way he envisioned the war ending: (1) unconditional surrender, since complete defeat will cause the disappearance of the myth of the German army's invincibility; (2) Germany will surrender all its rights and powers in simple and short terms; (3) such an agreement will be signed by the German high command and by the government existing at that time. Then the Allies, having accepted the surrender, will focus their attention on maintaining administrative structures; these will be controlled by the Allied military government, which in turn must eradicate national-socialism. With time the military government will be replaced by a civilian one.

Since Myron Taylor left the pope a note recapitulating his ideas, Pius XII instructed that a response be prepared by Monsignor Tardini, who actually redacted two notes giving his own opinions, the first on the phrase "unconditional surrender," and the other on the question of relinquishing power to a foreign conqueror. He took these to the pope on 10 December. The expression "unconditional surrender," as Tardini saw it, did not exclude the conqueror from preparing certain conditions nor the vanquished from knowing these beforehand, but such a phrase was causing fear in those who would even surrender to harsher conditions. And after emphasizing the danger of throwing the loser into a resistance of despair, Tardini enclosed in a final dilemma his complete aversion to unconditional surrender: "The conditions that the conqueror has already prepared for the conquered are either just or unjust. In the first case there is no reason why such conditions cannot be known beforehand; in the second case it is impossible to see how the human conscience can approve them."

Then, examining the phrase about relinquishing power to the conqueror, Tardini noted that according to democratic principles those holding power govern through the will of the people; governments can resign but they cannot hand over power to others. Likewise, military authority does not have the right to yield civil power to a foreign nation, and in any case the conqueror always has the moral obligation not to exceed the limits of human and civil justice.

Pius XII looked at both notes and then told Tardini to send Taylor the second one as having been drawn up by an expert. However, he should hold back the other note because Taylor considered "unconditional surrender" an incontestable dogma regarding which he had not requested any advice from the Vatican.

The other camp, however, was not yet so disposed; till the end of 1944 the hierarchs of the Third Reich were sticking to their dreams of hitting back, assured by new weapons prepared by their engineers and of which the V1 and the V2 gave only a slight idea. It was not till after von Rundstedt's offensive was halted in the second half of December that it became evident that the Reich had its back to the wall and, on his own, Ribbentrop sent out agents in various directions. They were to sound out the Allies on conditions for peace. On 17 February Wilhelmstrasse sent Weizsäcker a sixteen-page telegram. The diplomat was hardly enthused by this, so little so that it took two days before he spoke about the message to Father Leiber, Pius XII's private secretary. The German explained that he considered the text to be mere gibberish. And although he had to communicate it, he did not want to be considered its author.

The next day, 20 February, at quarter past noon, the ambassador appeared before Monsignor Tardini with a file of some ten pages. This was, he explained, the telegram that his assistants had taken thirty-eight hours to decode, and its ideas were those of the "Berliners," not his own. The points contained in it were as follows: Germany will continue to fight till its adversaries understand that they cannot conquer it. Russia intends to bolshevize all Europe, and Stalin is already engaged in organizing a Bolshevist German army. The time is approaching when Germany will have to choose between the two camps, and if Germany goes with the east, then England and the United States will not escape the Bolshevist tide. For the rest, Germany and Japan intend to have a role in the concert of the great powers; all that Germany wants is to keep its population within its boundaries; it also desires freedom for all European countries. Nazism has been misunderstood. The Jewish question can be settled by an agreement among the nations;

and as regards the church, a favorable evolution can be seen in Nazism. Cooperation among the great powers is necessary to stop perpetual war. Unconditional surrender appears unacceptable to Germans since they believe that millions of their compatriots will be deported for purposes of forced labor.

With his customary caustic humor Monsignor Tardini told the German diplomat "that this immense telegram" reminded him of Hitler's interminable speeches which, in addition to some true elements contained any number of paradoxes and plain foolishness. The prelate recognized the seriousness of the dual threat, namely, Nazism and Communism—the double face of materialism. However, it seemed impossible that Churchill and Roosevelt would negotiate with the Nazis. Who would believe that Nazism was misunderstood and that it wanted all Europe to be free, Tardini asked. As to the Jews, how often did the Holy See speak out against acts of cruelty, all to no avail? Regarding the church, Nazism had prohibited Catholic schools, destroyed Catholic organizations, closed convents, hunted down religious, and prosecuted, imprisoned, and executed so many priests. And today an evolution favorable to the church can be seen. Weizsäcker then asked whether the Allies were ready to "pay something" if Hitler would be eliminated and if negotiations were begun. Tardini responded that the Allies would not easily abandon the formula of unconditional surrender.

That very evening Monsignor Tardini sent his notes of the meeting to Pius XII, who returned them the next day. The pope did not see what could be done, but he nonetheless promised to meet with the Reich's ambassador.

While awaiting the papal audience, Weizsäcker went back to see Tardini on the morning of 25 February. He repeated the dilemma: Either the Allies take note of the Communist danger and then ease up on their action against Germany so that the Germans can rout the Russians and through negotiations arrive at peace; or Germany becomes Communist, to the great detriment of England and the United States. In Tardini's eyes, the German request was somewhat suspicious; what he saw was not a diplomatic proposal but a military plan of the Germans, who were seeking to obtain a relaxation of Allied pressure in the west so that Germany could concentrate its forces in the east. Consequently the Holy See could not pursue this. Apparently the same conclusion was reached by Pius XII, to whom Tardini, the evening of the meeting, sent his notes.

Nonetheless, when Pius XII received Myron Taylor on 28 February, the pope asked whether there was any possibility, however remote, of speaking with the Germans to conclude the war. Taylor excluded any possibility of having a meeting or a conversation, endorsing "nothing other than unconditional surrender." The next day at half past nine in the morning the pope received the ambassador from the Reich and was able to confirm that "after testing the ground," he had ascertained that "no conversation or discussion with the United States and England was possible."

POLAND AND THE COMMUNISTS

Among the pope's concerns as to the future, those pertaining to Poland continued to hold a very special place, and in London the Polish government-in-exile revived its concerns through Archbishop Godfrey, who was the apostolic delegate to England and the chargé d'affaires ad interim for Poland.

At the end of January 1944 Godfrey held a meeting with the Polish foreign minister, Tadeusz Romer, who explained that much tension existed between his government and the Soviets; he hoped that the Americans would strongly support the Polish government in London. Yet he expressed his fear of seeing a puppet Communist government established in Poland, one supported by the Soviets. Meanwhile the Poles continued to have confidence in Churchill and in Roosevelt, since their country's future would be an opportunity to verify whether the United Nations would remain faithful to the principles of the Atlantic Charter.

At the same time two Polish bishops, Karol Radoński and Zygmunt Kaczyński, had written to Archbishop Godfrey, who in turn sent their message to the Vatican with his report of 1 February. If the Soviet government's demands were accepted, then 51 percent of Polish territory with twelve million souls, eight million of these being Catholic, would fall under Russian domination. Besides, Russia had decided to annex Estonia, Latvia, Lithuania, part of Finland, and part of Romania. In such a case the Catholic Church would be eliminated from all these areas because Molotov had stated that he would tolerate only the Orthodox Church placed under state control. In addition, the two bishops warned that Moscow would establish a puppet government in Poland. The cardinal secretary of state informed the apostolic delegate in Washington of the Polish concerns relating to the eastern borders of their country. The question in itself was political, but so closely was the matter linked to religious questions that it should be of interest to Catholics in the United States; furthermore it also concerned a whole section of Europe, exposed as it was to the Communist threat. The Holy See was counting on American Catholics to influence the U.S. government's decision, upon which Europe's fate depended, and especially the future of the church in Poland.

At the beginning of June 1944 the Polish prime minister, Stanislaus Mikołajczyk, traveled to Washington in order to discuss the question of the eastern frontiers of his country. According to the Soviets, a condition for establishing diplomatic relations with Poland would be to recognize the Curzon line as the border between the two countries, a border differing but little from the Ribbentrop-Molotov dividing line. The Polish prime minister explained to the State Department that his country wanted to enjoy good relations with the Soviet Union, but that after the terrible suffering it had endured, Poland could not at the conclusion of the war find itself with reduced territory. Besides, it was necessary to exclude all foreign interference in the internal government. The minister did not hide his bitterness as he stated that the three major powers had discussed his country's future without Poland's participation. Through the intermediary of the apostolic delegate in Washington, Mikołajczyk had a message sent to the pope. The Polish people long for their country's reconstruction and "to this end place unlimited confidence in the protection of Your Holiness." In a cable sent on 12 June Cardinal Maglione reminded Archbishop Cicognani of a message sent on 1 February and repeated his instructions to interest American Catholics in the Polish question.

On 28 July Pius XII received in a formal audience a representation from the Polish army. General Sosnkowski, commander in chief of the Polish army, and General Anders, commander of the Polish unit in Italy, led a contingent of five hundred of their soldiers. Also present were the nuncio, Filippo Cortesi, and Ambassador Papée. In moving words Pius XII reminded them of the audience of 30 September 1939 granted to Rome's Polish colony at a time when their country was undergoing defeat under the assaults of the Nazi and Soviet armies. After five years of struggle, hope was stronger than ever, and the sovereign pontiff vigorously reaffirmed the rights of Poland:

Your right is so certain that we firmly hope that all nations will be aware of their debt to Poland, which has been the theater and all too often the playing field of their conflicts. We also hope that those who hold in their hearts a spark of a truly human and Christian feeling will be anxious to demand for Poland its rightful place according to the principles of justice and true peace.

Following the pope's example, the Scottish bishops issued a statement in favor of Poland, something that did not please the British public, which was still enthusiastic about the exploits of the Red Army. And when a visit from Churchill was announced in Rome, the Secretariat of State prepared a note on all unresolved matters; among these the Polish question was prominent. The Holy See was concerned about the future of so many Catholics and would be happy to have, thanks to the good offices of England, some real news on the religious situation in the Soviet-occupied zone; and it wanted to send there an ecclesiastic who could evaluate matters. In a forty-five-minute audience that Churchill had with Pius XII on 23 August, the pope mentioned problems in regard to Germany, Poland, Russia, Communism, and Italy.

Two days later the Secretariat of State received from Washington a response, hardly reassuring, regarding the Polish situation. Cordell Hull, the U.S. secretary of state, being questioned by Archbishop Cicognani, explained that when Poland was under German domination, at least some news was obtained through the clandestine movements; but under the Russians all communications were broken. It seemed that the Soviets did not disturb religious practice west of the Curzon line, but "one simply does not know what is happening to the east."

WARSAW UNDER SIEGE

There was a lengthy delay before the Secretariat of State received, on 17 October, a report from Archbishop Godfrey who had met with the Polish foreign minister at the end of August. At that meeting Tadeusz Romer spoke especially about the tragic situation in Warsaw, where the partisans, encouraged by the proximity of Soviet troops and by radio appeals, rose up against the Germans. But the Russian forces, both those on land as well as in the air, did not intervene in the conflict; only the RAF, which for this purpose had to fly thousands of kilometers, tried to support the insurgents. Romer also returned to the question of borders, explaining that the Poles wanted to postpone this discussion till after the war since "a government-in-exile is in no position to bargain in regard to its country's frontiers." Finally, there was fear that the Communists would install a straw government in Warsaw.

Archbishop Godfrey's report had not as yet arrived at the Vatican when on 16 August Ambassador Papée handed a message from President Raczkiewicz. The Germans were now destroying the Polish capital and exterminating its inhabitants, and so the president was asking the pope to intervene on their behalf. Upon receiving this appeal on 18 August, Pius XII observed: "What more can I say on behalf of Poland?" Meanwhile the pope had ordered that a reply be prepared when, several days later, Papée returned to the Vatican with a new entreaty. This time it was the mothers of Warsaw who were calling upon the pope, the mothers "of these children who are fighting and who are destroying tanks with bottles of gasoline." They blamed the Russian army, which had encamped for three weeks at the gates of Warsaw without taking a step forward.

On 31 August the pope, responding at length to the president of the Polish republic, expressed his desire to neglect nothing to save so many threatened human lives. The following day the Secretariat of State passed on to Myron Taylor and to Osborne the appeal from the women of Warsaw, and he asked them to bring it to the attention of their governments. Obviously it was Washington and London that could do something. Meanwhile the Polish president's appeal to the pope and Pius XII's response to Raczkiewicz were published in *l'Osservatore Romano* on 14 September. Pius XII also wanted to say something during a general audience of 15 September to the two thousand Polish soldiers present there, together with English, French, and American troops. His words, as reported by the same paper, were words of esteem and sympathy: "Know that Our heart has bled over the ruins of your great capital, within whose walls has unfolded one of the most sorrowful of tragedies but also the most heroic events of your country's history."

But toward the end of the month the Wehrmacht unleashed an attack prepared for by a terrible artillery bombardment. It reduced Warsaw's very center to ruins. And after sixty-three days of fighting, which the German commander did not hesitate to call heroic, General Bor's soldiers had to surrender on the morning of 2 October. On 15

November Pius XII again received the Poles from Rome; once more he publicly praised the heroism of Warsaw's defenders and proclaimed Poland's right to be recognized by all: "Once the dizzy storm of madness, of hatred, of cruelty, has passed, then the world as a terror-stricken witness of the extent of its disaster will begin to regain its equilibrium; it will recognize, it has to recognize the part Poland played in its preservation."

THE YALTA CONFERENCE

In addition to those who were actually present for this speech, the pope was obviously addressing the Allied governments, upon whom the future of Poland and the Baltic countries depended. According to another telegram from Cicognani, the Soviets were acting in Poland as if in a conquered land, introducing a new administration and deporting citizens en masse. The American bishops, in turn, recognized the gravity of the situation and publicly expressed their concern for the fate of Poland, the Baltic states, and other European countries. And because the American government did not seem to take seriously the consequences of the Soviet invasion, the bishops decided to speak to Roosevelt. On 15 December Monsignor Tardini again urged Cicognani to continue working for Poland. Complying with these instructions, the delegate found some State Department officials who were willing to second his efforts. In January 1945 the apostolic delegate received assurances from Cordell Hull that the pope's appeal on behalf of Poland had been sent on to Roosevelt. The American secretary of state let it be understood that he shared the views of the pope and his representative and confided to the archbishop that Roosevelt and Churchill, at their next meeting with Stalin in Yalta, would seek to agree upon a common plan.

What happened in Yalta was far from what the Holy See had in mind. Although the Polish question was discussed at length, the Red Army's presence in Poland gave the Soviets a strong position. Soviet Russia demanded that it be given all Polish territory up to the Curzon line, which the English diplomat bearing this name had recognized as the ethnic boundary between Russia and Poland, something the Allies had agreed to at Tehran. After a preparatory meeting of the foreign ministers at Malta on 1 February, the conference between Roosevelt, Churchill, and Stalin, accompanied by Stettinius, Eden, and Molotov, opened in Yalta, on the Black Sea, during the afternoon of 4 February 1945.

Discussion on Poland's future began on 6 February, with Roosevelt acknowledging the Curzon line as Poland's eastern frontier, although he suggested that the border be somewhat modified so that Lwów would remain Polish. In addition, he wanted the creation of a government composed of the principal parties of the country. Churchill was also in favor of the Curzon line as the eastern boundary, but he was more interested in Poland's sovereignty and independence than he was in its border. As to the formation of the government, he recommended the Poles he knew in London, namely, Mikołajczyk, Grabski, and Romer. Although Stalin intended to keep the Curzon line as Poland's eastern frontier, he did not want the government to include the people from London, one of whom had called the Lublin Committee a band of brigands. As Stalin saw it, the Lublin government, now installed in Warsaw, was the Polish government. So as to make some allowance for his allies, he permitted a few corrections to be made to the Curzon line and even said that some "émigrés" could be added to the new provisional government, which as soon as possible would hold an election to form a permanent government. Both Roosevelt and Churchill criticized the word *"émigré,"* with Churchill wanting to add to the government some democratic individuals from within Poland itself. In a rather forceful letter the U.S. president again told Stalin that he would not agree to the Lublin Committee under its present form. Knowing that this committee in no way represented the Polish people, England would not abandon the Polish government in London, which it had recognized throughout the five years of war; the English people would view doing so as treason. For his part, Stalin defended the Lublin Committee which, according to him, was being enthusiastically supported by the Polish people. Roosevelt asked Stalin how long it would take before there were free elections. Stalin replied: "Possibly within a month"; Stalin did not indicate that these elections would occur while the country was still under the Red Army's control. Churchill admitted that elections would, from the English side, remove all difficulty.

Discussions continued on 9 February and 10 February. On the evening of 10 February the final document was adopted. In it the Allies reaffirmed their "common desire to see the establishment of a Poland that was strong, free, independent, and democratic." The new government would be formed on the basis of the Lublin Committee, "reorganized upon a broader democratic base and including democratic leaders [taken] from Poland and from among Poles living abroad." Stalin allowed the Anglo-Saxons to replace the word *émigrés* by "Poles living abroad." This government would be bound to proceed as quickly as possible to free and open elections with universal suffrage and a secret vote; the Allies would grant it diplomatic recognition. As to boundaries, the Allies were considering that the eastern frontiers follow the Curzon line with several corrections of five to eight kilometers in favor of Poland. After consultations with the new government, Poland would receive new areas in the west. This western border, however, would not be determined till the peace conference.

Pius XII did not forget this Catholic country, which was passing from Nazi persecution to Communist oppression. From the time Russian troops entered Poland, all news from that country had completely ceased. The Vatican knew that numerous dioceses were without pastors, that seminaries were empty, and that the clergy had been dispersed. It was urgent that an ecclesiastic be sent there to gather information and to suggest appropriate action. Cicognani was told to ask the government in Washington to choose an American bishop, if possible one of Polish descent, to be a member of the Allied commission that was to go to Poland. But first Cicognani obtained from the Polish ambassador in Washington a document analyzing the situation of the eleven dioceses located east of the Curzon line. Then on 24 February he sent to the State Department a memorandum containing the questions and wishes of the Holy See. Personally visiting this department on 5 March, he repeated to Joseph Grew, an undersecretary, the Vatican's increasing concerns about the lack of news from territories occupied by the Russian armies and its desire to send there an ecclesiastic, preferably an American of Polish origin. Grew acknowledged the lack of news, but he believed that it would be very difficult to send an ecclesiastic into Poland since the new government had not yet been formed; nonetheless, he promised to speak to his direct superior, Edward Stettinius, about this. Cicognani consulted the archbishop of Detroit as to the person he believed capable of fulfilling such a mission, namely, prelate Thomas Noa from the Grand Rapids Diocese. The archbishop as well as his colleague in Chicago unreservedly approved the choice of Noa as well as the idea of conducting this mission.

THE FAR EAST

During these crucial weeks other regions, more distant, also required the Holy See's attention. Since Pearl Harbor the Far East was on fire. Thanks to the special legation of Japan, whose establishment had caused American indignation, the Holy See was able to bring some relief to prisoners in Japanese camps. In July 1944 the apostolic delegate to Japan, Archbishop Paolo Marella, sent a message to the Vatican that the country's authorities had decided to segregate those missionaries who were citizens of countries at war with Japan. Marella stressed that it was for reasons of the war itself that this decision had been made and that it did not precipitate any change in the government's attitude, which was always favorable to Catholicism. French Indochina was at the mercy of a Japan that looked favorably upon the government in Vichy, and so it was that Archbishop Drapier, the apostolic delegate to Indonesia, could tell the Vatican at the end of November 1944 that the situation in Indochina was tolerable. Yet he did not conceal his apprehensions concerning possible repercussions if French policy should change. Meanwhile, Marella continued to promote peace in his conversations with the Japanese authorities. In December he met with the vice-minister of foreign affairs, Renzo Sawada, formerly the Japanese ambassador in Paris and in Rangoon; Sawada was a Christian with an open mind and was good at heart. Marella, however, warned the Secretariat of State that the war would inexorably follow its course "and merely saying the word *peace* set into motion the police and the constables, with the most serious consequences." The vice-minister observed that for the Allies peace was to be imposed on the principle of racial superiority, whereas his government wanted to bring about an order founded on the complete equality of all people and all races. Marella's answer was that these principles "were none other than Christian principles, often stated and explained by the sovereign pontiffs Benedict XV, Pius XI, and Pius XII."

The Vatican was not under any illusions that it could seriously influence Tokyo's policy, but from the perspective of the western nations the question concerned the Holy See's participation in the peace conference that would conclude this world war. A century earlier, Pius VII's secretary of state was one of the conspicuous figures at the Congress of Vienna, seated as he was among the representatives of the major powers in the debates on the reorganization of Europe following the Napoleonic wars. On the other hand, at the end of the First World War Benedict XV was impeded from attending the Versailles conferences by a secret article in the 1915 agreement signed in London by the Allies and Italy. In 1945, now that the Roman question had been settled, nothing seemed to stand in the way of the Holy See's presence at an international conference, especially because on many points the views of Pius XII regarding international relations coincided with those of the Allies.

On 1 September 1944, in a radio message given on the occasion of the fifth anniversary of the beginning of the war, the pope referred to what would follow the conclusion of hostilities. The abyss of miseries into which humanity had been thrown by the spirit of violence and the primacy of force was an invitation to return to Christian principles. Pius XII approved those who "wanted to again find in other camps, till now separated and far distant from one another, collaborators, companions in life and in struggle." He also recalled that in his 1939 Christmas message he expressed his hope that an international organization would be created, "really capable of preserving the peace according to the principles of justice and fairness against any possible future threat." During an audience with Tittmann on the next day the pope informed the American that he had deliberately inserted into his address a mention of international organization so often spoken about by Myron Taylor. Two days later Taylor thanked the pope: "I was deeply moved when Mr. Tittmann informed me of what you said last Saturday, namely, that you accepted my suggestion regarding an international organization for peace and had inserted it into your address. This gives me infinite satisfaction."

The following 18 October Taylor, on Roosevelt's behalf, sent Pius XII a proposal for an international organization; the plan had been perfected during meetings held in September and October with representatives from the United States, Great Britain, the Soviet Union, and China. The schema foresaw a general assembly, a small executive council, and a court of justice; police power would belong to the executive council, which would have at its disposal forces that could intervene; however, using such troops would require the consent of the four principal nations. The question of arms control had been deferred till much later.

When the end of hostilities was near, the question of the pope's participation in the peace conferences became more urgent. The archbishop of Liverpool explicitly brought up the matter in his Lenten pastoral letter when he wrote that the League of Nations had been weakened by the absence of the pope. A discussion with Lord Cecil followed, and the topic assumed more prominence. On 2 April Pius XII spoke about it with Monsignor Tardini, who summed up the substance of the conversation. We must distinguish, said the pope, between a peace conference and a future organization on behalf of peace. As to a peace conference, the Holy See has not asked and does not intend to ask that it participate. And if it were invited, it would first have to study the question, and its participation would have no other purpose than to defend the principles of justice and fairness. As to a general organization of nations, if it were open to all states, both large and small, then the Vatican City State would have the right to take appropriate steps to participate in it.

ROOSEVELT'S DEATH AND THE END OF THE WAR

The study of these international problems was interrupted by some sad news: On 13 April the pope himself sent to Harry Truman, the new president of the United States, an expression of his condolences upon the sudden death of Franklin Roosevelt. Another cable, also signed by the pope, was sent to Roosevelt's widow. Meanwhile, the apostolic delegate presented the pope's condolences to other members of the administration. Certainly the pope had to have been deeply moved by Roosevelt's loss. Notwithstanding the disappointments and divergences that came between them, for example, in the discussion regarding Rome, on the status of religion in Russia, on "unconditional surrender," and on Poland's future, the personal relationship between these two men was always one of reciprocal respect and cordiality. Besides, Roosevelt knew how to choose in Myron Taylor a representative who was equal to the task. When one of Taylor's collaborators telephoned Monsignor Tardini to say that the ambassador would remain at his post after Roosevelt's death since Taylor was the "personal representative of the president and not of Roosevelt," Tardini remarked: "The reasoning is not very persuasive, but I thank God for the news, which I deem to be very good."

In Europe military operations were coming to an end. On 30 April Hitler, by his death, escaped the dissolution of the Third Reich.

On 7 May at two in the morning General Jodl at Reims reported the surrender of all German armed forces; the official announcement of this was broadcast on the afternoon of the next day. At noon on 9 May Pius XII addressed people everywhere in a radio message: "Finally we come to the conclusion of this war which has held Europe in the grasp of the most atrocious suffering and bitter sadness." After offering a prayer of thanksgiving that the war had ended and a prayer of inter- cession for the dead, the pope spoke to the people of his hopes for the future. Faithful to his initial desire to remain above all disputes and divisions, Pius XII neither condemned the vanquished nor praised the victors, but he urged all to participate in the work of reconstruction.

> The war has brought about an utter chaos of ruins, both material and moral, such as the human race has never experienced through- out its history. Today it is a matter of rebuilding the world. As the first element of doing so, We desire to see, after so long a wait and as circumstances allow, the prompt and speedy return of prisoners and internees, both combatants as well as civilians, to their homes, to their spouses, to their children, and to the noble works of peace.

The following day, on 10 May, three telegrams signed by the pope himself were sent out from the Vatican: one to the king of the Belgians, another to the queen of the Netherlands, and a third to the grand duchess of Luxembourg. Recalling the messages he sent them on this date five years earlier, Pius XII wanted to share in the joy of the independence and liberty that had been regained, a desire he expressed during the tragic hours of May 1940.

Conclusion

~·~

THE WORLD WAS AT PEACE in March 1939 when Cardinal Pacelli became Pope Pius XII. But, as he later said to the cardinals on 2 June 1945, what kind of peace was it? "We were reaching out for peace as someone at a bedside reaches out for a dying person where ardent love, even against all hope, confronts death's embraces." In fact, Pius XII did everything possible to avoid war: secret diplomatic initiatives, solemn addresses, moving appeals to peoples and governments. First, in early May he embraced the idea of a meeting to which would be invited the heads of the governments in Rome, Paris, London, Berlin, and Warsaw in order "to resolve among [them] by means of a conference the questions that threaten to unleash the conflict." The pope was not discouraged by the negative though friendly responses he received. During the following weeks he continued to insist that all provocations, especially between Poland and Germany, be avoided. He endeavored to dissipate the dangerous illusions that nourished Hitler and his entourage in power to attack Poland without any declaration of war. When the announcement of the German-Soviet pact brought the crisis to a head, Pius XII understood that the time had come to issue a final and solemn appeal on behalf of peace, as Bonnet and Halifax had suggested that he do. On 23 August at seven in the evening the pope sent a radio message to those responsible for peace and war: "Nothing is lost with peace. Everything can be lost with war."

Fifteen days after the Wehrmacht, despite all, had crossed Poland's boundaries, Pius XII defined his policy for this time of war in an address given on 14 September, when he received the credentials of Belgium's ambassador: "We will not cease to watch attentively so that We may give all the assistance within Our power and as opportunities allow: especially to motivate once again the people, today inflamed and divided, toward concluding a peace that is honorable for all...and then, for as long as this is not possible, at least to alleviate the terrible wounds that have been or will be inflicted in the future." This was the mission Pius XII took upon himself, a mission he pursued to the end.

The pope's first concern was to keep Italy out of the conflict. On 21 December, while receiving King Victor Emmanuel and Queen Helen at the Vatican, Pius used the occasion to congratulate warmly the Italian leaders who had kept their country out of the storm sweeping down upon Europe. And in order to give more force to his peacemaking words the pope himself, going beyond protocol, went to the Quirinal Palace for the purpose of visiting the Italian king and of renewing his praise of "the peace which has been protected by the wisdom of its leaders [who] make Italy strong and respected."

When Ribbentrop came to Rome in March 1940, Pius XII granted his request for an audience, doing so with the hope—although he was immediately disappointed—of saying something on behalf of peace. And when rumors of Italy's approaching entrance into the war became more persistent, the pope with Roosevelt planned a double intervention: a letter from the pope and a message from the president to the head of the Italian government persuading the latter to keep his country at peace.

At the same time he sent to London the proposals of the German generals who wanted to free themselves from Hitler but were requesting guarantees regarding an honorable peace for their country.

After the German attack on Belgium, Holland, and Luxembourg, Pius XII, who a few days earlier had informed the ambassador of France and the minister of England of this, sent three telegrams which, under the form of condolences to the three sovereigns, unequivocally condemned the invasion of the neutral states. Here the pope was responding to a French and English request. In this regard Pius XII explained to the cardinal archbishop of Munich the Vatican's position regarding the warring parties: not neutrality, which could be understood as passive indifference, something unbecoming the head of the church, but rather impartiality, which judges things according to truth and justice. On the other hand, Pius XII refused to yield to the demands of Italy's ambassador on behalf of the German and Italian soldiers participating in the campaign against Bolshevist Russia. The pope was well aware of the Bolshevist religious persecution, and he also had no illusions as to the intentions of the Nazis, who were only awaiting victory in order to finish things with the Catholic Church. The swastika was not exactly the crusaders' cross.

Myron Taylor, Roosevelt's personal representative, was better received than the Italian ambassador when Taylor came to ask Pius XII to allay the scruples of American Catholics in regard to the assistance the U.S. government was planning to furnish Russia: Honesty required an acknowledgment that Pius XI's encyclical against Communism did not have in mind the present situation.

Although the Reich was pretending to lead a crusade against Bolshevism, it carried out a ruthless persecution of the church and of the Polish people. The horrible events cited by Pius XII when receiving Italy's ambassador of Italy on 13 May 1940 were far from ending, and if the pope refrained from stigmatizing such deeds with fiery words, it was out of fear that this would worsen the fate of the victims. At that time the cardinal primate of Poland as well as the archbishop of Cracow were complaining that the pope was not speaking out on behalf of the Polish Church nor was he condemning its torturers. The same was stated in February 1943 by two Polish bishops who were refugees in England.

Pius XII and his advisers discussed the question of issuing a public statement against the persecution of the church in Poland. But already the encyclical *Summi Pontificatus* had recalled the past heroism and the present sufferings of the Polish nation; so well did the letter appear to embrace the Polish cause that French airplanes dropped thousands of copies of the document over western Germany. On many occasions the pope made discreet although not unclear references to the fate of Poland. Despite the fact that the Poles in exile wanted stronger words, those in Poland were indeed more cautious. And so Monsignor Tardini concluded: faced with a solemn condemnation, the occupying power would increase the oppression over the victims and would forbid even the little relief that the Holy See could still bring them. Instead, a letter signed by Cardinal Maglione was sent to Ribbentrop listing all the brutalities inflicted on the church in Poland by the Nazis. However, this letter was not accepted and remained hidden within the walls of chancelleries. Finally, speaking to the cardinals on 2 June 1943 Pius XII extolled the present sufferings and the past glories of Poland, and for this reason the dignitaries of the Polish Church expressed to him their warmest gratitude.

It was a little after the German assault on Russia that the persecution of the Jews increased. As early as August 1941 the pope was asked to intervene on behalf of the Jews in Croatia. In March 1942 the

Holy See's chargé d'affaires in Slovakia warned the Vatican that the deportation of the Jews from that country was imminent. The heads of the Jewish communities in Europe and in America appealed to the Holy See and its representatives to do something for their fellow Jews who were either in danger of deportation or who had already been deported from Germany, Slovakia, Croatia, Romania, France, or Hungary. Uncertainty reigned as to their lot, but with time suspicions of a tragic destiny became stronger. In a letter to the pope on 19 December 1942 Ambassador Papée affirmed that the Jews were "being put to death in places especially prepared for this purpose." On the following 5 May the Secretariat of State received a message sent by the World Jewish Congress to the British and American governments warning that the campaign of exterminating the Jews had reached its highest point. It was on this date that the Secretariat of State summarized in a short but impressive note the communiqués it had received on the fate of the Jews: There was talk of death camps, of victims by the hundreds being shut up in chambers where they were gassed to death, of victims being stuffed together in airtight vehicles. What was the exact meaning of this information which caused the Allied governments and even Jewish circles themselves to be uncertain as to what they should or could believe?

In his 1942 Christmas message Pius XII denounced the cruelty of the war then in progress and the violations of those international conventions that should have limited its horrors; further, he recalled "the hundreds of thousands of people who, through no fault of their own and at times only because of their nationality or race, are destined to be killed or are allowed simply to waste away."

In his consistorial address on the following 2 June 1943 the pope again mentioned those who were turning to him because, due to their nationality or race, they were "destined, even without any fault of their own, to exterminating imprisonment." He also warned that "whoever carries the sword must use it in accord with God's law."

As clear as such references were for those willing to listen to them, these allusions were not the explicit and strong condemnations that some were asking him to issue. But in the same talk Pius XII explained that every word of these public addresses "had to be considered and weighed with a deep seriousness in the interest of those who are suffering."

Pius XII henceforth observed this reserve despite the requests, more or less disinterested, that were addressed to him. This disappointed those who believed that resounding statements would be an effective way of opposing the massacres of the Poles, the executions of hostages, and the extermination of the Jews.

The pope had given thought to the possibility of public statements, but it was not without deliberation that he clearly chose silent action. In several letters to the German bishops he shared his hesitations and his doubts. For example, on 20 February 1941 he wrote: "When the pope wanted to cry aloud in a strong voice, waiting and silence were unhappily often imposed; when he wanted to help and to bring aid, patience and expectation [were required]." This was repeated on 3 March 1944: "Frequently it is with pain and difficulty that a decision is made as to what the situation demands; prudent reserve and silence or, on the contrary, candid speech and vigorous action."

The motives that inspired the choice of Pius XII are clear; the Red Cross spelled them out in a short formula: Protests gain nothing, and they can harm those whom one hopes to assist. The only way to help the Jews, answered the State Department, was to win the war. And after the conflict had ended, many authorized voices, coming from various horizons, shared the pope's opinion. As an example of someone who had an opportunity to do a documentary study of the mentality of the Nazi leaders, one could cite Robert M. W. Kempner, the former United Nations' delegate to the Tribunal of War Crimes at Nuremberg. He wrote: "Any propaganda attempt undertaken by the Catholic Church against Hitler's Reich would not only have been a provoked suicide, as Rosenberg has now said, but would have hastened the execution of still more Jews and priests."

Furthermore, Pius XII had to consider that a public statement on his part would have furnished ammunition to Nazi propaganda, which would in turn have presented the pope as an enemy of Germany. In the expert hands of a Goebbels, a pontifical speech could become a choice weapon against Christianity. It could unsettle the faithful—not all of whom were unaffected by the successes of the regime—in their confidence in the church and its leader. Pius XII was taking into consideration German Catholics, not the regime and its leaders, for the pope had no illusions as to the deep-seated intentions of the hierarchs of the Third Reich. Persecution of the church only made the war worse, and such persecution continued on till these last months, said Pius XII on 2 June 1945, "when its adherents, once the military victory has been obtained, still flatter themselves that they have the power of settling things once and for all with the church. Authorized and indisputable witnesses have informed Us of these plans."

Such reserve was completely contrary to any indifference regarding the victims. While the pope was silent in public, his Secretariat of State was exerting pressure on the nuncios and apostolic delegates in Slovakia, Croatia, Romania, and Hungary, telling them to intervene with governments and national episcopates in order to undertake relief actions whose efficacy was recognized at the time by repeated thanks from Jewish organizations. The Jewish historian Pinchas Lapide did not hesitate to estimate that about 850,000 people were thus saved.

While Pius XII was receiving appeals for help from the Poles and the non-Aryans threatened with extermination, the war was continuing on all fronts with its destruction and massacres. In his 1942 Christmas message the pope called for an effort to lead society "to the juridical order willed by God and from which flows the inalienable human right to juridical security and to a concrete sphere of right that is protected from every arbitrary attack." The following months were indeed far removed from this ideal, for at this time the Anglo-Americans issued their Casablanca statement on the unconditional surrender they were demanding from the enemy and which they were attempting to impose by weakening the people's morale through massive bombings of German cities. "What we for a long time have heard regarding inhuman horrors," wrote Pius XII on 30 April 1943, "and which absolutely goes beyond the real needs of war, can only seize a person with amazement and fright." And once again on the following 1 September he addressed both parties. Like Benedict XV in 1917, he invited the combatants to ask the question: "Does the continuation of the war, and of a war like this, conform to national interests that are reasonable and justifiable before the Christian and human conscience? Can anyone even say that it does?"

The Anglo-Americans responded that any conversation had to be preceded by the elimination of Nazism and by the unconditional surrender of the German army. It was not Pius XII's intent to preach an unsatisfactory peace. On the typed text of his 1943 Christmas message he added with his own hand: "Naturally, concluding such a peace would in no way signify the abandonment of the guarantees and sanctions necessary when being confronted by attempts to employ force against what is right." But he thought that loudly broadcasted demands for unconditional surrender would only prolong, and uselessly so, the destruction and the mass killings.

On 2 June 1944, when the Allies were at the gates of Rome, the pope publicly took a position against the idea of unconditional surrender, which, by leaving the defeated side to believe that there were no alternatives other than complete victory or total destruction, would give it a courage born of despair and thus prolong the destruction and the killing. But at the end of the month Roosevelt's representative again told the pope that unconditional surrender remained a policy of the U.S. government. It was on this point that the pope collided with Anglo-Saxon intransigence, and as a result he did not give Taylor the note prepared by Monsignor Tardini on this subject. A repeated protest, even done privately, would only offend the U.S. representative and make any further steps impossible.

It was also at this time that the Poles were asking the pope to intervene with the western Allies against Soviet Russia's demands. He did his utmost to interest the State Department and Catholic opinion in the United States on what was happening to Poland, but at Yalta, despite Roosevelt's and Churchill's initial intentions, Poland and eastern Europe were abandoned to the Soviets.

Pius XII's attention extended to the war in all its breadth and under all its aspects. Countries under military occupation, countries suffering from starvation, the civilian population, the elderly, the women and the children who perished by the thousands during the bombing of German cities, the Poles who were destroyed, the Jews who were deported and murdered, the combatants who fell on the first line of battle on both sides of the front, prisoners separated from their spouses and children, mothers, married couples, and children separated from these captives—all were the objects of his concern and, insofar as he could do something for them, of his tender care. To all these evils Pius XII wanted to bring the remedy of peace.

While awaiting the peace that he desired above all else, the peace that was the focal point of everything he said and did, Pius XII never relaxed his efforts to alleviate the sufferings brought about by the war.

It is not surprising that the pope and Vatican diplomacy, with the resources available to them, obtained only limited results. But perhaps what is most surprising is that, in spite of all, the Holy See was able to give hope and consolation to so many families worried about what was happening to their family members who were prisoners. Vatican efforts brought material relief into any number of camps and cities with starving populations. And finally, through the sustained dedication of the Holy See to the cause of human justice, a considerable number of lives were saved.

Although it is difficult to total up all the results, it is nonetheless permissible to come up with an idea of the totality of the Holy See's charitable and humanitarian activity, namely, that carried out by Pius XII himself during the Second World War. The very mass of documents by itself stands as an eloquent testimony of the intensity of the care that the pope showed on behalf of the human problems that the war brought about throughout the world. Society's secularization notwithstanding, the Catholic Church always remained conscious of its humanitarian mission, which was intimately joined to its religious one. This resulted in Pius XII's determination to extend his charitable work to all the victims of war, regardless of nationality, race, religion, or political party. This universality was not the fruit of any political calculation or interest. Nothing was more opposed to the pope's intentions than to use human suffering as an opportunity to increase his prestige and power. Pius XII proceeded silently, with discretion, at the risk of appearing inactive or indifferent. And yet the work of assisting the war's victims was his favorite undertaking. His experience as nuncio in Bavaria during the First World War had accustomed him to disappointments, refusals, and failures. Consequently, he did not nourish any illusions as to the extent of his influence, even if others, supplied with good intentions or, on the contrary, with hostile intentions, ascribed to him unlimited power. Moreover, his action, completely independent and often spontaneous, was not isolated; on the contrary, it was coordinated with the efforts, often more effective, of other humanitarian groups like the International Committee of the Red Cross or various Jewish organizations, which for a long time were dedicated to helping the Jews dispersed throughout the world. The Holy See's efforts to relieve humanity's sufferings not only encountered misunderstandings and misconceptions, but also positive resistance, whether in the name of military needs or even as the result of undisguised passions of hatred and fanaticism. Confronted with all these obstacles, the Holy See displayed an obstinate tenacity and a perseverance worthy of the noble purpose it had chosen for itself as defined by Pius XII in April 1941, "to make the war more humane, to alleviate its evils, to assist and console its victims."

Several years later Pius XII returned to these years of fire and sword in a speech to nurses given in May 1952. He asked the question: What should we have done that we have not done?

The pope was saying that he was conscious of what he had accomplished to prevent the war, to alleviate its sufferings, to reduce the number of its victims—everything he thought he could do. The documents, insofar as they allow one to probe the human heart, come to the same conclusion.

As for results, to affirm that the pope himself or some other person in his place might have been able to do more is to depart from the field of history in order to venture into the undergrowth of suppositions and dreams.

In concluding these pages on Pius XII and the war, it seems appropriate to recall how he was remembered by two men who knew well both the pope and the war. Shortly after the pope's death on 9 October 1958, Field Marshal Montgomery wrote in the 12 October issue of London's *Sunday Times:* "He was a great and good man, and I loved him." And above we saw how General de Gaulle, describing his Vatican audience of 30 June 1944, wrote in his *War Memories:* "Pius XII judges everything from a perspective that surpasses human beings, their undertakings and their quarrels."

Pope Pius XII's high ideals, transcending as they did opposing interests and rival passions, will always make difficult the task of understanding his policy and personality.

Further Sources

~.~

What follows is not a bibliography on this subject, which the reader can find in many of the works given below. Rather, it is essentially a listing of the published documents and memoirs used as sources.

PUBLISHED DOCUMENTS

Acta Apostolicae Sedes. Vols. 31–37 (1939–1945). Vatican City: Typis Polyglottis Vaticanis, 1939–1945.

Akten zur deutschen auswärtigen Politik (1918–1945), Aus dem Archiv des deutschen auswärtigen Amtes. Series D, E (1937–1945). Göttingen: Vandenhoeck and Ruprecht, 1956.

English: *Documents on German Foreign Policy (1918–1945): From the Archives of the German Foreign Ministry.* Washington, D.C.: U.S. Government Printing Office, 1949.

Churchill, Winston S. *The War Speeches.* 2 vols. Ed. Charles Eade. London: Cassell, 1963–1965.

Der Notenwechsel zwischen dem Hl. Stuhl und der deutschen Reichsregierung. Ed. Dieter Albrecht. Vol. 2, 1937–1945. Mainz: Matthias-Grünewald-Verlag, 1969.

Documenti diplomatici italiani. Series 8 and 9 (1935–1943). Rome: Libreria dello Stato, 1954.

Documents on British Foreign Policy 1919–1939. Edited by E. L. Woodward and J. P. T. Bury. Series 3, vols. 5–7. London: H.M. Stationery Office, 1952.

Documents pontificaux de Sa Sainteté Pie XII. 20 vols. Saint-Maurice, Switzerland: Éditions Saint-Augustin, 1939–1958.

Foreign Relations of the United States, Diplomatic Papers, 1939–1945. Washington, D.C.: U.S. Government Printing Office, Superintendent of Documents, 1956.

MEMOIRS AND ARTICLES

Chadwick, Owen. *Britain and the Vatican during the Second World War.* New York: Cambridge University Press, 1986.

Charles-Roux, François. *Huit ans au Vatican, 1932–1940.* Paris: Flammarion, 1947.

Chaunu, Pierre. *Les Enjeux de la paix. Nous et les autres. xviiie–xxe siècles.* Paris: Presses universitaires de France, 1995.

Chélini, Jean, and d'Onorio, Joël-Benoît, ed. *Pie XII et la Cité.* Aix-Marseille: Tequi, Presses universitaires, 1988.

Ciano, Galeazo. *Diario.* Vol. 1 (1939–1940). Milan: Rízzoli Editore, 1946. English: *The Ciano Diaries 1939–1943.* Ed. Hugh Gibson. Garden City, N.Y.: Doubleday, 1946.

Duroselle, Jean-Baptiste. *Histoire diplomatique de 1919 à nos jours.* Paris: Dalloz, 1953.

François-Poncet, André. *Au palais Farnèse. Souvenir d'une ambassade à Rome 1939–1940.* Paris: Fayard, 1961.

Gaulle, Charles de. *The Complete War Memories of Charles de Gaulle.* Tr. J. Griffin and R. Howard. New York: Simon & Schuster, 1972.

Graham, Robert A. *The Pope and Poland in World War Two.* London: Veritas, 1968.

————. "La missione di W. d'Ormesson in Vaticano nel 1940." *Civiltà Cattolica,* 124/4 (1973): pp. 145–48.

————. "L'enciclica *Summi Pontificatus* e i belligerenti nel 1939." *Civiltà Cattolica,* 135/4 (1984): pp. 137–51.

Henderson, Sir Neville. *Failure of a Mission: Berlin 1937–1939.* New York: G. P. Putnam's Sons, 1940.

Lapide, Pinchas E. *The Last Three Popes and the Jews.* London: Souvenir Press, 1967. U.S. Edition: *Three Popes and the Jews.* New York: Hawthorn Books, 1967.

Leiber, Robert. "Pius XII," in *Stimmen der Zeit* 163 (1958–1959), pp. 81–100.

Maccarrone, Michele. *Il nazionalsocialismo e la Santa Sede.* Rome: Studium, 1947.

Martini, Angelo. "La Santa Sede e gli ebrei della Romania durante la seconda guerra mondiale." *Civiltà Cattolica* 112/3 (1961): pp. 449–63.

————. "La fame in Grecia nel 1941 nella testimonianza dei documenti inediti vaticani." *Civiltà Cattolica* 118/1 (1967): pp. 213–17.

Nobécourt, Jacques. "'Silence' de Pie XII." *Dictionnaire historique de la papauté.* Paris: Fayard, 1994.

Schambeck, Herbert, ed. *Pius XII. Zum Gedächtnis.* Berlin: Duncker und Humblot, 1977.

Taylor, Myron C. *Wartime Correspondence between President Roosevelt and Pope Pius XII.* New York: Macmillan, 1947.

Weizsäcker, Ernst von. *Erinnerungen.* Munich: P. List, 1950.

Index

294